Issues and Events to Come in the New Millennium

The Destruction of the U.S. Constitution and Our National Sovereignty

Volume I

By David E. Smith Jr.

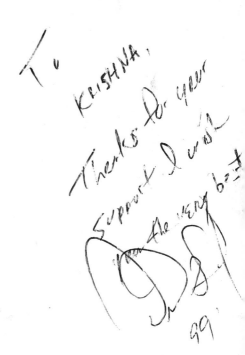

David E. Smith

Destech Press Publishing

Destech Press Publishing, Inc. Peekskill, NY 10566
©1998 by Destech Press
1st Printing
All Rights Reserved
Publication Date: 02/1999
Printed in the United States of America

Contacting the Author

David E. Smith Jr. is available for speaking engagements and book signings.

Destech Press Publishing Inc.
Suite 3
13 South Division St.
Peekskill, NY 10566
Ph: (914) 739-8053
Fax: (914) 739-8007
E Mail: destech@pcrealm.net

Web: www.destechpress.com

David E. Smith

Acknowledgements

I would like to express special gratitude to all those
who helped me make this book become a reality.

Dedication

To the Creator, My Family, Ancestors, Friends and to
the Entire Human race.

Table of Contents

Preface

Thank you for the purchase of my third book. I believe that it is my duty as an author to write material that is relevant to the to times of today.

This is a book that was not designed to be a complete authoritative guide to all events happening around the world, but a book that hopefully sends a message to all people who are ready, willing and able to recognize that they need to be prepared for the coming catastrophes that awaits us all as a people. According to the science of numbers, this is the period of Revelations. This is an era where people will face reality one way or the other.

Our civilization is now entering a New Age, a New Age that approaches approximately every 2000 years. As the wheel of the zodiac of twelve constellations rotates, we now enter the Age of Aquarius. The Age of Aquarius represents a devastating and catastrophic change in the social order, and moreover, a change in the geology of the earth. Christianity is now in its last chapter, and will cease to exist, as Revelations is the last chapter in the Bible. A new higher level of worship will be pronounced to the Creator unknown or unrecognized by most people.

This by no means does this represent the end of the world, but 1999 is actually the year where the Age of Aquarius actually makes a transformation and begins a new era. According to the science of numbers or Numerology, the number nine represents a number of completion as explained later in the book.

As an author, or in other words a messenger, I understand the fact that I will not be able to convince everyone that something tragic is coming to affect us all. Like Noah and his Ark, most people still go around and believe that such a boat or ark existed.

Well, if we were to correctly interpret the meaning of the story, it would be similar to what many have been brainwashed to believe.

Noah was an ordinary man with a vision. Noah was a man that saw a catastrophe on the horizon, and warned the people of his community. No, he did not collect two gorillas, two zebras, two rhinoceros, two cobra snakes, two scorpions and two giraffes to sleep with him on his ark. Furthermore, a question that one may ask themselves is, would you sleep on a boat for forty days and nights with unloadable cow dung and a possible broken jar that once contained scorpions or snakes? I would think not.

What this story is actually depicting, is a man that warned others and properly gathered his food and stored it away. Noah collected gold and silver, water, blankets and other amenities for survival. He then built a large fortress with the help of those that believed him, and completed it in time before the great deluge or flood.

When the catastrophe came, people outside the fortress began to believe what Noah actually told them. When they approached the fortress asking to be permitted to enter, the doors remained shut. Those people eventually perished.

After this book is finished and when the mainstream distributors and press read the content, I will probably become "fair game" from the powers that be to suppress this information. I may not be a master in all things that I know, and I may only have basic knowledge of biology, geometry, and psychology; but I do know one thing, I am continually mastering the art of Tricknology. This book, I promise for most of you, will be unlike any book many of you have ever read. It is a book that gives you the applicability to fill in the blanks, while making you think at the same time.

I cannot cover everything in one book, so this may only be volume one. However, I tried to cover enough to let you know that there is a serious series of events about to occur that you need to be aware of, and protect yourself from.

I must admit that overall, many people unfortunately conduct themselves like cattle. They follow the Piper or the Shepherd as if they are their only compass to survival. Take a look at some of the cities around the nation, such as New York. The mayor of the city, Rudolph Guiliani practically tells people where they can cross the street. Practically every point of entry into the city, is monitored by surveillance cameras and electronic monitoring devices. Officials in the city know when people are coming and going; using license plates and all for reference. If a person is a ticket scofflaw or a deadbeat dad, they can pick them up at any toll booth like clockwork, and in the morning they are rounded up. People are creatures of habit, and tend to use the same route to travel to work each day. Where will it stop? It is practically a police state now, whereby the mayor does not even condemn four white police officers who shot an unarmed black man forty one times. This police state is only concerned with control of the people.

This book is meant to be a wakeup call. Unfortunately, many people and churches continue to sleep. The only donation that will benefit many of them, if they do not see the light soon, are pillows so they can rest their heads while they unknowingly await the coming catastrophes.

Many churches do not realize that they are entitled to be separate from the State and still benefit from most grants and tax deductions they have now under a 501 (c)(3). Presently, many churches are nothing more than an entity of the State. In other words, if they decide to get into politics or the State is not in favor of what they are doing, the State can come in and audit their books or practically just shut them down.

There is no excuse for most churches in this country to fall under this Not for Profit Corporate status. Many pastors are aware, but refuse to do anything about it. I have spoken to a few of them, but they choose to remain clueless. Many of them treat their congregation like cattle and just collect tithes. Ask them why they are not preparing for Y2K and a host of other events, and see what many of them will tell you. Oh, make sure you keep up on your tithes before you address that question.

You see, I am not interested in bashing any church, even though it may sound that way. However, I want to protect you the reader, from the tragic events that are soon to come. Very soon! Challenge your pastor, for you may save many people in the process. Understand what the term **Saved** really represents. The Creator gave you life, what more can one ask for? The Creator expects you to think for yourself. Prepare for the worst, and be saved from it. It is all written! Do not expect a man to fall through the clouds when the major catastrophes come to pass and save you. Wake the hell up!

I have placed some of my thoughts in this introduction for those that may never read the entire book, but will make note that they need to prepare for something coming their way. I used the church here, because the government will use it and make it the downfall of many people. People need to stop being sheep and once again think for themselves. I am not saying to stop believing in your faith, but think for your self.

Enjoy your reading, and do not hesitate to send your comments to me. May the Creator bless you and work with you in all your preparation for the future.

CHAPTER ONE

What is Y2K?

Y2K is a serious problem.   Y2K represents (Y =Year, 2=2, and K= Kilo or Thousand). The coined term is the "Millennium Bug". Let us set the record straight, this is not an actual computer virus that can spread from computer system to computer system, continually destroying anything in its path as the media may have you believe. Y2K is a design flaw in our technology that was actually created intentionally. Furthermore, none of the big computer companies such as IBM, Oracle, Intel or Microsoft have or will have a quick-fix solution that will fix more than 100 million computers world-wide in time as we approach the year 2000 and beyond.

"The technotronic era involves the gradual appearance of a more controlled society. Such a society would be dominated by an elite, unrestrained by traditional values."
Zbigniew Brezhinsky, National Security Advisor to Pres. Jimmy Carter and advisor to 4 other presidents. Exec. Dir. of Trilateral Commission.

There are a host of complicated problems such as the "two-digit" problem and the "fixed date" problem. During the years of the 1950's through the 1990's, computers have been programmed to count up to the year 1999. The next century is quickly approaching and many pre-programmed computers in lay terms, need to correspond and rotate like a turnstile to recognize the year 2000. A simple process you say? Well, not exactly. Computers work just like a counter that needs to go from 1997 to 1998 to 1999 to 2000, right? Wrong! Computers will not understand the turn of the century due to the fact that many of them for instance, were programmed to use the last two digits in the advancement from year to year. This means that, the number '96' (the last two digits) instead of 1996 will advance forward, '97' instead of 1997, '98', '99', and then either back to '00' or the counter will not advance at all. The counter will not go to 2000 if it does advance, but turn over to the year 1900, and many lines of code will actually be reading the incorrect date.

As for embedded chips, they read a "fixed date." This means that the number '19' was never used due to the fact that the embedded chip were made to assume that a '19' was present before each number. However, when the computer tries to convert from the number '99' to 2000, it will read the date to be 1900; thus reading and operating with the incorrect date. This is a problem that affects the entire global infrastructure.

Every country industrialized or not, and practically everyone living, in some manner or form will be affected by a tremendous fault in computer technology. In industrialized nations, whether they are international or national, their local banks are controlled by thousands of networks of computers that are dependent upon each other. This is a financial structure that people depend upon daily. When one of these computer networks stop operating, millions of people are affected. When a series of systems stop working, a domino effect becomes evident and hundreds of millions people are affected. When most of the systems go down during the incoming of the new millennium, every industrialized nation on earth will suffer a potential global structural and financial collapse.

To make things a little easier to understand, think about small level scenarios. Automated teller machines will be inoperable, whereby many people who wish to withdraw money from their accounts come day one of the year 2000, will not be able to do so. Compounded with this problem, are signed presidential Executive Orders limiting the amount of funds that can be withdrawn from the banks. Bank vaults may not open when necessary, and due to the counter problem, vaults may open on a Saturday and close for the weekend on Thursday.

A Typical Scenario

You go out to a party on that Friday night which is actually December 31, 1999. You party joyfully with your friends, and sing the whole night through. After the party is over, January 1, 2000, Saturday morning comes around and you go to the ATM machine. Now, we take you, Mr. or Ms. John Doe, and say okay you had for example $10,000 in your bank account on the 31st of December. You've been mentally conditioned to believe in the banks, their commercials and information statements claiming that everything will be alright. The banks told you that there may be a few disruptions, but they are for the most part Year 2000 compliant.

You go to the ATM machine and the ATM machine registers an amount of zero in your account. Everything has been wiped out of the account. You had $10,000 in that account, but now you're without money on Saturday, Sunday and Monday is a holiday. Tuesday you go running to the bank like millions of others, to get money after you've experienced starvation over the weekend. With too many people approaching the banks, they may not open their doors until a few days later when they are sure there will not be a run on the bank. That is when too many people go to the bank and withdraw money; an amount that the bank does not have on demand. Banks work on a "fractional reserve" system.

With bills to pay, no food or necessities to keep you afloat until the shortage of your personal money supply dilemma subsides, your bank tells you that your money is not there. To make things worse, the bank informs you that there is no record of it ever being there. You show them your checkbook but your checkbook is not authenticating documentation to prove that you had that money in the bank. Neither is your savings book enough to prove that you had that money in the bank. So you bring a bank statement, but the last bank statement that you will have had, most likely will be dated December 8th or so, and the next one to come would be around January 8th. Therefore, you still don't have any proof. Now what?

Again, if you are like millions of others that will run to the bank on the following Tuesday, you cannot be guaranteed that the bank will actually open up. Their computers will have to be repaired and since they are operating on a "fractional reserve" system, and even if your money is still recorded in the bank records, each branch must protect themselves of successive withdrawals from people trying to take advantage of the chaos.

Therefore, all machines inoperable will need to be repaired, while you are out on the street in a frenzy. The volume of people wishing to withdraw money will be very high, and most likely the bank may not have enough cash on hand to meet your demand. Further, with the implementation of Executive Orders, do not fool yourself to believe that you will be able to withdraw all of your money one day or even one month in advance. You may need to consider seven to nine months in advance.

Of course that is not all. Within 3 days or so, there will be a limited fresh food available anywhere in the United States. Six days later, there will virtually be no food at all at the retail level. This all possible, compliments of Y2K system failures.

Intentionally Created?

In fact, this was a problem that dates back to the late 1950's or perhaps a little earlier. The excuse then, and the excuse now is that much of this Y2K complexity was due to a lack of foresight of the year 2000 and limited technology. These are excuses used by major company manufacturers that were involved, and technology experts who study the problem. Excuses that can be table-designed for debate, but we will never get to the bottom of this problem unless we put this debate to the side for another discussion. Although, the excuses manufacturers and experts provide must be mentioned for reference of knowledge as to why this problem ever came into existence.

One of the claims that manufacturers and experts use, is the fact that at the time of manufacture, the cost of memory or electronic storage space was too expensive. This was to justify the fact that they programmed computers to have the last two digits operate in order to save space; leaving us with an end of '99'. The number '99' just happens to give you a sensation of the end or completion if you really think about it.

This thought process of saving money sounded very plausible, which in effect led to the shortening of the dates by all companies over a period of time. However, it is interesting to note that all other manufacturers decided to follow suit; manufacturers that were supposed to be independent of each other. This so-called ingenious idea, gave them what they considered a green light to eliminate the number '19' and just use the last two digits. Manufacturers and experts claim that it was necessary and evident that the computer languages used in the programming of their computer systems, would not last for 30 or more years due to rapid technological advancement.

Furthermore, in the analyzation of this programming problem, is the issue that programs were not expected to last. The decisions were not entirely left in the hands of the programmers to place the proper coding in business and personal machines. It was not the programmers who never foresaw that their programs would be used in 30 years. I find it difficult to believe that all these manufacturers did not do their research or in their research they did not anticipate future complications or legal ramifications if the systems were to last past the year 2000. Companies of the past and today, spend much of their energy and time planning, and this is something that they supposedly all left out of thought; especially when the same problem was happening in the 1960's going into the 1970's when using the last single counting digit. Further, it is hard to believe that not one of the manufacturers had vision to spend the extra money in case their systems lasted beyond the year 2000.

Do you truly believe that each and every manufacturer did this by mistake or accident? Why are there so many computers that were manufactured in the 1990's going to be non-compliant? Should we as a people not ask the Intel Corporation, the computer chip maker that helped convince many companies and individual people through consistent advertisement, to have Intel computer chips inside their computer? Why is Apple Computer the only company that possesses a computer system that is compliant, while all other systems are scrambling for a solution? Think about it.

The Utilities Factor

Regional and local telephone companies are controlled by computer networks that route communication from point to point. The same as if a phone call were made from point A to B. With Y2K, phone systems will no longer be used for business and pleasure purposes, but for emergency purposes only. Emergency meaning to make 911 calls only; limiting your ability to immediately communicate with anyone else accept your local authorities. If the domino effect interrupts the flow of communication, expect not to make any phone calls for a while; possibly days or even months. You probably ask the question, can this really happen? Let us now focus our attention on the area of energy.

Executive Order 10997

SECTION 1. Scope. The Secretary of the Interior (hereinafter referred to as the Secretary) shall prepare national emergency plans and develop preparedness programs covering (1) electric power; (2) petroleum and gas; (3) solid fuels; and (4) minerals.

These plans and programs shall be designed to provide a state of readiness in these resource areas with respect to all conditions of national emergency, including attack upon the United States.

(a) The term "electric power" means all forms of electric power and energy, including the generation, transmission, distribution, and utilization thereof.

The utility companies however, will experience power grid failures that will obstruct everything from lights to nuclear plants. Power grids operated by major utilities and smaller private companies will most likely go down. When the people affected begin to immediately complain, and not by phone of course, the power companies will be pointing at each other or blaming Y2K. With proper emergency planning such as the one provided for in the above executive order, the government will tell the people that, since power utility computer networks are not operating correctly, they must alert you as to when they will power up in the morning and, when they're going to power down at night. Basically telling you, when you may wake up in the morning and when you may go to sleep at night. Is this control over the masses or what? I don't think you want to sleep on this issue, no pun intended.

The primary concern that should be recognized here, is that

important electrical power systems will go down. These are the root to the seeds of growth in any industrialized nation. However, if this country started to use fusion energy years ago like it should have, instead of being suppressed by the power elite who control the use of fossil fuels, one mile of ordinary rock could energize vast areas of this country for approximately four years. It is less expensive and small areas could produce it without the help of large utility plants.

Once the computer networks fail, the power generated from these plants will shut down electricity in regions all over the world. We are not talking about a plant here or there, but many electric or nuclear generating plants. It is almost like the telephone companies, "We're all connected!"

The longer a utility company remains powered down, the longer it takes to power up. Equipment must constantly be exercised in order to assure that all components are efficiently producing needed electricity. Massive plants have no room or time for cobwebs in their systems. Any commercial enterprise that is dependent upon electricity, and it is hard to think of many that are not, will find themselves out of business in a very short period of time. We are talking about a few days to a few weeks before such businesses come to the reality that they can no longer afford to operate. For most companies, it will be only a few days.

Imagine the scenario for home owners in any industrialized nation, sitting in the dead of winter with no heat because there is no electricity. Many risk death from the possibility of freezing to death. We may not be totally set back to the stone ages, but we will surely be placed into the Dark Ages! Do you have any candles?

About 20%- 40% of energy supplied in the United States alone comes from local nuclear generated power plants. For these facilities, it is critical for them to be Y2K compliant, and yet many have not achieved or come close enough to say they are actually in the final testing stage. By the time that this book is finished or at least read, hopefully they will all be close to compliant. If there are any facilities that claim compliance, ask them for a statement in writing. Surely, they will not give it to you because of the liability implications.

There are approximately 108 nuclear plants nationwide, and all have been warned by the Nuclear Regulatory Commission that they need to be compliant or face the possibility of closure. Let us take it a step further, whereby tests are conducted, and nuclear plant officials say that things are all okay. However, because of oversight, whether it be human error or computer error, a local plant may face a possible meltdown; exposing millions of people to deadly radiation. The question then becomes do you depend on their testing methods and wait to see what the end result brings about, or do you pack up your bags and find another location until you believe that things are operating as normal?

If 10% of power is cut off for an extended period of time, it can create problems; but 20 – 40% can cause major catastrophes. I am not trying to make things sound dim, no pun intended, but one must realize that they must prepare for the worst case scenario. There are many reports circulating about Y2K and energy plants, but you must prepare for any, and I mean any possible flaws that can affect your life drastically. Many of you heard the term before, "If you need something accomplished, don't depend on anyone else but yourself, for it will be you to blame." If things turn out to be fine, then the only thing that you can say to yourself is thank God nothing happened, and at least using the brain that I was blessed with, "I was prepared for the worst that never came". You will not be comfortable if you find yourself caught short because you depended on someone else to hopefully tell you the truth and think and act upon their so-called common sense.

Even if the power grids do not go down overnight, they will eventually stop running off of any reserved power. As noted before in the failure of power grids, you cannot expect equipment to just sit around for a long period of time inactive. Parts can rust, parts can bind up, all because they need to be in continuous operation in order to work properly. For those that have old cars or appliances that have not been in operation for while can understand that fact. If airlines, autos, banks and railways that depend on electricity do not function, such plants will not even be able to obtain supplies.

Many plants need supplies and replacement parts of some sort, whether large or small, every day that they are in operation. Remember how big these facilities are. Power grids are crucial! Society cannot change over to solar power over night, and still it is not nearly as efficient since many things are modified and dependent upon current generated from such power plants.

If you may be missing the point, then let me give you an example. If your local power region goes down due to a lack of compliance, then you can be sure that areas that share the same power grid will go down that are located more than a thousand miles away. Do not forget the domino theory. This will happen whether the other interdependent computers are located on the same grid are compliant or not. It is more than just putting out fires in different locations, it is having systems being set properly in each region to correspond with computers in other regions. In August 1996, there was a major blackout in the Western Power Grid that affected more than eleven states and millions of people. The same thing can happen once again; but with a more devastating effect.

Right now it is not important whether or not they are making the issue of power a primary concern. You now know, and it is up to you to prepare for what other people will not be prepared for. There is only one word for this, and that is the word CRITICAL! Remember, there is not one compliant plant in this country, and there are less than 400 days and 230 Federal days remaining. If these plants go down, they need to be brought back up through resources. If trains around the country stop operating, then fossil-fuels such as coal will not make it to the plants to generate necessary power.

Efficient and Compliant Equipment is Crucial

Subcontractors and thousands of vendors will not be able to adequately supply the plants with necessary materials, because their supply chain has been severely interrupted. This means no replacement parts for heavy equipment and/or computers, let alone miscellaneous supplies that employees need to make transactions with vendors and financial institutions. In order to imagine some of the integral parts that effect the operation of a plant, and if one these things fail, then all systems risk failure simultaneously. Here are just a few:

1.   *security computers*

2.   *plant process (data scan, log, and alarm)*

3.   *safety parameter display system computers*

4.   *radiation monitoring systems*

5.   *dosimeters/readers*

6.   *plant simulators*

7.   *engineering programs*

8.   *communication systems*

9.   *inventory control system*

10.   *technical specification surveillance tracking system*

In hospitals, all major medical facilities will result in interdependent component failures such as EKG machines, X-ray machines, respiratory monitors and other systems that possess embedded computer chips.

Manufacturing Systems such as water and sewer will not be able to direct water to the proper facilities and residences that require it.

Basically:

1.   Consumable water will not be available.

2.   Plumbing equipment will not operate properly, making it difficult to dispose of waste to avoid vermin and disease.

3.   Oil refineries and their equipment will not be able to route oil to the proper storage facilities for commercial and residential heating.

4.   Transportation providers and their equipment for aviation, railways, autos, and marine crafts will become static.

Executive Order 11003

SECTION 1. Scope. The Administrator of the Federal Aviation Agency (hereinafter referred to as the Administrator) shall prepare national emergency plans and develop preparedness programs covering the emergency management of the Nation's civil airports, civil aviation operating facilities, civil aviation services, and civil aircraft other than air carrier aircraft. These plans and programs shall be designed to develop a state of readiness in these areas with respect to all conditions of national emergency, including attack upon the United States.

Air traffic control systems will not be able to navigate airplanes in the proper direction due to radar malfunctions, reservation systems will not be able to track customers and airplane cabin systems will not be able to keep the planes on course. What will the emergency plans consist of? Problems such as these give rise to the above executive orders.

The FAA has major Y2K problems at US airports. Toward the mid or possibly end of 1999, the probability that a lot of other airports run by airline regulators overseas will encounter tremendous problems. In short, the disruption in global air traffic will be very detrimental to world-wide business activity. It is not so much the importance of leisure travel, even though tourism is important, but the delivery of goods and services that play a more critical role in business.

The FAA does not directly oversee the functions of the commercial application software, and are not responsible for any updates. Therefore, they are dependent upon outside vendors to be compliant, and presently such vendors are not. Data sensitive systems are critical to control towers around the world, and any glitches can create some of the most tragic accidents this country or the world has ever seen. As for commercial and military building networks and systems, security systems will not operate properly; providing a breakdown in safety measures that protect employees and patrons. The government is presently preparing to place one half of our armed forces under U.N. control, and all citizen-owned guns banned; hence the myth that gun control is crime control. When you have no weapons to protect your individual self, do you honestly believe you can trust the men who possess the power of the gun to behave accordingly in times of peace or war? How much do you really trust the next man? A security breakdown can mean chaos. Security access will be denied to all, or if not functional, a threat of attack on infrastructure may be evident.

As for communications and security:

1.   Many telephone companies will not be able to route calls, especially emergency calls, because of the fact that their communication switches will be inoperable.

2.   Satellites will not be able to transmit data from point to point, which can consist of critical and strategic weaponry deployment; medical information in emergency cases; and weather tracking.

Embedded Chips

Many people believe that this is just a software issue and can be corrected with a "Bill Gates Fix-it Software Solution". This is not the case. For example, the hardware may contain an embedded chip that is incapable of holding or updating a date in the year 2000 or beyond. Micro and macro computers world-wide suffer from this problem; a problem very difficult to rectify. Computers have many different components that allow them to function properly and with any particular computer system in the world today, the Y2K problem may originate at any level of operation.

A problem could be in the computer hardware, in the operating system, in the language tool that the program was created in, or in the "middleware" which coordinates data and programs for other purposes. Basically, since the date is something used in all levels of computing, systems will most likely become inoperable; making them useless no matter at what level they may fault. One must understand the importance many of these systems have that contain embedded chips. They are too numerous to guess where the problems may turn up in each system. These systems are very old, and naturally the chips would be just as old. Not only are there many systems, but these systems must be disassembled which can take a tremendous amount of time, and then the chips must be located. Once located, embedded chips do not just pop out, but must be removed with special instruments.

Many of these chips are obsolete, therefore many of them cannot be replaced. Technology has rapidly advanced. Embedded chips have become obsolete, and now these older chips are just riding out their time. Many systems today that are more than two years old have fallen into the category of being obsolete.

Such systems cannot easily be reprogrammed, and programmers would find it very difficult to work on these legacy systems. Many of the systems were coded with programming languages that are not really used that much today. Therefore, the main problem of reprogramming the systems with legacy proprietary languages, is practically impossible. Many programmers that once knew the languages are no longer available for work. Many of the programmers are nowhere to be found, retired, or deceased. Younger programmers are busy learning archaic languages, but there is just not enough time.

Chips cannot just be taken out and others that are 2000 compliant just popped in. The chips must be coded properly with programming language that corresponds to the function that the machines were specifically designed for. Overall, programming takes a lot of time.

Programming and Y2K

Many companies with legacy systems have to be coded with millions of line codes. They are not simple sentences, but lines that are divided into thousands of individual programs that operate different components to make the computer function properly overall. These programs divide each component up to perform a different task, and must be done with accuracy to avoid the computer from receiving any inaccurate information.

The long, boring and tedious job of the programmer, is to write instructions for each of these chips line by line. This is not written in English, but in symbols and brackets. As each line is written, a separate task is specified within the entire set of instructions to the computer. As each line is composed, the programmer then types a summary written in English informing any one who follows behind their work, what the code line purpose is, making the computer perform the way it does. Each brief summary is called a "tag" or "documentation".

However, not all programmers in the past followed the discipline of the specific task of documentation; making compliance even more difficult. This could have resulted from laziness, time constraints or specific instructions that informed them that it was not necessary. Whatever, the original people who may have written the code initially, or those that know the language and follow behind the work of others will have problems reading the work. More than one programmer had usually worked on the same task, and trying to decipher a programming language after a period of thirty years is not easy.

In short, before programmers have the language compiled or read by the computer, many inconsistent changes will result and patches implemented to try to alleviate what will be a problem. Although, most computers will not function properly unless they are coded accurately.

There are many software languages such as PASCAL, COBOL, FORTRAN and BASIC for instance, that run on computer mainframes to keep the flow of productivity. There are hundreds of languages and not enough programmers which compounds the problem of not enough time. Although software engineering tools which automate the process are becoming increasingly sophisticated, the work is still very substantial and no tool can entirely automate the process. Besides which, the correction of the system is only part of the job. Extensive testing is required to be sure the system processes information correctly. This is not just for day to day operation, but also so that it can handle transitional situations, such as bank accounts in 1999 and converting to the year 2000.

Companies and government agencies that operate nationally and internationally will affect the lives of millions. Partial compliance in any network doesn't pass muster. They need to be 100% operable. The networks that must function perfectly, include companies and government agencies that are critical to the national, and in some cases, international infrastructure.

The End Result

Military arsenals, railroads, satellites, airlines, traffic facilities and computerized barges all contain non-compliant embedded chips that will force these devices or machines to operate ineffectively. Telephone companies will have switching problems and line disruptions, and eventually, they will all merge as if they are coming together because of a crisis. The same thing will happen with financial institutions and other agencies and big businesses; not to mention oil companies. Their possible excuse about coming together will be the same as all the other major companies merging. Y2K! Many computer operating systems such as Win95, Win98, NT, Unix etc. will experience simultaneous interruptions in their calendar and clock functions that are found on desktops, and networks. Servers as well as operating systems in mainframe computers will not go unscathed. There are more than 100 million computers and counting, with no time to compromise.

Everything such as financial institutions, utilities, government agencies, medical facilities, law enforcement, restaurants and retail establishments recognize that there is not enough time to have their systems compliant or those they do business with to be in compliance. Thus, expect many corporate mergers and acquisitions to take place in all of these areas, while many new companies will be created and many other companies filing under bankruptcy protection. Many things will be changing, whether people want to recognize it or not. To be saved as the bible points out, basically is to be prepared. That is what the Creator gave people brains for; to think with!

Unfortunately, many companies and government agencies are unorganized. Many lack a solution, let alone a plan to deal with the problem. If there is a plan, many have yet to implement it. It has been estimated that more than $600 million dollars will be spent to cope with the problem, but no assurances of success can be made. There are few industry alliances working to solve the problem collectively. Fixing and responding to the Y2K problem requires a cooperative approach, and unless this is done, many companies or agencies will be out of business. It is terrible to note, however, there are many companies still unaware of the problem or its devastating effects. Even more tragic, is the fact that there is no global campaign to assure awareness of the Y2K problem. Many people in this country are still unaware. Many people may even perish because of ignorance.

You think it won't happen? A fictitious crisis you say? This problem is so large in proportion that it poses a serious catastrophic threat to any and all nations that use computers. We are not just talking about industrialized nations of the world, but the entire world will be affected by something so simple, yet so complex in application. In effect, a global depression is inevitable.

Some claim it will be a global recession, however, I must differ. I differ because many authors and or the media wish to sugar coat the truth of the impending crisis. I also differ because of the true history of this country spells out what lays ahead for not only the U.S. but for the world as a whole. It is very difficult to place a percentage on how much of a chance it is that such an event will occur, and for how long; but the evidence I will place forward before you will help you come to your own conclusion.

Furthermore, this depression will not last for only a year or so, but will be one that will continue on for many years for some nations, while others will prosper. This is not a book that is totally fatalistic. By no means do I wish for this to be the case. However, this is a time that you must learn to handle the truth.

This is the Information Age. The United States, has become so dependent upon computers from personal to global economic activities, and unfortunately that it will be affected, most likely for the worst. Information is a valued commodity, and there are few personal or economic activities that can take place without it. Hence, computers that have made the gathering of information so much easier, that it will be very difficult to go back to the manual way of completing tasks.

One must understand that those in key positions in the US government are just waiting for that opportunity to take advantage of the lack of preparedness that they so skillfully helped to create. Their ultimate deeds loom in the dark shadows waiting to shine. After all is said and done, one will realize that it may not have been in the best interest of the country. People truly need to be able to read between the lines. Information Warfare assessments for example, tell people that the military concern is an external threat from terrorist outside the country. The real threat is right here before the American peoples' eyes.

When systems fail, that is when the final assault upon our livelihood begins. Everything from transportation to banking will disrupt lives. Don't let explosions fool you and media convince you of outside terrorism. One must be wise and see through all the smoke that will allow the power elite to achieve their goals. These failures will have the same effect as bombs created by terrorists.

In conclusion, there are many books available on the topic of Y2K. However, most tend to fault in their information as to who created it and when it is likely to strike. Y2K problems have already started, and the culprits of this problem know that it is too late to fix it. Therefore, they know that we can talk about it all we want, but the final assault upon our U.S. Constitution and National Sovereignty has already begun. The only challenge the people of this country have left is proper preparation. For it is written, that many people will miss this Ark also.

CHAPTER TWO

Executive Orders

An **executive order** is an order or regulation issued by the President or some administrative authority under his direction for the purpose of interpreting, implementing, or giving administrative effect to a provision of the Constitution or of some law or treaty. To have effect of law, such orders must be signed and published in the Federal Register. After a period of 15 days, the Executive Order becomes law.

A number of events, major or minor could precipitate what the President may consider a national crisis. For instance, a financial stock market crash could bring about a run on the banks. The President could then invoke "Emergency Banking Regulation No. 1", which would restrict your right to withdraw on your bank account, and "...prohibit withdrawals of cash in any case...that such withdrawal is sought for the purpose of hoarding." Most likely, before such a catastrophe would be incurred, the President has implemented such an order already months in advance. The Y2K problem is a prime example of a coming crises.

The following Executive Orders were combined by Richard Nixon into E.O. No.11490, which activates all of the following under national emergency conditions:

  * EO 10995 provides for the control of the communications media

[Example] Whether it is the threat of a real attack from another country or a domestic attack, the Global Positioning Satellite (GPS System) failure will contribute to such a threat. The date is August 21, 1999 at 11:59 p.m., when the system is scheduled to shut down; and a time extension is not possible. This satellite works in conjunction with the Atomic clock, and synchronizes network computers all over the world. When this satellite's 13 computer chips cease to function, the entire system will become useless. Therefore, not only will the stock market cease to operate, jeopardizing all of your investments, but all telecommunication systems will shut down. Both major and minor component failures such as beepers, cell phones, telephones, modems and most major computer networks in airports, rail lines, utilities and financial institutions that have some relation to telecommunications will create chaos unimaginable.

  * EO 10997 provides for the control of the power, fuels, and minerals

  * EO 10998 provides for the control of all food and farms

* EO 10999 provides for the control of all transportation, highways, etc.

* **EO 11000** provides for the mobilization of all civilians into work brigades under government supervision

* EO 11001 provides for control of all health, education, and welfare

* EO 11002 designates the postmaster to operate a national registration of all persons

* EO 11003 provides for control of all airports and aircraft

* EO 11004 provides for relocation of any populations

* EO 11005 provides for control of railroads, waterways, and public storage facilities

Laws can be implemented in the form of Presidential Executive orders, National Security Council memos, National Security Decision Directives and/or secretly or fraudulently introduced bills. These orders allow for the total control by the government to seize any and all of the above with military force in order to assure peaceful regulation. In other words, to prevent anticipated chaos from the people (masses). Congress in the form of the House and Senate is required to publish the laws that are made. This can be accomplished by having them published in the Congressional Record and the Federal Register. Citizens may contact their Congressmen or obtain them from the Government Printing Office. Pending or passed legislation of National

Security Directives are powerful, hidden and dangerous tools. More than 300 were written during the Reagan Administration, with no more than 50 ever leaking out to undergo public scrutiny. Most Americans have never heard of these subversive weapons that are a major force in the destruction of our U.S. Constitution. (Note: The U.S. Constitution was suspended in 1933 and there is no document on record of it ever being reinstated.)

During the Bush Administration, at around the hour of 3:00 a.m., the Senate Intelligence Authorization Act for Fiscal Year 1991 (S.B. 2834) was brought to a vote by Senator Sam Nunn and passed. Unfortunately, only about ten United States senators were present. The opposition was nowhere to be found at such time. It is a devastating Bill. This bill is very difficult, if not impossible to find through simple research, but thanks to informative authors such as William Cooper, such information has been made available to the public.

The President was given the power to initiate war, appropriate public funds, define foreign policy goals, and decide what is important to our national security. In "Oversight of Intelligence Activities," Title VII, S.B. 2834 it authorized the following:

♦ The President has the power to initiate covert actions.
♦ The bill prevents Congress from ceasing the President's initiation orders of covert operations.

- The bill allows the President to use any federal "departments, agencies, or entities' to function and/or fund a covert operation.
- The President was given the power to use any other nation or private contractor or person to fund or operate a covert action under his discretion or discretion to those he so authorizes.
- The bill has changed the meaning of covert actions to mean operations "necessary to support foreign policy objectives of the United States."
- The bill officially claims the right of the United States to under-handedly interfere in the internal "political, economic, or military affairs" of other countries in direct and flagrant violation of international law.
- The President is required prepare and deliver a written finding to the Intelligence committees of the Congress, and allows the President to omit "extremely sensitive matters."
- The bill authorizes the President to claim executive privilege practically at any time.

If the public does not act soon to disclose such bills and

classified National Security Directives, the overthrow of the U.S. Constitution is inevitable. You are probably asking yourself what are some the agencies that would help in such a diabolical plan? It is just too big of a conspiracy right? Ask FEMA.

FEMA

The Federal Emergency Management Agency (FEMA) is an agency located at Mount Weather just outside of Washington D.C. This agency has a complete parallel government with other Federal departments on site. They include the following: Agriculture, Commerce, HEW, HUD, Interior, Labor, State, Transportation, Treasury, FCC, Selective Service, Federal Power Commission, Civil Service Commission, and the Veterans Administration. Two privately owned corporations also exist, and they are the Federal Reserve Bank and the U.S. Post Office. Further, there is also standby government facility called the Office of the Presidency that includes a different President and a complete set of cabinet officers. FEMA is always ready and waiting for a national crisis 24 hours a day. If and when the President executes an Executive Order for Marital Law and suspends the Constitution, FEMA is prepared to take over local, state, and federal government. It does have the power to take control, and no plan to restore the Constitution has ever been found. Martial Law is "temporary complete control by military authorities imposed on a civilian population when civil unrest, economic crises, a major disaster, war, or other national emergency threatens the public safety as determined by the Commander –in-Chief or the Secretary of Defense."

FEMA official, John Brinkerhoff, made it clear that "Martial law suspends all prior existing law, functions, systems and programs of civil government. By 'all' one means all courts, mails, garbage collection, fire fighting, agriculture, aviation control, schools toll bridges – in a word, all."

According to the U.S. Marine Corps Training Manual FM-21, civilian population control measures may include

a)   establishing restricted areas;

b)   imposition of curfews;

c)   relocation of civilians, including limiting the nature and amount of personal items civilians are allowed to bring to relocation zones;

d)   disarming of civilian population;

e)   supervision of all harvesting, distribution and sale of food;

f)   searches of individuals, vehicles, and dwellings;

g)   offering bribes, rewards and inducements for civilians who will inform the authorities as to the possession of illegal weapons, restricted articles, or unauthorized food that may be in the possession of other civilians;

h)   establishment of clandestine intelligence networks for covert inspection and enforcement of all rules and regulations posted by military or civilian authorities;

i)   restrictions on communications and transportation, radio transmitters may be included among the restricted articles, mail censorship may be imposed, printed matter such as books and newspapers may be established where strict control may be exercised and individual persons may be searched;

j)   all meetings and assemblies will be carefully observed, special permits may be required to hold public meetings, entertainment and sporting events, and religious service;

k)   registration of all civilians may be ordered. Civilian records, business payrolls, and similar sources may be searched to insure that no person escapes registration.

A one-world government would require a world law, a world court, and for enforcement, a world army. With many of the Executive Orders on record, our Constitution and National Sovereignty is in trouble. We need to maintain the ability to defend our nation and ourselves. [Read the Second Amendment of the U.S. Constitution as part of a solution.]

The Communist Manifesto

This is a document created by the Illuminati and was later copied and credited to Karl Marx. This document represents an evil and opposing philosophy of our U.S. Constitution. When the communist philosophy is practiced, citizens unknowingly forfeit their rights for the sake of what evil represents as the "common good," and always ends in a police state. Control is the key concept here.

1.   Abolition of Private Property

2.   Heavy Progressive Income Tax

3.   Abolition of all Rights of Inheritance

4.   Confiscation of property of all Emigrants and Rebels

5.   Central Bank

6.   Government Control of Communications and Transportation

7.   Government Ownership of Factories and Agriculture

8.   Government Control of Labor

9.   Corporate Farms, Regional Planning

10.   Government Control of Education

CHAPTER THREE

The Federal Reserve Bank

"A disordered currency is one of the greatest political evils. It undermines the virtues necessary for the support of the social system, and encourages propensities destructive to its happiness. It wars against industry, frugality and economy, and it fosters evil spirits of extravagance and speculation. Of all the contrivances for cheating the laboring classes of mankind, none has been more effectual than that which deludes them with paper money."

Daniel Webster, Congressional Record (March 4, 1846)

Knowing the truth about the Federal Reserve Bank and how it was conceived is quite disturbing and almost hard to believe, since many Americans have been conditioned to believe that this bank is an arm of the federal government. When a person has been conditioned long enough to believe a lie, they eventually begin to believe the lie to be the truth. The chains of mental slavery have gripped our nation so tightly, that for many people, they have reached a point of no return from their mental bondage. They will continue to live and die with the mental chains; for they should be considered cowards if they have been given the true knowledge, but refuse to take any actions to release themselves.

The Great Corporate Swindle of Our Nation

"Knowledge will forever govern ignorance, and a people who mean to be their own governors must arm themselves with the power which knowledge gives."

James Madison

It was Frank Vanderlip, an agent of the Rockefeller family, who admitted in his memoirs years later that secrecy was of utmost importance for what he and other international bankers were about to do. The task was difficult, however if their objectives were accomplished successfully, the entire nation's economy would be at their mercy.

"Those who create and issue credit and money, direct policies of government, and hold in the hollow of their hands the destiny of the people."
The Right-Honorable Reginald McKenna, Midland Bank of England, Secretary of the Exchequer

The diabolical idea of a quest for total control of a nation's economy had been in the making for many years prior to the creation of the Federal Reserve Bank. In the years of 1913 and 1914, the years of planning to develop a central bank in this country came to fruition. It all started when confidential invitations were distributed by Senator Nelson W. Aldrich to the following individuals: Frank A, Vanderlip, President of the Rockefeller-owned National City Bank; Benjamin Strong of Morgan's Bankers Trust Company; Paul Warburg of Kuhn, Loeb and Company; A. Piatt Andrew, Assistant Secretary of the Treasury; Henry P. Davison of J.P. Morgan and Company and Charles D. Norton, President of First National Bank. Together, they were to all join the Senator in secrecy at a J.P. Morgan resort near Savannah, Georgia called Jekyll Island. Here, with these seven men, the Federal Reserve Bank was conceived.

"Centralization of credit in the hands of the State, by means of a national bank with State capital and an exclusive monopoly."
5th Plank of the Communist Manifesto, by Karl Marx (1848)

The Federal Reserve Bank turned out to be nothing more than the birth of a private Central Bank. However, it was created with the name "Federal" to intentionally deceive and down-play any suspicion as to how these seven men designed a system used by communists in order to usurp the money of the American people without question.

"Capital must protect itself in every way...Debts must be
collected and loans and mortgages foreclosed as soon as
possible. When through a process of law the common people
have lost their homes, they will be more tractable and more
easily governed by the strong arm of the law applied by the
central power of leading financiers. People without homes will
not quarrel with their leaders. This is well known among our
principal men now engaged in forming an imperialism of
capitalism to govern the world.
"Civil Servants Year Book, "The Organizer", Jan. 1934

These seven men decided to promote this unlawful scheme as a
"Regional Reserve" system with what was initially four branches
at the time and has since been increased to twelve throughout the
country: whereby New York was decided to be the key
headquarters.

"By law, the seven members of the Federal Reserve Board are
appointed by the President for a term of fourteen years each. In
spite of the incredible length of these appointments,
nevertheless, they are supposed to create the illusion that the
people, acting through their elected leaders, have some voice in
the nation's monetary policies. In practice, however, every

President since the beginning of the Federal Reserve System has appointed only those men who are congenial to the financial interests of the international banking dynasties. There have been no exceptions."

The Capitalist Conspiracy, G. Edward Griffin

Influential Key Players

The power that the "illuminati" or so-called "billionaire bankers" had in the early days are the same they still possess today. Their power affects the masses, and is used in such a way to keep them in such a powerful position forever. It was J.P. Morgan who created an artificial panic in 1907, and through his influential control in the stock market, he was later instrumental in leading the nation into WW1 without the country ever knowing it. The outbreak of war was brewing for years, and when Morgan believed that the loans he made to the British government were in jeopardy, war was declared. All financial manipulations in America were for self-interest; J.P. Morgan's loans were just an example. Many lives were lost because of what was in part one man's personal interest and not one of a nation's interest. It was this amount of power that helped convince legislators to pass the Federal Reserve Act.

"God would not have created sheep, unless he had intended them to be shorn."

J.P. Morgan

Morgan continued his reign of power by financing socialist groups that would help lead the way to bringing about a One-World Government. To accomplish this in part, actions were necessary to centralize many key national financial institutions. Another powerful individual that had a great influence in accomplishing this major deception of the people was that of Colonel Edward Mandel House. House was educated in Britain and was the son of a representative in England with major financial interests in America. House never served a day in the military and only received the title Colonel as an honorarium.

So powerful was House, that it was said that he controlled President Wilson from behind the scenes. Documenting some of the facts about House, we can look at a book he authored titled Philip Dru - Administrator.

"...our Constitution and our laws...are not only obsolete, but even grotesque."

Colonel Edward Mandel House

In this book written by House, he made a thinly fictionalized account about establishing "socialism as dreamed by Karl Marx." This book not only established his view of socialism, but his real life view for the constitutional passage of the 16th Amendment allowing for a graduated income tax and a central bank like the Federal Reserve. With a central bank, House noted that it would be easy to create "a flexible (inflatable paper) currency."

His plan, and to use his own words, "a conspiracy," would seek to achieve:

- The establishment of a central bank;

- A progressive graduated income tax; and

- Control of both political parties in the U.S.

If the reader is able to read The Communist Manifesto by Karl Marx, the reader will find that a central bank and graduated income tax are two of the ten planks listed in Marx's book.

"Banking institutions, paper money, and paper speculation are capable of undermining the nation's stability and could be a danger in time of war. The Constitution does not empower the Congress to establish a National Bank. Rather than trust the nation's currency to private hands, the circulating medium

should be restored to the nation itself to whom it belongs."

Thomas Jefferson

The Federal Reserve Act

"The Federal Reserve Banks are privately owned, locally controlled corporations"

Lewis vs. U.S., 680 F.2d 1239, 1241 (1982)

On December 22, 1913 by a vote of 298 to 60 in the House, and 43 to 25 in the Senate, The Federal Reserve Act was passed.

"This act establishes the most gigantic trust on earth... When the President signs this act, the invisible government by the money power, proven to exist by the Money Trust Investigation, will be legalized...The new law will create inflation whenever the trusts want inflation..."

Charles A. Lindbergh, Sr.

Another Congressman who was aware of what these men really did to the nation, brought about these famous words and five attempts on his life. Unfortunately, the fifth attempt was successful. The congressman declared:

"...we have in this country one of the most corrupt institutions

the world has every known. I refer to the Federal Reserve Board and the Federal Reserve Banks... This evil institution has impoverished and ruined the people of the United States... Some people think the Federal Reserve Banks are United States Government institutions...They are not government institutions. They are private credit monopolies which prey upon the people of these United States for the benefit of themselves and their foreign customers..."

"In this dark crew of financial pirates there are those who would cut a man's throat to get a dollar out of his pocket."

"Every effort has been made by the Federal Reserve Board to conceal its powers, but the truth is...the Fed has usurped the government. It controls everything here (Congress) and it controls all our foreign relations. It makes and breaks governments at will.

"The Federal Reserve (Banks) are one of the most corrupt institutions, the world has ever seen. There is not a man, within the sound of my voice, who does not know that this Nation is run by the International Bankers".

"... The Fed has cheated the Government of the United States and the people of the United States out of enough money to pay the Nation's debt.... The wealth of these United States and the

working capital have been taken away from them and has either been locked in the vaults of certain banks and the great corporations or exported to foreign countries for the benefit of foreign customers of these banks and corporations. So far as the people of the United States are concerned, the cupboard is bare."

Congressman Louis T. McFadden, Chairman of the House Banking and Currency Committee

"From a legal standpoint these banks are private corporations, organized under a special act of 'Congress, namely, the Federal Reserve Act.   They are not in the strict sense of the word, 'Government banks'."

William P.G. Harding, Governor of the Federal Reserve Board.

The power of this private banking institution quickly gained ground and eventually brought the country to its knees. During the periods of 1923 - 1929 the Federal Reserve Bank, which continues today, to have control over our nation's money supply. The bank during the 1920's inflated the supply of money by sixty two percent, actually devaluing the dollar. This in turn sent the stock market to steeply climb upward. Eventually these same private bankers or international bankers that made up the Federal Reserve tightened the noose on the money supply; creating an economic collapse known as the Great Depression.

This in fact happened despite warnings of a stock market crash in the House and Senate. The brakes were never applied to avoid such, and in 1929 the crash of the century struck. The pillage of America began in earnest during the Depression. The Fed deflated (reduced) the money supply, forcing thousands into bankruptcy and foreclosure.

"It (the depression) was not accidental. It was a carefully contrived occurrence... The international bankers sought to bring about a condition of despair here so that they might emerge as the rulers of us all."

Louis T. McFadden, Chairman of the House Banking and Currency Committee

Soon after McFadden left office, Congressman Lindbergh went on to become Chairman. As the Congressman stated:

"From now on depressions will be scientifically created. Using a central bank to create alternate periods of inflation and deflation and thus whipsawing the public for vast profits, had been worked out by the international bankers to an exact science."

Charles A. Lindbergh Sr.

The Federal Reserve Bank then became responsible for issuing notes instead of coins as a form of legal tender. Federal Reserve Notes, under the Constitution are not considered valid money.

Article 1, Section 8, Clause 5 says that: *[Only] Congress has the power to..."coin money, regulate the value thereof...and fix the standard of weights and measures.*
United States Constitution

According to Article 1, Section 10, Clause 1 of the Constitution: "No state shall make anything but gold and silver coins a tender payment of debts." Therefore, since Federal Reserve notes are only paper, then they should not be considered constitutionally sound money. Some say that carrying around gold and silver coinage is too heavy and bulky; and it is a sound goldsmith theory as to why we should carry around paper as money. Although, through the manipulation of currency with one such method as "fractional reserve banking," Federal Reserve notes are no longer backed by gold or silver. Due to this fact, this should enlighten you as to what appears to be qualified substitutes for constitutionally sound money, (paper dollars) are not. Gold, silver and notes that could produce such metals on demand, have now been replaced with more worthless paper notes. These notes are nothing more than promises to pay money; and unfortunately now considered a medium of exchange. Further, bankers of today use computer book entries,

an easier method than printing money and distributing it from
hand to hand or vault to vault. With this method, it is even
easier to inflate an amount of money in an account without a
precious metal backing.

*"Private fortunes, in the present state of our circulation, are at
the mercy of those self-created money lenders, and are
prostrated by the floods of nominal money with which their
avarice deluges us."*

Thomas Jefferson to John W. Eppes, 1813. ME 13:276

The same bankers who corrupted the system, continue to corrupt
the lives of the American people. They systematically place all
Americans in debt with usurious interest. Americans are in so
deep, that for most, there is no chance for them to ever pay their
way out of debt.

*"Those few who can understand the system (check book money
and credit) will either be so interested in its profits, or so
dependent on it favors, that there will be little opposition from
that class, while on the other hand, the great body of people
mentally incapable of comprehending the tremendous
advantage that capital derives from the system, will bear it
burdens without complaint, and perhaps without even suspecting
that the system is inimical to their interests."*

Rothschilds Brothers of London

The Federal Reserve Bank is a Powerful Corporation

The Federal Reserve Banks are a privately owned consortium controlled by major stock-holding banks. This small group decides the fates of hundreds of millions of people by their financial policies and maneuvers. The Fed is a bank that has never been audited, and has resisted all attempts to do so. There were in fact people other than congressmen who tried to battle the Federal Reserve Bank, but their attempts failed. Take Lt. Col. Archibald Roberts who was the Director of Committee to Restore the Constitution, began a campaign on March 30, 1971, testifying before legislators in Wisconsin about the improprieties and fraud surrounding the Federal Reserve Bank, but was unsuccessful in achieving positive action.

"In the U.S. today, we have in effect, two governments...we have the duly constituted government...then we have an independent, uncontrolled and uncoordinated government in the Federal Reserve System, operating the money powers which are reserved to the Congress by the Constitution."
Congressman Wright Patman, Chairman of House Banking Committee (in the 60's)

You will never find the Federal Reserve Bank listed in phone directories under "government offices". It is a private corporation owned by approximately 300 Class A stockholders. The controlling interest is held by less than a dozen international bankers, whose names, until recently, were one of the best-kept secrets of international finance:

Rothschild Banks of London & Berlin

Lehman Bros. Bank of N.Y.

Lazard Bros. Banks of Paris

Former Kuhn, Loeb Bank of N.Y.

Israel Moses Sief Banks of Italy

Chase Manhattan Bank of N.Y.

Warburg Bank of Hamburg & Amsterdam

Goldman, Sachs Bank of N.Y.

"Slavery is likely to be abolished by the war power and all chattel slavery abolished. This I and my European friends are in favor of, for slavery is but the owning of labor and carries with it the care of the laborers, while the European plan, led on by England, is that capital shall control labor by controlling wages. The great debt that the capitalists will see to it is made out of the war, must be used as a means to control the volume of

money. To accomplish this the bonds must be used as a banking basis. We are now waiting for the Secretary of the Treasury to make this recommendation to Congress. It will not do to allow the greenback, as it is called, to circulate as money any length of time, as we can not control that. But we can control the bonds and through them the bank issues."

From a Secret Agent - 1862

It's All About the Money

It is not a secret as to how our nation's money is created. It is only a secret to those who do not wish to research how it works. It can basically be described in a nutshell.

"As we have advised, the Federal Reserve is currently paying the Bureau approximately $23 for each 1,000 notes printed. This does include the cost of printing, paper, ink, labor, etc. Therefore, 10,000 notes of any denomination, including the $100 note would cost the Federal Reserve $230. In addition, the Federal Reserve must secure a pledge of collateral equal to the face value of the notes"

William H. Ferkler, Manager Public Affairs, Dept. of Treasury, Bureau of Engraving & Printing

The Bureau of Engraving and Printing prints the money. The Federal Reserve then buys the bills from the United States Mint for 23 dollars per 1000 notes for a total cost of 230 dollars per 10,000 notes. Next, they deposit this money at face value into their own account. They then purchase US Treasury obligations such as T-Bills, T-Bonds, and T-Notes and pay the money they just received right back to the US Department of Treasury, which distributes it into the economy. The Federal Reserve Banks, previously having nothing, now have the full face value of the money printed in their account. The Federal Reserve then secures a pledge of collateral equal to the face value of the notes. Additionally, they will receive the interest which will be paid on this money.

"Give me the power to issue a nation's money; then I do care not who makes the law."

Mayer Amschel Rothschild, I--1744-1812

It is not our Congress that determines the value of our current dollar. The value of the American dollar is determined in secrecy by officials of the Federal Reserve Bank. Presently, this country exchanges notes that are promises to pay money, because the Federal Reserve Notes are not money. Furthermore, instead of minting its own money, the government believes in borrowing its national currency and paying usurious interest to a private bank; namely the Federal Reserve Bank. The Federal Reserve Bank was unconstitutionally given the power to print money. This Central Bank should not be printing money for us, but the government should be printing the amount of money it needs backed by gold and silver, from its own National Treasury.

"Congress cannot delegate or sign over its authority to any individual, corporation or foreign nation."
16th *Corpus Juris Secundum*, Section 141

Congress does in fact have the power to take back the authority granted the Federal Reserve. There are easy ways of doing this, and after doing some of your own research, you the people should rain on the bankers parade by going straight to Congress and forcing your representative not to "sell out" in representing the United States of America.

"The general rule is that an unconstitutional statute, whether federal or state, though having the form and name of law, is in reality no law, but is wholly void, and ineffective for any purpose, since unconstitutionality dates from the time of its enactment, and not merely from the date of decision so branding it. No one is bound to obey an unconstitutional law and no courts are bound to enforce it."
16th *American Jurisprudence*, Section 25, 2nd *Edition*.

(Doesn't the above statement make you think about Gun Control Laws in each state and the Second Amendment's Right to Bear Arms. Remember, the Constitution, unless amended is the Supreme Law of the Land.)

The fiat dollar is no longer backed by gold. What was once called "fractional Reserve banking" turned into what is called "zero reserve banking." At this time, all of the precious metals that could be used for the U.S. monetary system is now stored securely in vaults five floors beneath the Federal Reserve Bank of New York. Such precious metals have been stolen by the private bankers of the Federal Reserve. America no longer owns gold for national spending and only full faith and credit of the American people backs the fiat dollar.

"Our public credit is good, but the abundance of paper has produced a spirit of gambling in the funds, which has laid up our ships at the wharves as too slow instruments of profit, and has even disarmed the hand of the tailor of his needle and thimble. They say the evil will cure itself. I wish it may; but I

have rarely seen a gamester cured, even by the disasters of his vocation."

Thomas Jefferson to Gouverneur Morris, 1791. ME 8:241

A question one may ask as to why this country should worry about the use of gold coins as the monetary medium of exchange? One of my answers are that many countries around the world still refuse to use paper money, and there may come a time that you or a family may need to travel afar. Another answer would be, that this precious metal remains a constant medium of exchange and cannot be devalued by the government; a method of reducing your spending power. Thus, when the Legal Tender Act was implemented, the U.S. Treasury began issuing certificates and notes to any people who chose to trade in their coins in order for them to conduct large business deals or make substantial payments in a less cumbersome manner. These certificates and notes were actually considered dollars equivalent to the amount of gold or silver that was traded in to banks or their local goldsmith. Therefore, a person was able to take such certificates or notes and redeem their value in gold or silver coinage. In other words, such notes and certificates were "worth their weight in gold." All had changed when the international bankers came on to the scene.

"We are now taught to believe that legerdemain tricks upon paper can produce as solid wealth as hard labor in the earth. It

is vain for common sense to urge that nothing can produce but nothing; that it is an idle dream to believe in a philosopher's stone which is to turn everything into gold, and to redeem man from the original sentence of his Maker, 'in the sweat of his brow shall he eat his bread.'"

Thomas Jefferson to Charles Yancey, 1816. ME 14:381

People understood the fact that certificates and notes passed around as money were figuratively not worth anything. They were nothing more than promissory notes that gave assurance that a certain sum of dollars were available on deposit at the goldsmith institution or bank, that issued the promissory notes initially. However, whenever the notes were presented by the holders to either of the two institutions, or bearer on demand, the value printed on the face of the note was expected to be redeemed.

The interest amount owed to the national and international bankers are not only usurious, but so numerous in size that the money the Federal Government collects in taxes is totally usurped by the interest payments alone; leaving nothing to actually spend on the necessary services such as roads, buildings, transit systems etc.

Let's use an example to show you how silly the deeds Congress performs is by giving away its power to create money. Say there is no money left for necessary federal projects because all of the citizens' money has gone to interest payments. Now, suppose the Federal Government must now have money created. They quickly make a call upon the corporation known as the Federal Reserve Bank. Without a second thought, and since the Federal Reserve Bank is a private corporation in business solely to make a profit, it does not act in the interest of the people. It is the Federal Reserve Bank that hurriedly creates the money and lends it to the Federal Government with a promise in writing to pay it back along with a usurious interest fee.

Piracy In Effect

"... The merchants were the powers of the earth, and their sorceries deceived all nations."
Revelation 18:23

After an agreement to pay the sum certain interest fee along with the requested loan amount of say for example $10,000,000, Congress then notifies the U.S. Treasury Department and orders them to print $10,000,000 in U.S. Bonds. These bonds are then exchanged for the borrowed amount in cash (which in reality may only cost them about $10,000 in total to print by the Federal

Reserve Bank.)

"Let us see how a bank creates a mortgage lien on a house: A man who owns a building lot and has $20,000 needs an additional $75,000 to build a house. If the banker finds the collateral sufficient, he may credit the man's checking accounting with $80,000 – minus several 'points' for expenses – against which checks can be written to pay for construction. When the house is completed, it will have a thirty-year lien at 12 or 15 percent. After working 30 years to liquidate the debt, the owner will have paid perhaps $300,000 for something that did not cost the bankers a dime in the first place. This is the magic of fractional reserve banking."

The Battle for the Constitution, Dr. Martin A. Larson

The Federal Government can now move forward with their spending plan, whatever it may be, and in some cases it may be salaries for all Federal employees. Yes, the Federal government can go ahead with their spending plan using the sweat off your back; the taxpayer.

"If all the bank loans were paid, no one would have a bank deposit and there would not be a dollar or coin or currency in

circulation. This is a staggering thought. We are completely dependent on the commercial banks. Someone has to borrow every dollar we have in circulation. If the banks create ample synthetic money, we are prosperous; if not, we starve. We are absolutely without a permanent money system. When one gets a complete grasp of the picture, the tragic absurdity of our hopeless position is almost incredible, but there it is. It is the most important that our present civilization may collapse unless it becomes widely understood and the defects remedied very soon."

Robert Hemphill, former Credit Manager, Fed Bank of Atlanta (In testimony before the Senate)

Now you should ask yourself should such transactions be legal? This country has slipped so far into indebtedness that not only might the U.S. declare bankruptcy again, even though it is already still in the state of bankruptcy currently, this may be the final chapter of the U.S. Constitution since the bankers will become the authoritative role players. Why you might ask, because they know and will later own this beautiful country outright; disposing of anyone who is not ready, willing and able to work for little or no wages. I will let you be the judge of what the word disposal means. My definition may be too shocking.

"In the case of the federal government, we can print money to

pay for our folly for a time. But we will just continue to debase our currency, and then we'll have financial collapse. That is the road we are on today. That is the direction in which the 'humanitarians' are leading us. But there is nothing 'humanitarian' about the collapse of a great individual civilization. There is nothing 'humanitarian' about the dictatorship that must inevitably take over as terrified people cry out for leadership. There is nothing 'humanitarian' about the loss of freedom. That is why we must be concerned about the cancerous growth of government and its steady devouring of our citizens' productive energies... I speak of this so insistently because I hear no one discussing this danger. Congress does not discuss it. The press does not discuss it. Look around us – the press isn't even here! The people do not discuss it – they are unaware of it. No counter-force in America is being mobilized to fight this danger. The battle is being lost, and not a shot is being fired."

Congressman William E. Simon, in a speech to the House of Representatives (April 30, 1976).

The National Debt is recorded publicly in the amount of approximately $7,000,000,000 (trillion) dollars, at close to 10% interest per annually. The true figure may be around thirty to forty trillion dollars. In any event, most if not all of the income taxes you pay, are towards interest payments. That would amount to about $700 billion dollars per year. You are paying this money to people you don't even know.

"We are now in chapter 11. Members of Congress are official trustees presiding over the greatest reorganization of any bankrupt entity in world history – the United States Government. We are setting forth hopefully, a blueprint for our future. There are some who say that it is our coroner's report that will lead to our demise."
Congressman James Traficant, House Record 1303 (March 17, 1993)

As a citizen of the United States, you are paying interest to the same bankers that you borrowed money for your car, house, boat, or business. Think about the long term they give you to pay the money and usurious interest fee, and how much you actually are paying for that car, house, boat or business.

"A great industrial nation is controlled by its system of credit. Our system of credit is concentrated. The growth of the Nation and all our activities are in the hands of a few men. We have come to be one of the worst ruled, one of the most completely controlled and dominated governments in the world--no longer a government of free opinion, no longer a government of conviction, and vote of the majority, but a government by the

opinion and duress, of small groups of dominant men."
President Woodrow Wilson

A note: Just before the death of President Woodrow Wilson, it was reported (though I have not seen documented proof) that he claimed to have been "deceived" and that "I have betrayed my Country", whereby he was referring to the Federal Reserve Act that was passed during his term as President. However, it is also fair to note that no documentation of these words have ever been found.

"Banking was conceived in iniquity, and was born in sin. The Bankers own the Earth. Take it away from them, but leave them the power to create deposits, and with the flick of the pen, they will create enough deposits, to buy it back again. However, take it away from them, and all the great fortunes like mine will disappear, and they ought to disappear, for this would be a happier and better world to live in. But if you wish to remain the slaves of Bankers, and pay the cost of your own slavery, let them continue to create deposits."
Sir Josiah Stamp, (President of the Bank of England)

A Problem of Indebtedness and Debauchery

To overcome this financial problem, and open up the way for the war to be prolonged so that the fullest financial and political benefits could be derived from it, "the bankers secretly devised a scheme by which their (loan) obligations could be met by fiat money (so -called Treasury Notes)."

*"There [is a measure] which if not taken we are undone...[It is] to cease borrowing money and to pay off the national debt. If this cannot be done without dismissing the army and putting the ships out of commission, haul them up high and dry and reduce the army to the lowest point at which it was ever established. There does not exist an engine so corruptive of the government and so demoralizing of the nation as a public debt. It will bring on us more ruin at home than all the enemies from abroad against whom this army and navy are to protect us." **Thomas Jefferson to Nathaniel Macon, 1821.***

An increase in un-backed paper money can lead to many things, but the commonly known problem is staggering inflation. Inflation has and can once again ruin lives just through the devastating effects that are incurred to their savings, checking deposits, mortgages, insurance, mutual funds, bond holdings etc.

"Conspiracies to seize the power of government are as old as the institutions of government."
Franklin Delano Roosevelt

This planned debauchery of money by the international bankers had an added impact, one which fitted in perfectly with their plans to destroy the 'old world order' in order to make way for the Illuminati's New World Order. International bankers had come to the conclusion that money and/or deposit loan accounts are the root of all power. So much power that, they have been able to convince people to surrender their money or actual wealth created by sweat and labor, in turn for a promise by the international bankers for more money. Basically, people would put up their real property or savings such as a 401K, IRA, Keogh, Mutual Fund, etc. as collateral; for a piece of paper that is nothing more than a promissory note: in other words an IOU.

"To preserve [the] independence [of the people,] we must not let our rulers load us with perpetual debt. We must make our election between economy and liberty, or profusion and servitude. If we run into such debts as that we must be taxed in our meat and in our drink, in our necessaries and our comforts,

in our labors and our amusements, for our callings and our creeds, as the people of England are, our people, like them, must come to labor sixteen hours in the twenty-four, give the earnings of fifteen of these to the government for their debts and daily expenses, and the sixteenth being insufficient to afford us bread, we must live, as they now do, on oatmeal and potatoes, have no time to think, no means of calling the mismanagers to account, but be glad to obtain subsistence by hiring ourselves to rivet their chains on the necks of our fellow-sufferers."
Thomas Jefferson to Samuel Kercheval, 1816. ME 15:39

No longer is there real compensation for work completed, but paper stating the promise to pay. There are no hard assets or what may be considered tangibles given in return for a person's labor. The American people have been conned for years, and are still in a state of unawareness. Times have not changed, and the people have no idea of what is available in Gold Reserves, (est. at a little more than $12 billion dollars). People still continue to accept fiat paper that has been created without an actual secured backing of reserves. In other words, more paper was printed than what the bankers actually had in reserve. If all the people who became aware of such debauchery, and demanded coinage for their notes at the same time, bankers would not be able to provide it. A scam can only go on only for so long. However, it has thus gone on long enough for other countries to lose faith in business with our paper economy nation. The bankers created such a tremendous confidence in the promissory notes that people in the past, as they do today, have become overconfident and believe this economy will last forever. Failing to realize that bankers at any time can make money unavailable, pull the plug on the economy, and collect collateral through common law or admiralty contracts signed by parties contracted with them. The bankers would even foreclose on the collateral put up by the laborer just to satisfy the debt. It is the bankers who create fiction (paper money) and foreclose on real tangible assets. If you, a taxpayer in this country tried to conduct the same activities as the bankers, you would be criminally prosecuted.

*"That we are overdone with banking institutions which have banished the precious metals and substituted a more fluctuating and unsafe medium, that these have withdrawn capital from useful improvements and employments to nourish idleness, that the wars of the world have swollen our commerce beyond the wholesome limits of exchanging our own productions for our own wants, and that, for the emolument of a small proportion of our society who prefer these demoralizing pursuits to labors useful to the whole, the peace of the whole is endangered and all our present difficulties produced, are evils more easily to be deplored than remedied." --**Thomas Jefferson to Abbe Salimankis, 1810. ME 12:379***

Greed

"[The] Bank of the United States... is one of the most deadly hostility existing, against the principles and form of our Constitution... An institution like this, penetrating by its branches every part of the Union, acting by command and in phalanx, may, in a critical moment, upset the government. I deem no government safe which is under the vassalage of any self-constituted authorities, or any other authority than that of the nation, or its regular functionaries. What an obstruction could not this bank of the United States, with all its branch banks, be in time of war! It might dictate to us the peace we should accept, or withdraw its aids. Ought we then to give further growth to an institution so powerful, so hostile?"
Thomas Jefferson to Albert Gallatin, 1803. ME 10:437

It is the obsession with wealth by the public and their total confidence in paper promissory notes, which do not equal the value of actual coinage or property, to allow paper money to be printed without limitation. Money printed without limitation creates inflation without proper backing of gold, silver, platinum, etc. The same holds true of such printing of money that is not backed by proper real production of goods and services. Look

at all the 20, 30 and 50 billion dollar deals that the big companies
are flaunting and boasting about; money that is not even
available.

*"Whereas I charge them, jointly and severally, with the crime of
having treasonably conspired and acted against the peace and
acted against the peace and security of the United States and
having treasonably conspired to destroy constitutional
government in the United States."*
**Congressman Louis T. McFadden Chairman of House
Banking and Currency Committee**

The big international bankers can therefore position the economy
at will through warfare, restriction on resources or technology,
or just outright temporarily pull the plug on the stock mark.
When the latter happens, people begin to panic and sell off. A
depression is easily created, and the rich buy everything in the
stock market for a song and a dance; scooping up stocks for
practically nothing. As they buy up, the economy terribly
suffers, and they become richer than ever before. Many cannot
see that the time is due for them to do it again; this time
permanently separating the classes of wealth.

"I believe that if the people of this nation fully understood what Congress has done to them over the past 49 years, they would move on Washington, they would not wait for an election... It adds up to a preconceived plan to destroy the economic and social independence of the United States."

Senator George W. Malone, speaking before Congress about the Federal Reserve Bank (1962)

In summary, these problems should be addressed and can be met. Once again we turn to the quote of one of the most loyal presidents this country has ever had.

"In order to be able to meet a general combination of the banks against us in a critical emergency, could we not make a beginning towards an independent use of our own money, towards holding our own bank in all the deposits where it is received, and letting the treasurer give his draft or note for payment at any particular place, which, in a well-conducted government, ought to have as much credit as any private draft or bank note or bill, and would give us the same facilities which we derive from the banks?"

Thomas Jefferson to Albert Gallatin, 1803. ME 10:439

CHAPTER FOUR

INTERNAL REVENUE SERVICE

"Our tax system is based upon voluntary assessment and payment, not upon distraint."
U.S. Supreme Court in Flora v. United States, 362 U.S. 145

All individuals who file a tax return waive their Fifth Amendment Rights. The Government cannot require individuals to waive their Fifth Amendment Rights. Therefore, the Government cannot compel individuals to file income tax returns.

Thanks to the research of well known author William Cooper, many revelations were made regarding this taxing entity known as the Internal Revenue Service. The re-birth of the Internal Revenue Service came about in the year of 1953. The original name was the Bureau of Internal Revenue which was changed by the Secretary of the Treasury.

"Single acts of tyranny may be ascribed to the accidental opinion of a day. But a series of oppressions, begun at a distinguished period, and pursued unalterably through every change of ministers (administrations), too plainly proves a deliberate systematic plan of reducing us to slavery."
Thomas Jefferson

No congressional records or authorizations from the President to make the change from the BIR to the IRS has ever been found. Apparently after more research, it was revealed that it is possible that the Secretary exercised his authority as the trustee of Puerto Rico Trust #62 (Internal Revenue) (see <u>31 USC sec. 1321</u>) whereby it is a fact that the Secretary operates as the Secretary of Treasury of Puerto Rico.

In fact, neither did the constitution nor Congress create the "Bureau of Internal Revenue." (see Federal Register at 36 F.R. 849-890; 37 F.R. 489-490; and in Internal Revenue Manual 1100 at 1111.2). The IRS is nothing more than a [PRIVATE TRUST]. They are not a Federal Agency and no one has ever been given access to find out who owns it, only the owners know who own the agency. They do not have any Delegation of

Authority among the Several States (The United States).
Information reveals that both the IRS and the Bureau of Alcohol,
Tobacco and Firearms are not found listed as government
agencies or affiliated with the United States Department of the
Treasury. Research has proven valuable, and you may do a little
research on your own and find the same thing if not more. You
can find more information located in the index of Chapter 3, Title
31 of the United States Code.

"Our federal system is, in short, utterly impossible, utterly
unjust and completely counter-productive. The present system
of taxation reeks with injustice and is fundamentally un-
American. It has earned a rebellion and it's time we rebelled!"
President Ronald Reagan, Williamsburg, Virginia (May 1983)

Thus, Americans have not been giving their money for taxes to
an agency that is an arm of the federal government. This is the
same agency that harasses people, garnishes paychecks, seizes
property etc. (Plank no.1 of the Communist Manifesto is
"abolition of private property". Private property can represent
homes, savings, pensions etc). In many cases it is
unconstitutional, and the use of many of their methods are
criminal. A criminal complaint was filed with the attorney general
of Oklahoma, W.A. Drew Edmondson. The complaint was filed
against an Enid-based revenue officer, whereby at no time did
the Internal Revenue Service make claim denying the allegation

that they were in fact an agency of Treasury, Puerto Rico. A short time thereafter, further criminal complaints were filed with a United States district court for the District of Northern Oklahoma, grand jury in Tulsa. Attorney General Edmondson, the United States Attorney Office and the Internal Revenue Service have received filings of the criminal complaints, and not one of the three mentioned have denied the allegations regarding the complaints. (United States of America v. Kenney F. Moore, et al, 95 CR-129C).

It was the founding Fathers of this country that created a constitutional Republic as our form of government. The United States Constitution gives limited powers to the federal government. Any powers that were not given to the United States, are reserved to the States respectively or to the People of the States. The States or then considered the Union, was formed to be the servant of the People and not the People servants of the Union. In Article VI, Clause 2, our founding fathers stated that the United States Constitution is the Supreme Law of the Land!

"Who would believe the ironic truth that the cooperative taxpayer fares much worse than the individual who relies upon his constitutional rights."
Federal Judge Cummings in United States v. Dickerson, 413

F.2d 1117 (1969)

The IRS and Taxing

"Nobody owes any public duty to pay more than the law demands. Taxes are enforced extortions, not voluntary contributions."

Justice Felix Frankfurter in Atlantic Coast Line v. Phillips, 332 U.S. 168, 172-73

It is the Constitution that delegates authority to Congress to lay and collect taxes to pay the debts of the government; not a private trust such as the IRS. Congress has been granted authority to collect via DIRECT TAXES, which are subject to the rule of apportionment among the States of the Union. This means for example that if Congress said that tax for the year is $100.00, then everyone that is a U.S. Citizen or Permanent Resident Alien, regardless of income is required to pay $100.00 for the year.

The second class of taxes is INDIRECT TAXES, which include imposts, duties and excises, subject to the rule of uniformity. Therefore, the government is not, and I repeat, not allowed to deviate from the two classes of taxes mentioned above and tax U.S. Citizens or Permanent Resident Aliens of the United States

of America, DIRECTLY. It is a master/servant relationship that
was intended by the founding fathers and the People were and
are to be the master of the government. (<u>Article 1, section 2,
clause 3 of the U.S.C.</u>)

This Court in the past and is continuing to stray away from this
scope of limitation and are acting as a "social engineer"
amending and changing Constitutional meanings. In other words,
the Court has taken it upon themselves to go beyond the scope
of just interpreting the laws. The only method of lawfully
altering, abolishing or changing the Constitution in any way, is
through Article 5 of the Constitution. However, the American
People have been indoctrinated with the words of so-called
experts in the media that it is an old and out dated document;
and that justifies any changes to laws that are within the scope of
the Constitution.

In 1916, the U.S. Supreme Court ruled that the 16th Amendment
did not change the United States Constitution. The Court said
that <u>Article 1, section2, clause 3, and Article 1, section 9, clause
4</u>, was not repealed or altered; and the U.S. Constitution cannot
conflict with itself. The Court went on further to say that the
16th Amendment merely prevented the "income duty" from being
taken out of the category of Indirect Taxation.
(<u>Brushaber v. Union Pacific R.R. Co., 240 US, p.16</u>)

As you can see, the Court noted that the Constitutional Amendment was not valid. Therefore the 16th Amendment of the Constitution which was never properly ratified by ¾ of the States to begin with, and represents an "Income Tax Amendment" on its face, was found to be null and void because the Constitution was not in fact changed. Two great authors who spent time investigating these facts are Bill Benson and Red Beckman. Their research is worth mention because it was not only extensive, but exhaustive. In their book, <u>The Law That Never Was</u>, Vols. 1& 2, demonstrates the fact of the invalid ratification of the 16th Amendment. This is not to say that this amendment may not have any relevance or bearing on us today, however, upon your own research you will be able to make a positive determination.

The 16th Amendment was never properly ratified. This has been proven in court. Two of the 36 states that had allegedly ratified the amendment were California and Kentucky, however, no record of California's vote can be found recorded. As for the state of Kentucky, legislators voted against it 22-9. Therefore, not enough states voted in favor of the amendment and that constitutes that it is invalid. (U.S.C. Article V).

"A proper regard for its genesis, as well as its very clear language, requires also that this [16th] Amendment shall not be

extended by loose construction, so as to repeal or modify, except as applied to income, those provisions of the constitution that require an apportionment according to population for direct taxes upon property real and personal. This limitation still has an appropriate and important function, and is not be overridden by Congress or disregarded by the courts."
Eisner v. Macomber, 252 US 189, 206

If the 16th Amendment was considered to be valid, it was the U.S. Supreme Court that held that it did not in fact create any new powers of taxation. The U.S. Constitution provides for the government to operate without personal income taxation. That is why the founding fathers stipulated that imposts, duties, and excises would provide the necessary funding for government expenditures.(Article I, Section 8, Clause I).

This is where personal income taxes go:
"100% of what is collected is absorbed solely by interest on the Federal Debt and by Federal transfer payments. In other words, all individual income tax revenues are gone before one nickel is spent on the services taxpayers expect from their government."
The 1984 Grace Commission, Report to President Reagan
When you receive your cancelled check back from your bank after paying taxes, note that it will often state: "Pay any Federal

Reserve Bank, for debts incurred by the U.S. Government."
Therefore:

"To lay with one hand the power of the government on the property of the citizen, and with the other to bestow it on favored individuals... is none the less robbery because it is done under the forms of law and is called taxation."
U.S. Supreme Court in Loan Association v. Topeka (1874)

those persons and entities that are responsible for withholding of money for income tax purposes are, according to section 7701(a)(16), those only authorized for sections:

1441 - NONRESIDENT ALIENS; 1442 - FOREIGN CORPORATIONS;

1443 - FOREIGN TAX-EXEMPT ORGANIZATIONS; 1461 - WITHHOLDING AGENT LIABLE FOR WITHHELD TAX.

IF YOU DO NOT FALL WITHIN ANY OF THESE CATEGORIES, THEN YOU MAY BE A VOLUNTEER INCOME TAXPAYER!

"The Criminal Investigation Division enforces the criminal statutes applicable to income, estate, gift, employment, and

*excise tax laws involving United States Citizens Residing in
Foreign Countries and nonresident aliens subject to Federal
income tax filing requirements. "*
**Internal Revenue Manual, Chapter 1100 Organization and
Staffing, section 1132.75**

1.   Are you a United States Citizen residing in Foreign
      Countries or
2.   A nonresident alien?

**IF NOT, YOU SHOULD NOT BE SUBJECTED TO THE
CRIMINAL INVESTIGATION DIVISION AT ANY TIME!**

*"If an individual gives you [the domestic employer or
withholding agent] a written statement in duplicate, stating that
he or she is a citizen or resident of the United States, and you
do not know otherwise, you may accept this statement and are
relieved from the duty of withholding the tax. "*
IRS Treasury Regulation 1.1441

**IF YOU ARE A NON-FEDERAL EMPLOYEE THIS
APPLIES TO YOU!**

It is also important to note that the only way a United States
citizen or permanent resident alien, living and working within a

State of the Union, can have taxes directly deducted or withheld from his/her pay, is by voluntarily making an application (Form SS-5). This form is used to obtain a Social Security Number, and then entering that number on an IRS Form W-4 and signing it, permits withholding of "Employment Taxes". This also includes "Form W-4 Employee's Withholding Allowance Certificate".

Obtaining a social security number is voluntary and there is no federal law or regulation that requires workers to have a Social Security Number or sign a W-4 to qualify for a job. Therefore, you do not have to place your social security number on the W-4 form; you do not have to sign it, and you should still be paid. This is, if you fall within the guidelines stated above.

"The general term 'income' is not defined in the Internal Revenue Code."
U.S. v. Ballard, 535 F2d. 400

Income is not everything that comes in. It is not my advice to you, however it is up to you to further your research to find out if you are a volunteer taxpayer.
"We must reject in this case… the broad contention submitted in behalf of the Government that all receipts – everything that

comes in – are income within the proper definition of the term
'gross income...'."
Southern Pacific company v. John Z. Lowe, Jr., 247 US 330,
335

However, there is a definition of gross income according to
Section 61(a) of the Internal Revenue Code. In this section, it
states:

(a)   General Definition – Except otherwise provided in this
       subtitle, gross income means all income from whatever
       source derived including (but not limited to) the
       following items:

1)   Compensation for services, including fees, commission,
      fringe benefits, and similar items;

2)   Gross income derived from business;

3)   Gains derived from dealings in property;

4)   Interest;

5)   Rents;

6)   Royalties;

7)   Dividends;

8)   Alimony and separate maintenance payments;

9)   Annuities

10)   Income from life insurance and endowment contracts;

11)   Pensions;

12)   Income from discharge of indebtedness;

13)   Distributive share of partnership gross income;

14)   Income in respect of a decedent; and

15)   Income from an interest in an estate or trust.

The information that was provided may or may not be enough to convince you the reader, that something is seriously wrong. Not paying income taxes does not make you a criminal, but a person who decided to exercise their right as a United States Citizen to be free from the true criminals of taxation; that is the IRS. They prey upon fear: your fear and constant letters and phone calls. Unconstitutional seizure of property makes them nothing short of a Gestapo and perpetuators of a Communist or Totalitarian State. The IRS, like the Federal Reserve Bank, believe in a One World Government.

You are being placed in perpetual debt voluntarily, and you may understand more by doing some of your own research. Hopefully this information will help you to start your journey that will educate as to what your true rights are as a citizen.

CHAPTER FIVE

A NEW WORLD ORDER

"My people are destroyed for lack of knowledge; because thou hast rejected knowledge, I will also reject thee, ..." **Hosea 4:6**

In order to achieve a desired totalitarian state, or what may be soon called a dictatorship in America, one must control anything and everything that affects the actions of the masses (the people) in a significant way. This means that control must be established through financial, political and military influence; and there can be no competition by opposing forces to those that wish the desired totalitarian state. In effect, there must be only one military, concentrated ownership or control through influential leadership in corporations that conduct the nation's major manufacturing facilities, financial institutions, commerce, natural resources and transportation entities.

"The real rulers in Washington are invisible and exercise power from behind the scenes."

Justice Felix Frankfurter, U.S. Supreme Court

The Council on Foreign Relations and The Trilateral Commission, are the so-called "elite" organizations that have implemented silent weapon technology upon the people in order to achieve the objective of a One World Government. These two groups among others such as The Round Table Group, Committee of 300, Club of Rome and the Bilderberg Group to name a few, hold positions of power, and have determined that there is an overpopulation here on earth. By using the law of natural and biological warfare selection, they believe they can dominate the masses of a nation: or the entire world if a larger amount of people choose not to use their intelligence. Their philosophy is that people are no better off than a herd of animals who lack the ability to reason. The people are nothing more than a burden, ripe and plump for slavery through world domination.

"To achieve world government, it is necessary to remove from the minds of men their individualism, loyalty to family traditions, national patriotism, and religious dogmas."
Brock Chisolm, Director, UN World Health Organization

A quiet war has been waged against the American people in order to obtain their definition of a One World Government and peace established through initiated chaos. It is all about taking the wealth from the lower class, those who are undisciplined, unworthy and irresponsible, and placed into the hands of the few that are disciplined, worthy and responsible. Thus the power elite seek control of all people.

"...His [the individual's] freedom and choice will be controlled within very narrow alternatives by the fact that he will be numbered from birth and followed, as a number, through his educational training, his required military or other public service, his tax contributions, his health and medical requirements, and his final retirement and death benefits." **Professor Carrol Quigley of Harvard, Princeton and Georgetown**

Control means obtaining a monopoly on everything important to the people. This could be done in a city, state, nation or world depending upon what level of a totalitarian government is desired to be established. People must come to understand that "Community" as in "Communism" is not an enemy of the multi-billionaires, but a form of government that is applauded by them. This type of government would control the masses of people in a nation by controlling all aspects of livelihood such as wages and prices of products that are considered necessities. In order to accomplish these aims, the conspirators have had no qualms about fomenting wars, depressions and hatred. They want a monopoly which would eliminate all competitors and destroy the free enterprise system.

"In politics, nothing happens by accident. If it happens, you can bet it was planned that way."

President FDR

This country was not founded by our forefathers on Socialist government principles, therefore, the goal to subvert the U.S. Constitution had to be accomplished by conspirators in disguise of top patriots. Through simple research, one can find a vast amount of information regarding the plans of the billionaire conspirators to undermine the nation's sovereignty and create a One World Government. Once again, it is suggested that you conduct your own research to find additional merit in what the author writes. Thus a great starting and reference point for the researcher would be the reading and understanding of the document that represents the Supreme Law of the Land. I refer to the U.S. Constitution.

Organizations of Influence

The American contingent was led by Col. House and became known as the Council on Foreign Relations (CFR). It was founded on July 29, 1921, backed by Rockefeller and Carnegie Foundation money. It included many of the same people who established the Federal Reserve. Its quarterly journal, <u>Foreign Affairs</u>, had called for world government as far back as

December, 1922. It was CFR member James Warburg (whose father Paul Warburg merged his Manhattan Bank with Rockefeller's Chase Bank), a former aide to FDR, who expressed this to the Senate Foreign Relations Committee this on Feb. 17, 1950:

"You shall have world government, whether or not you like it, by conquest or consent."
James Warburg

As to publications:

"...building a new international order (which) must be responsive to world aspirations for peace (and) for social and economic change...an international order with states labeling themselves as Socialist."
CFR Publication, Study NO.7, Nov. 25th, 1959

Another organization, which possesses tremendous strength, power and influence is the Trilateral Commission. The Trilateral Commission was formed in 1973 by David Rockefeller (grandson of John D. Rockefeller). David Rockefeller has also been a director of the CFR since 1949. The Trilateral Commission was the brainchild of Columbia University professor Zbigriew Bzrezinski, who, in his book "Between Two Ages", advocated an economic alliance among the western industrialized nations. Rockefeller was responsible for hiring Bzrezinski, and making him the executive director, and established a tri-lateral alliance encompassing Japan, North America, and Western Europe. Its first meeting was held in Tokyo Oct. 21, 1973.

Bzrezinski believed that America is in obsolescence, whereby he advocated a Marxist government that entails central planning. Bzrezinski was quite candid in his book. This former National Security Advisor to President Jimmy Carter believed in developing limitations on the sovereignty and outwardly acknowledged his advocacy for a One World Government. President Carter was a student of Bzrezinski.

"The two men met for the first time about four years ago, when Mr. Bzrezinski was the executive director of the Trilateral Commission and had the foresight to ask the then obscure governor of Georgia to join its ranks. Their initial teacher-student relationship blossomed during the campaign and appears to have grown closer still."
March 1, 1978 New York Times Article

Another influential person among many is Henry Kissinger. Kissinger is mentioned here because he was and still is one of the most powerful and influential members of the Trilaterals and the CFR. Kissinger, also a strong One World advocate, believes plausibly that by controlling energy, especially oil, one can control nations and their financial systems.

By placing food, oil, and the world's monetary system under international control, Kissinger is correct in that a world government can become a reality. The Trilateral Commission has more than 300 members divided up among Japan, North America, and Western Europe. If you would like to request any information from this commission to verify members, you can write to them at The Trilateral Commission, 345 East 46th Street, N.Y., N.Y. 10017.

The Trilateral's goal is a world government, the same as that of the CFR. The first 35 members of the Trilateral were also members of the CFR. They both have as members, some of the most elite names in finance, industry, media, labor, academic circles, and government. The difference between the CFR and the Trilateral is the fact that the Trilateral is an elite group, who has been chosen to speed up the process of a One World Government through the control of food, energy, and an international monetary system.

The CFR and Trilateral influence in government as mentioned before, is very strong. CFR control in government actually began to create a strong hold in the year of 1939. This was done by establishing within the U.S. State Department, a "Committee on Post-War Problems"; the group (staffed and funded by the CFR) that designed the United Nations. (More information regarding the U.N. can be found contained in State Dept. Publication 2349-"Report To The President On The Results of the San Francisco Conference").

Since WWII, the CFR has filled key positions of government and banking in virtually every presidential administration since then. By controlling the candidates we vote for in presidential elections, the CFR is assured their goal of world government. Since Eisenhower, every man who has won the nomination for either party (except Goldwater in 1964 and Reagan in 1980) has been a member of the CFR:

Democrats
* John W. Davis(1924)
* Adlai Stevenson (1952,56)
* John F. Kennedy (1962)
* Hubert Humphrey (1968)
* George McGovern (1972)
* Jimmy Carter (1976,80)
* Walter Mondale (1984)
* Michael Dukakis (1988)

* William Jefferson Clinton (1992)

Republicans
* Herbert Hoover (1928,32)
* Wendell Wilkie (1940)
* Thomas Dewey (1944,48)
* Dwight Eisenhower (1952,56)
* Richard Nixon (1960,68,72)
* Gerald Ford (1976)
* George Herbert Walker Bush (1988,92) (who was also a director of the CFR 1977-1979)

Since its inception in1973, Trilateral members have also filled key positions. One of the first members of the Trilateral Commission was Jimmy Carter, whose administration had 19 Trilateralists including:

Vice President Mondale
Secretary of State Vance
Secretary of the Treasury Blumenthal
Secretary of Defense Brown
National Security Advisor Bzrezinski

These five positions were made up of One World Government advocates. Were these members of the National Security

Council serious in their oath of office to uphold the Constitution? One may conclude to think not. Note all of the following positions below:

1) Nearly all of the undersecretaries of State;

2) Nearly all of the undersecretaries of Treasurer;

3) The Panama Canal Treaty negotiator;

4) The Salt Treaty negotiator;

5) The Ambassador to the United Nations Andrew Young;

6) The Ambassador to Italy, Richard Gardner

"The Trilateral Commission doesn't secretly run the world, the Council on Foreign Relations does that."

CFR past President and Assistant Secretary for East Asian/ Pacific Affairs (State Dept.) and special envoy to Red China - Winston Lord

The CFR domination of just the last three Administrations reveals:

347 under Reagan;

382 under Bush, and

387 under Clinton

The following CFR members hold top positions in our current Administration:

President Bill Clinton

Vice President Al Gore

Secretary of State Warren Christopher

Deputy Secretary of State Clifton R. Wharton

CIA Director R. James Woolsey

National Security Advisor W. Anthony Lake

Deputy National Security Advisor Samuel R. Berger

Secretary of Defense Les Aspen

Chrmn., Intel. Adv. Bd. William J. Crowe

U.N. Ambassador Madeleine Albright

Sec. H.& H.S. Donna E. Shalala

OMB Alice M. Rivlin

Secretary H.U.D. Henry G. Cisneros

Secretary of the Treasury Lloyd M. Bentsen (former CFR)

Secretary of the Interior Bruce Babbitt

Supreme Court Justice Ruth Bader Ginsberg

There are more than three hundred others as well. The most prominent of these are the Bilderbergers (of the Bilderberg Group, est. in 1954), and they are largely responsible for the unification of Europe through the Treaty of Rome (1957).

The Holdings of the Powerful Elite

Currently, David Rockefeller is the honorary chairman of both the CFR and the Trilateral Commission, as well as (through his Chase Manhattan Bank) a top stockholder in the Federal Reserve. The Rockefellers play a key role in America's financial and political life. The Rockefeller influence goes back to the 1800's, when John D. Rockefeller was refining nearly 90% of all crude oil in the country, and frequently worked in concert with Wall Street banker J.P. Morgan. By the turn of the century, John D. Rockefeller purchased the Chase Bank and brother William bought the National City Bank of New York. In 1913, these banks became part of the Federal Reserve System.

There are just too many of the so-called elite to mention, and too many financial holdings to list. A choice between the Rothschilds, Rockefellers or the J.P. Morgan family were among the top three of my list for selection. The Rockefeller family whose house I personally had the privilege to visit on a few occasions, helped me make a final decision as to which family to concentrate for portrayal in this book. (The Rothschild Family is a research project in itself. The Rothschild Family had a net worth of 7.5 billion dollars in 1848. Most people were going to the movies for 5 cents in the 1930's. Just imagine what the family wealth has accumulated to in this present day.)

According to the Sept. 16, 1916 New York Times, the Rockefeller oil holdings alone were worth more than $500 million; a conservative estimate. For those that are old enough, I am sure that you remember going to the movies for five cents. Imagine that wealth then, and what it has multiplied to today. Bill Gates of Microsoft cannot even count that high. By 1930, the 200 largest corporations, under the Rockefeller and Morgan influence, held over 49% of the assets of all 40,000 corporations in the country. This is a feat that can easily be achieved when a family owns a large financial institution such as a banks. Remember, banks make loans and possess collateral.

AT&T (controlled by J. P. Morgan) had greater assets than the total wealth in 21 states. The influence of the Rockefeller and Morgan groups were so great during that period of history, that they could affect the economic life of the country to a large degree and almost control its political life on the Federal level. America's entry into W.W.II enhanced all of the above, and Rockefeller's wealth continued to be funneled into the tax-exempt foundations. This in turn, allowed for the Rockefellers to unload up to half of their income into their foundations and deduct these donations from their income tax.

"The foundation pays no capital gains tax and no income tax, so those funds can continue to multiply."
Nelson Rockefeller

In the 1970's, Congressman Wright Patman's Report in the Congressional Record concluded in his findings that Rockefeller's power was so tremendous that, in direct stock, the family presently owned more than:

Exxon - 156.7 million shares;

Rockefeller Center – 98 million shares;

Standard of California - 85 million shares;

IBM - 72.6 million shares;

Chase Manhattan Bank - 18 million shares.

Other companies in which they have 10 million or more shares in:

Mobil Oil;

Eastman Kodak;

General Electric;

Texas Instruments;

Minnesota Mining & Mfg.; along with significant portions of about 50 other major American companies.

Their security holdings revealed that the family controls:

Chase-Manhattan Bank;

City National Bank of New York;

Former Chemical Bank which is now merged with Chase

Manhattan.

There are many others, and these are just a few of the top names.

The Chase Manhattan Bank deals in many foreign countries as

well as corporations: well over 100 countries with about 50,000

affiliated banks.

As the reader can see, their financial holdings run deep. A look

at the interlocking boards of directors in the insurance industry,

at the time this data was compiled, the Rockefellers controlled 3

of the 4 largest insurance companies in the world. These

companies are Metropolitan Life, Equitable Life, and New York

Life. The assets of these three at that time was $113 billion. They

control others as well, but the former three top the list.

In short this amounts to 25% of all the assets of the 50 largest

banks, and 30% of all the assets of the 50 largest life insurance

companies in the world. This is tremendous leverage

economically and politically. Congressman Patman went on to

find that if a stockholder controls 5% or more of the stock in a

corporation, whereby the stock is widely held, the stockholder has in effect, minority control. In analysis of those corporations that the Rockefeller family has 10% control, or 5% and at least two members of their board of directors; the following control of these corporations results:

Exxon, Mobil Oil, Standard of California, Standard of Indiana, International Harvester, Inland Steel, Marathon Oil, Quaker Oats, Wheeling-Pittsburgh Steel, Freeport Sulphur, and International Basic Economy Corporation. Corporations. The problem that the Congressman acknowledged is that such influence is difficult to trace.

Stock ownership through trusts and foundations are the following:

Texaco, IT&T, Westinghouse, Boeing, International Paper, Sperry Rand, Xerox, National Cash Register, National Steel, American Home Products, Pfizer, Avon, and Merck (the largest integrated producer and distributor of pharmaceuticals in the country.)

As to transportation companies, the Rockefeller influence continues and includes Penn Central, TWA, Eastern Airlines, United Airlines, National Airlines, Delta, former Braniff, and Consolidated Freightways. Those they control through interlocking boards of directors are: Allied Chemical, Anaconda Copper, DuPont, Monsanto, Olin-Mathison, Borden, National Distillers, Shell, Gulf, Union Oil, Dow, Celanese, Pittsburgh Plate Glass, Cities Service, Stauffer Chemical, Continental Oil, Union Carbide, American Cyanamid, American Motors, Bendix, and Chrysler.

The list goes on from major financial centers to major department stores. With all of companies above, think about the ones that have gone bankrupt at the taxpayers expense and those that were bailed out at the taxpayers expense. Also, this information should point out the fact that it is utterly impossible for an individual to start up one of the above companies and become a Fortune 500 company in this lifetime. The Rockefeller family is just one of the powerful influentials that will be sure to intervene if any corporation threatens to undermine their wealth. Furthermore, if you thought Bill Gates had money, now you know he has nothing in comparison to this family. Oh, do not lose sight of the fact of their investments in Microsoft as well.

The Rhodes Scholar & Adam Weishaupt

From time to time, you may have heard about individuals who were Rhodes Scholars. The media usually portrays them as men who have achieved great academic scholarship. Of many names, immediately one happens to come to mind, and he is President William Jefferson Clinton. He is one of many Rhodes Scholars, however, President Clinton did not graduate. There are many other scholarships, and I thought I would mention this scholarship to show readers how many Americans have been conned into believing that scholars of this program were to be elected, and have been elected in the so-called best interest of Americans. Below, I identify through research, what type of people that Americans have chose to elect.

I will only touch upon the man who was the founder named Cecil Rhodes and his evil intentions, to let the reader know that there were and still are individuals who truly believe in achieving the objective of a totalitarian state. President Clinton is only one of such leaders who has studied under the philosophy of this man.

Cecil Rhodes, was a gold and diamond magnate, and a well known racist. Rhodes was a man who concentrated his efforts on achieving a New World Order. According to Sara Millin, Cecil Rhodes biographer, she noted that "the government of the world was Rhodes simple desire."

Rhodes, in the mid 1890's, had a personal income of at least one million pounds of sterling silver a year, which equated to approximately five million dollars. He would spend so freely for his unknown or so-called mysterious purposes. Rhodes was found to be usually overdrawn on his account.

In the book the <u>American Rhodes Scholarships</u>, Frank Aydelotte noted that Rhodes did in fact have a commitment to the conspiracy to establish a World Government. To solidify his commitment, Rhodes constructed a series of wills. Aydelotte mentioned that: "The seven wills which Cecil Rhodes created between the ages of 24 and 46 constitute a kind of spiritual autobiography ... Best known are the first and the last, which established the Rhodes Scholarships..." Cecil Rhodes was part of a secret society; a society he mentioned in his first will. In other wills, Rhodes is considered an acknowledged racist, and not only against particular races but groups of people that did not subscribe to his one world government theories.

The secret society that Rhodes was a member of, was the same one as the one originated by who some called the "Human Devil," Adam Weishaupt. Weishaupt founded the Order of the illuminati May 1, 1776, the same day as Law Day acknowledged by the American Bar Association. This society was created to formulate and execute plans for a New World Order or One World Domination. Rhodes was responsible for what was called the Reign of Terror, and the techniques used to carry them out could easily be compared to the same theories prescribed by

Communism.

Another secret society that Adam Weishaupt was a member of was the Society of Jesus (the Jesuits), and used this society as his model for planning a Revolution. Weishaupt later began to encrypt his plans and wrote his code in Masonic terms. The New World Order as noted earlier in the book, is a global re-structuring of governments to achieve a totalitarian state whereby, the world's wealthiest families will place the majority of the masses on earth in servitude under their complete control. This is to take place all behind the false front or veil of the United Nations; an organization that people were made to believe was an organization to establish peace around the world.

In order for this plan to work effectively, many people must die under the illuminati creation of disease, famine, war etc. The goal is for at least 2.5 billion people to be eliminated by early 2000. Population control is already in effect through drugs, liquor, murder, fluoridated water, mayhem and free medicine offered by your government. Now these demagogues who planned all this chaos are accelerating the pace.

Presently, we are in the period of revelations, and no one man or group of people can stop what is actually written in many different Holy Scriptures. The worst must come to pass, and people can only prepare themselves for the worst while they hope for the best.

POPULATION CONTROL IN THE UNITED STATES

Many people today, do not realize that they are and have been victims of subconscious manipulation. Such manipulations are so powerful, that before a person ever realizes that they have succumbed to the tools and techniques of the people responsible for their implementation, it is too late. An example of this would be, if a person has been lied to all their lives about a particular topic or event, that person not only believes that lie, but will even act upon that lie as if it were the truth.

A way to break this mental chain of slavery is to read and evaluate both commercial and non – commercial material, and avoid techniques the mass media uses to profess their Tricknology. Once one knows how it works, the same techniques used to chain your subconscious mind can be used to set it free; and it will not be an overnight process.

Once a man's brain has become enslaved by another man, there is nothing that the man responsible for the programming cannot make him do mentally or physically. Imagine how many people have been programmed in one way or another; whether it is a historical belief, fashion, luxury, cultural, cult or idea. Unless the subconscious programming is pointed out with opposing facts and the programmed person chooses to use reason, then such facts will be recognized and understood as truth. The chains will not be broken. A man that believes he is free mentally and/or physically from bondage, are those people that are indoctrinated in the worst way, and are even more enslaved than they actually know.

It should be recognized or acknowledged again, that breaking the chains are not easy, because repetition and distraction from possibly learning the truth will create a conditioned response in people who have been subjected to the repetitive programming. If one has ever studied the martial arts or watched a professional gymnast, they will see that repetition and focus brings about perfection of their art. If their repetition was combined with distraction, they may know the moves they are supposed to perform, but if they do not understand them, the martial artist may be killed in the street, and the gymnast may be injured on the parallel or asymmetric bars. The wrong move without reasoning or proper timing creates actions with recklessness.

The TV, Radio and Movie Factor

Adults and children need to have their access to television minimized at all costs. Experiments have been conducted proving how television actually shuts down the conscious mind, while the subconscious continues to work as antennas of reception. The conscious mind is placed into a trance - state and is actually suspended during viewing and up to three hours after the television is shut off. The most tragic and most powerful instillation of influence takes effect upon those that watch television just before they go to sleep. The television screen appears static, but it actually flickers and the brain registers this. Surely there have been times that you have caught yourself staring blankly at the television screen, losing all sense of time and place. At this stage, when you stop conscious thinking and your mind goes blank, then your mind is in its most suggestible state. At this time, the mind is primed for mental programming. Surely you have heard of subliminal messages?

The nationwide suppression of these facts by all the 'leading' newspapers, places added emphasis on the famous words of John Swinton, editor of the New York News at the annual dinner of the American Press Association in 1914.

"There is no such thing as an independent press in America...Not a man among you dares to utter his honest opinion...We are the tools and the vassals of the rich behind the scenes. We are marionettes. These men pull the strings and we dance. Our time, our talents, our lives and our capacities are all the property of these men -- we are intellectual prostitutes. "

John Swinton, Editor of New York News

Information Control

"Who controls the past, controls the future: who controls the present controls the past. "

George Orwell

In George Orwell's book 1984, originally titled 1948, the primary means of oppression is the absolute control of information. Orwell indicated that all published material is constantly changed so that history fulfills the wishes and aims of the government. Keeping true knowledge away from the people helps create control of a people. Information control is nothing more than a silent weapon that interferes with the pre-destined social lives of the people. A prime example would be soldiers of war or law enforcement officers, that are brainwashed to believe that all the enforcement they are doing is for the good of the government and the people. There are so many officers that do a great job in their line of work, however, if they only were to become aware of the evil objectives that are and will soon be placed upon them. One cannot blame many of them for the lack of knowledge, for many of them just follow orders and have been recruited at a very young and impressionable age.

"A general state education is a mere contrivance for molding people to be exactly like one another; and as the mold in which it casts them is that which pleases the predominant power in the government,...it establishes a despotism over the mind, leading by natural tendency to one over the body, "

John Stuart Mills

Education of the younger generation is generally used to condition their minds as to what evil programmers plan for later, thus eliminating the difference between propaganda and teaching. Propaganda cannot work effectively without education; especially incorrect facts. The mind is conditioned with vast amounts of information posing as "facts" and "knowledge" dispensed for ulterior motives. The "educated" and "intellectuals" are the most vulnerable to propaganda because they absorb the largest amount of secondhand information and consider themselves to be "above " the effects of propaganda. They are the hardest to convince that they have not been educated, but indoctrinated; especially if they attended schools that are considered Ivy or elite. Lacking the principles of street knowledge and common sense makes them no better off than a person who received no education at all. To be indoctrinated with lies all of your life can easily create a student's demise.

War has been waged amongst the common people, and with the use of silent weapons, the destruction of livelihoods are easily conducted. Reactions made by such weapons do not make center-grabbing attention, but a quiet noise that is methodically planned. The damage it creates can be mental or physical, and it is planned that way to interfere with every day social life. The only person(s) that would be familiar to the end result is ones who initiated the crisis or situation.

Once it is recognized and acknowledged that people are undisciplined, and due to a lack of mental awareness, fail to comprehend silent weapons. Therefore, when such weapons are used against the masses, it is hard to fight. One reason is the fact that it is hard for the masses to believe that such a weapon(s) would be used against them and secondly, the egos of the people convince them that they cannot be overtaken by such.

Such weapons are hard to fight, especially when people do not know when they are being attacked by them. Also, it is even more difficult when the masses do not know who to run to for help; let alone notify authorities of a weapon they cannot see, feel or comprehend on a conscious level. The weapons are not tangible. After a while, silent weapons overcome and win by making the public adapt to it, and people eventually live with such impediments that such weapons create.

Monopoly of the Mass Media

"We are grateful to the Washington Post, the New York Times, Time Magazine, and other publications whose directors have attended our meetings, and respected their promises of discretion for almost 40 years...It would have been impossible for us to develop our plan for the world if we had been subject to the bright lights of publicity during these years."
Bilderbergers' (European-based globalists) meeting in Baden Baden, Germany, David Rockefeller

In order to obtain control the masses in a country, cult or bonafide organization, control of the media is important. To achieve a One World government, Totalitarian State or Autocracy, it is a must! A monopoly of all means of communication, especially without the masses or public knowing makes it very easy to create propaganda; a way of thinking; scientific experiments; a method of thinking; or the reason not to think at all. It should be noted that not all communication mediums need to be controlled by the hands of the few just the communication mediums that reach the most people in numbers. Through the power of suggestion and manipulation, people can be led to believe something that is not true. This is especially the case when information is carefully timed and presented by what is perceived to be an accepted and respected authoritative source. Observe the media and how they find qualified experts for everything and anything.

"All they know about public policy is what we tell them."
David Brinkley (CFR), to a meeting of the American TV/ Radio Broadcasters Association about the American People

Among the communication corporations represented in the CFR and Trilateral are these:

CBS
NBC
ABC
PBS

CNN (A United Nations entity. Notice how Ted Turner is supposedly donating One Billion dollars to the U.N. Actually, that is nothing more than a repayment of money contributed by the U.N. initially. It is not because Turner believes that such a donation will bring about peace.)

Washington Post

New York Times Co.

Wall Street Journal

Newsweek

U.S. News and World Report

Time, Inc

Associated Press and Reuters (both of which local papers rely upon)

CFR members who are TV news personalities include:

Dan Rather

Tom Brokaw

David Brinkley

John Chancellor

Barbara Walters

Diane Sawyer

Robert McNeil

Jim Lehrer

Daniel Schorr

"We hold these truths to be self-evident, that all men are created equal; that they are endowed by their Creator with inherent and inalienable rights; that among these, are life, liberty, and the pursuit of happiness; that to secure these rights, governments

are instituted among men, deriving their just powers from the consent of the governed; that whenever any form of government becomes destructive of these ends, it is the right of the people to alter or abolish it, and to institute new government, laying its foundation on such principles, and organizing its powers in such form, as to them shall seem most likely to effect their safety and happiness."

Declaration of Independence as originally written by Thomas Jefferson, 1776. Papers, 1:315

CHAPTER SIX

INVESTING IN A DEFENSIVE EQUITY STRATEGY

This chapter is dedicated to what I believe to be your best equitable strategy for turbulent economic times ahead. Companies large and small will not only experience a tremendous downturn in their profits and stock value, but many will outright be going bankrupt! Not to mention, that for every persons faults is another man's riches. Therefore, it can be said that there will also be a wealth of opportunity for those that prepare for the worst. As for those who don't, then most likely they may consider themselves an asset of the state and directed under the auspices of their control possibly for the rest of their life.

The strategy that you must learn to possibly adapt to, in this so-called apocalyptic time is that of Lord Rothschild. The time that he buys is when there is "blood in the streets." In other words those who are prepared for the coming storm, will not invest, but di-vest funds out of their accounts and buy tangible assets such as gold and silver and other precious metals as discussed in a later chapter. This can only be done through breaking the chain of mental slavery which encompasses confidence in fiat money or paper money that is not actually backed by gold reserves. It is only paper that you own, and is used as a monetary unit. Actually to be more specific, paper that is nothing more than an IOU; something due you as your confidence is built upon the premise that it will be paid to you. This is nothing different than your paper note debt to a banker.

Since the stock market will eventually topple, corporation stock will drop to an all time low; employee vested funds will be depleted, not by the employee, but by the negative fluctuation in the market. In other words, usurping years of vestiture and savings. For many employees, it will be like starting from day one. For those that have invested in gold and silver, your money will be highly valued. Below, are the things you would want to do to make wise investments.

An Equity Strategy for the Future

Here are some of the chosen industries I believe are safe investments immediately after a stock market crash:

Bottled Water Companies

The ultimate necessity in maintaining life is water. There is no other source on earth that can replace it. It is necessary for your vitality. It can keep you going alive by providing you with necessary minerals, prevent dehydration and even be used as a cooking source to prepare any of the necessary foods you require for further nutrition.

Soap Companies

People will still be concerned about their hygiene as well as the cleansing of their immediate surroundings; whether they live in a house or in an apartment. These companies should have products that include cosmetics, toothpaste and heavy duty industrial cleaners.

Large Food Manufacturers

People have to eat, therefore manufacturers will face a heavy demand for more food, and hopefully if resources are available, they will be fulfilling a lot of orders. Usually, these manufacturers have the largest and best resources for obtaining and delivering food products.

Tobacco Companies

Expect a larger increase in nicotine addiction. It is already big around the world, and with a depression of this magnitude there will be a lot of smoking going on. People used tobacco before the economic downturn and surely will not stop; if anything, they will be more dependent after the downturn. Thus, a new generation of tobacco users will emerge bringing greater profits for the tobacco companies.

Pharmaceutical Companies

This is one of the largest drug dependent countries in the world. A country that continues to advertise "Just Say No to Drugs." The drug campaign are for those drugs the FDA was given authority to deem illegal. Drugs for just about every ailment are manufactured by these big companies; whereby Rockefeller has a controlling interest in approximately four of the major companies. With tobacco usage on the rise, expect more drugs made to help find a cure for cancer.

I believe that it is fair to just make a note of a few things. One thing to notice is that there are drugs made for most ailments; which consists of cures from your head to your toe. Whether or not you would like to believe that certain diseases or ailments have cures already established, you should think about how evil such companies can be.

There are cures for some forms of cancer for instance, but the economic effect that it would have on the companies that promote remedial drugs, and non-profit organizations that provide so many jobs would be devastating. Of course profits would be lost. The question is, if you weigh the good with the bad, would an announcement of cures be in the best interest of the world?

Information Technology Companies

The largest information technology companies have many resources; especially resources that helps them contain, maintain, distribute and sell information. Almost all aspects of our daily lives uses information technology. Just because there will be a Y2K and 10 2K problem does not mean that information will stop all together; especially information technology.

Entertainment Companies

People need to keep their minds off their troubles and what better ways over the centuries have proven to be a great outlet. Many people cannot or refuse to face reality, and will choose to fantasize. Whether it is Disney World or just television movies, it is more than likely that people will turn to these industries for relief in what they are experiencing as rough times. Disney World is a prime example of a model One World Government. However, not everyone will be so happy when things truly begin to become apparent, nor will Mickey Mouse be waiving in your face with that big old grin. Most people will only be able to identify with Goofy when all is said and done.

Trade Industry

Towns and cities must rebuild infrastructure from causes stemming from the Y2K breakdown, terrorist disasters, government disasters, domestic and possibly international warfare.

Hospitals

Many people use, and will use hospitals because of the need of medical attention. Most hospitals that are modernized are computer dependent and quick rebuilding will be necessary to alleviate the chaos that will result because of the total technology failure in the hospitals.

Casinos

People will always gamble; that is as along as they believe in hope. Knowing that the odds are against them because the odds favor the house, investing in companies such as these indirectly makes you a part of the house.
Get it!

Private Transportation and Freight Service

Information, goods and services need to go from point to point and companies will still be operating. Things may not be business as usual, but these services should, at least the larger ones, should become very busy.

In Summary

Once again, these types of companies are just a few of many industries that I believe will aid you in making sound investments. I am not an investment advisor, but my research as a writer brings me to these conclusions.
Stocks will eventually rise again. You may not be able to buy as much as the next person, but being a wise investor can bring you to a higher standard of living than many people without money at all. The key here however, is discipline! I am not an expert, but through research and common sense, I mention just a few of these areas to help you build, rebuild and/or maintain good sound investment strategies. You must remember, that after some of these events occur, you must make decisions for yourself and your family. Your concern is not what people are saying about where you invest, it is what you believe to know what is best investment for you and your family.

It is important that you make sound judgements, and not place yourself on a frolic from your plan. I am not telling you to sell everything, but make sure what you have is tangible and all the required paperwork, if necessary, is available to secure your assets. It is necessary to protect everything you have that you consider important.

Avoid any debt instruments, such as agreements for extended
bank credit, bonds, loans, mortgages, investment or retirement
plans. You need liquid assets for now. Property is not always
the safest purchase either; at least in the year of 1999. If you
owe money on your property and the dollar value is worth
nothing, then you will have it taken from you by your once
friendly banker. The first plank of the Communist Manifesto is
the Abolition of Property! Furthermore, if you own a house
theoretically, because the mortgage debt was paid off, you
certainly should not be duped to believe the property is actually
yours and solely yours. Stop paying taxes on it, and you will see
what I mean!

After reading material from Dr. Yardeni, Chief Economist,
Deutsche Morgan Grenfell, he is a person who takes more of a
globalist view and approach to the oncoming problems. I believe
that some of the sectors he mentions for investment are quite
sound at his web site www.yardeni.com. He does not offer
explanations as to why you should invest in these industries, but
if you think about them for a while, you will probably come to
some logical conclusions.

Furthermore, Dr. Yardeni's suggests that people invest in
Temporary Personnel, Security Services and Utility companies.
For Capital Goods, the suggestion was made to invest in

Aerospace/Defense, Packaging & Containers, Basic Materials and Energy companies. As for Technology, companies that provide Personal Computers, Computer Services and Networking. In the distribution sector, invest in companies that provide Semiconductors and Equipment including such manufacturers. I agree with these suggestions in part, and may soon favor a globalist view. However, I do not believe the selection process by the power elite is fair and just, because U.S. citizens have not chosen them. Before I accept such a view, the process must change, and change drastically.

CHAPTER SEVEN

THE POWER OF GOLD AND SILVER

"If the American People ever allow private banks to control the issue of their currency, first by inflation and then by deflation, the banks and the corporations that will grow up around them will deprive the people of all property until their children wake up homeless on the continent their Fathers conquered."
Thomas Jefferson

Introduction:

Gold and silver are both very valuable precious metals. It is in your best interest to avoid your conscious mind telling you that you do not need it. This is what the power-elite want you to believe. In this chapter, the words of gold and silver are used interchangeably. In other words, when gold is mentioned solely, I am usually speaking of all precious metals, unless a metal is specifically mentioned and addressed.

"All the perplexities, confusion and distress in America arise

not from defects in their constitution or confederation, not from a want of honor or virtue so much as down-right ignorance of the nature of coin, credit, and circulation."

James Madison

In order to get a full understanding of why it is important to buy gold and silver coinage, one needs to be educated with the definitions of some basics terms.

What is Currency?

Currency is coined money and such bank notes or other paper money as are authorized by Law, which do in fact circulate from hand to hand, as a medium of exchange.

Black's Law Dictionary 6th Edition.

What is Money?

Money is "a medium of exchange." In lay terms, it is a medium of exchange that is termed anything that can be used in the act of an exchange of goods or services and has a common basis of measurement. According to the dictionary, usually, it is seen as the ordinary acceptance of coins and paper currency that is used in the medium of exchange, and does not embrace notes, bonds, evidences of debt, or other personal or real estate. Further, it is also considered A medium of exchange authorized or adopted by

a domestic or foreign government as its currency."
Black's Law Dictionary 6th Edition

What is a "Note"?

A note is, an instrument containing an express and absolute promise of the signer to pay to a specified person or order, a definite sum of money at a specified time or on demand. Federal Reserve Notes therefore, are not "dollars", or in other words, not "money".
Black's Law Dictionary 6th Edition

What is Legal Tender?

All coins currency of the United States, (including Federal Reserve Notes, and circulating notes of Federal Reserve Banks, and national banking associations), regardless of when issued, are legal tender for all debts, public and private, public charges, taxes, and dues.
Black's Law Dictionary 6th Edition

What is Inflation?

The increase in money supply or cash receipts without a gold or silver backing.

According to Article 1, Section 10, Clause 1 of the United States Constitution: "No State shall make any thing but gold and silver coin a tender payment of debts." The fact is, Federal Reserve notes have replaced money as the circulating medium of exchange.

According to the Constitution, Federal Reserve Notes are nothing more than what is considered Legal Tender, and are not in fact lawful money.

The Monetary State of Our Nation

In industrialized nations, this is the Age of Electronic Banking. By now, most of you that either reside in or visit an industrialized nation, have been introduced to some form of electronic banking. Whether it is the use of Automated Teller Machines (ATM); stock market trading; or buying stock with electronic money over the Internet (cyber dollars), most of you, if not all have been exposed. With "Smart Cards", like the one made available by Chairman David A. Rockefeller's Chase Manhattan Bank, it is easier to access funds from a bank or any other financial institution; not to mention that valuable and personal information is also made available for easy access.

Over the years, there has been a reduction in the circulation of $100 and $50 bills. The power elite have eroded the use of hard currency and are continuing their focus on convincing the public that a cash-less society, a society we presently live in, is what the country needs. No longer is the U.S. dollar bill or any other paper currency produced in this country redeemable in gold or silver. Gold was banned in 1933 and silver coins were no longer minted after the year of 1964. Thereafter, coinage has contained copper combined with other junk alloys; and in essence people are carrying nothing more than mere slugs in their pockets. U.S. paper currency is no longer backed by gold or silver either; essentially making the Federal Reserve Notes worth zero.

Interestingly enough, take a look at any federal reserve note or "paper dollar denomination" in your pocket and read the following words: "This note is legal tender for all debts public and private." Many years ago, it read "Pay to the Bearer on Demand" and "Redeemable in Gold, on demand, at the U.S. Treasury or in gold or "lawful money" at any "Federal Reserve Bank.

In 1932 these words disappeared, but the public still has confidence that these notes can be redeemed in such lawful money. Many other currencies can, such as the (ECU) European Currency Unit, but not this nation's money. Therefore, this country has not only been duped by the "Invisible Hand," but the people are only passing Federal Reserve Notes back and forth which represent nothing more than mere IOUs.

This demonstrates the point that you are actually living in a cash-less society at the moment, and many people do not know or understand this fact. Furthermore, many people don't care. Isn't it strange that many countries around the world that do not even accept U.S. paper currency? The only thing that keeps it viable here in the U.S., is the fact that the public has not lost confidence in it yet. However, history repeats itself, and all things must come to an end. Remember the Great Depression in 1929?

At Barclays Bank in Britain, a senior executive made statements to consumers that actually warned them to sell their homes, stockpile their cash and buy gold in case of a global economic collapse caused by the millennium computer bug. This is from the Sunday edition of the LONDON TIMES (March 29, 1998). It is not the Millennium Bug that is the concern of this chapter, but notice what this senior executive is telling people to buy. He is telling them to buy gold, a tangible asset that can be used in good times or bad.

In a crisis such as an electronic bank failure; a nationwide recession; a devastating depression that is worse than this country has ever experienced in 1929; or a global economic collapse, it will be gold and silver that will weather the storm. Gold is a true currency and tangible asset.

Precious Metals and Fiat Paper

"To emit an unfunded paper as the sign of value ought not to continue a formal part of the Constitution, nor even hereafter to be employed; being, in its nature, pregnant with abuses, and liable to be made the engine of imposition and fraud; holding out temptations equally pernicious to the integrity of government and to the morals of the people."
Alexander Hamilton

Gold is a precious metal that is universal in monetary usage. No matter the age of time, it consistently maintains its value and is made available only to those who demonstrate access to resources to obtain it. It is considered scarce, easily measured and defined.

Whether it is gold, silver, platinum or palladium, these precious metals among others, represent the only real sound money used in the world, whereby their value cannot be diminished. Once a coin leaves the mint, it has value that is solidified; for instance, by weight. As for Federal Reserve notes or fiat paper as it is more commonly called, they can easily be devalued by printing more notes; what people today believe to be money. Printing more notes only create economic problems, and inflation is a prime example of just some of the problems this activity causes.

"Paper is poverty,.... it is only the ghost of money, and not money itself."
Thomas Jefferson to Edward Carrington, 1788. ME 7:36

It is the fiat paper in this society that is actually worthless. It is nothing more than debt created through the use of bank credit, bank notes and bonds over and above the amount of actual gold reserves that are available to support it. However, as mentioned before, no longer is U.S. money backed by gold reserves. The debt is created through the simple process of continually printing an abundance of paper on a printing press, or with the help of modern technology, a computer book entry. Bankers continue to claim and convince people that such paper or electronic book entries have value.

Both fiat paper and electronic money (electronic book entries) are easily expandable; easily given a fictitious value; easily manipulated; and easy to obtain in an abundance. The only difference between electronic money and fiat paper is that, with a simple digital bookkeeping entry, a banker can create more money (debt to the holder) without the use of a printing press. This is the bankers' dream come true. This is how they survive as huge financial institutions - off of fictitious money that is created almost as if a magic wand had been twirled. As you can see, the average worker does not have the ability to do the same; and sadly accepts debt without truly rebelling against the bankers in strong numbers with other people who understand their plight.

"It is a [disputed] question, whether the circulation of paper, rather than of specie, is a good or an evil... I believe it to be one of those cases where mercantile clamor will bear down reason, until it is corrected by ruin." **Thomas Jefferson to John W. Eppes, 1813. ME 13:409**

The Demonetization of Gold

With gold, silver, and other precious metals, they can not be easily demonetized because it is very difficult to manipulate their values. Gold is a standard, and has a universal value. Therefore, those with tremendous wealth who wish to possess or maintain their power status, and have access and control of gold do not wish to have such precious metals to be obtained by any other;

whereby it would stand in the way of their "One World Government" objectives.

Since paper money can easily be manipulated, it can place the masses (people) and foreign countries who abide by the bankers terms, at ease from the bankers' verbiage. Words communicated to them stating that the so-called money that they seek is available. It is the same as a calming effect as to what the bankers' decide to do with their electronic money and fictitious value upon it, to make the public believe in the value of their book entries.

"...the surest way to overthrow an existing social order is to debauch the currency."
Vladimir Lenin

In the U.S. a debauched currency has already been accomplished. The ruling elite continues telling you, the public, that gold is obsolete. That is shear nonsense! Take the Wall Street Journal article dated August 7, 1998, "Finding a Safe Harbor in Choppy Market." Here, it was noted that "gold used to be the portfolio hedge of choice in tough times. Now, some call it obsolete." This was a two page article with only one paragraph that mentioned gold. In that paragraph, it was also stated by a so-called expert metals analyst, that in the last decade, "gold has lost most of its glitter." Further, that gold can no longer be considered a safe haven. His final analysis was that "tremendous returns in the stock market has rendered this non-interest bearing commodity somewhat obsolete."

The government and those with tremendous wealth know the value of gold, but publicly try to dissuade private ownership. That should tell you something! You are being told such disinformation because those that have financial and/or political power, want to keep their power. Therefore, they do not wish to have gold act as a discipline. Only paper money promises "something -for- nothing" and not gold or silver. Gold and silver are true constants. Paper is not!

"The trifling economy of paper, as a cheaper medium, or its convenience for transmission, weighs nothing in opposition to the advantages of the precious metals... it is liable to be abused, has been, is, and forever will be abused, in every country in which it is permitted."
Thomas Jefferson to John W. Eppes, 1813. ME 13:430

It is the international bankers who are a part of the Council on

Foreign Relations and the Trilateral Commission that have so
skillfully crafted the war on gold. So skillful, that they have been
successful in duping and convincing people who possess fiat
paper and any debt that can be termed illiquid to replace their
gold and silver for more worthless paper; whereby the people fail
to demand gold as real compensation for their wages. You see,
gold cannot create income because its value for the most part
remains constant, except in extreme market conditions.
However, market conditions are never constant and gold will
always prevail. It undoubtedly is a safe means of protecting your
wealth.

Greed and Gold

Most people want more and more money in life and greed is only
a part of the equation. When prices go up, people want and not
necessarily need more money in order to purchase what may or
may not be a necessity. High price material items are an example
of possible non-necessities as opposed to basics for hygiene,
shelter and food. The learned conditioning of obtaining luxuries
has clouded the minds of many. Greed has people buying value-

less name-brand items to satisfy their fantasies, desires or whatever; making them feel as though they truly possess something of value.

When prices go up, people usually do not earn enough to obtain their desired product immediately, so they try to locate a source that will provide them with what appears to be a "money store". Any lending institution like a bank or mortgage company is a prime example of a "money store". People then, as collateral put their few real possessions, such as property, wages, and other liquid investments on the line to receive in return more worthless fiat paper. More fantasy money! Like drugs, many products can be termed a temporary fix. Meanwhile, not the high from drugs, but the debt they incur almost appears to last forever.

If gold were used instead of being substituted with fiat paper, then most people would be forced to live within their means. The collapse of a fiat system only promises collection of collateral by the lender, since the borrower has no real value but only fictitious money they borrowed in the first place in order to pay off that debt. Property (collateral) is as good as gold! The lender would be happy to take the property; which just happens to be the first plank of the Communist Manifesto (Abolition of Property), and still collect a monetary amount.

One person alone cannot save the world, and it is important that you protect what is yours until and while you are able to destroy the "Invisible Hand" that runs our government. It is not the government itself, but a small group of the power elite who run the government and look to debauch our monetary system in order to keep the gold for themselves. War, domestic in nature, may be the only way "we the people" will be able to fight for and defend the U.S. Constitution that the forefathers of this country so masterfully designed.

Our forefathers did not intend for greedy money-mongers to distort, disrupt, corrupt and abolish our constitution for their own personal gain. It is the New World Order philosophy adhered to by the members of the United Nations, Council on Foreign Relations, Bilderbergers and Trilateral Commission to name a few that is about to pull the greatest caper involving chaos along with the re-distribution of wealth in American history. According to the occult sciences, this is the period of 'revelations', and all evils will come to the forefront; for this is all written in many religious books.

*The name of the **Trilateral Commission** was taken from the alien flag known as the Trilateral Insignia. Majesty Twelve was to survive right up to the present day. Under Eisenhower and*

Kennedy it was erroneously called the 5412 Committee, or more correctly, the Special Group. In the Johnson administration it became the 303 Committee because the name 5412 had been compromised in the book.

The Value of the Note

In the early 1900's, a United States Note or "Gold Certificate" was issued, this currency was actually able to be redeemed for gold coinage that was on deposit in the United States Treasury. This was sound paper currency. United States Notes were at one time commonly referred to as "Lincoln Greenbacks." These notes, made it possible for this country to have money and not pay any interest to International Bankers; one of the reasons that President Lincoln was assassinated.

Silver certificates had the same effect as gold at one time, whereby silver certificates were once redeemable in silver. One silver dollar would be given in return for a one dollar silver certificate. The government has since reneged on its promise to pay silver upon demand, making the silver certificate worth nothing. Instead of United States Notes, Federal Reserve Notes are now passed around, with no true value whatsoever.

"Paper money expansionism will not work...but even highly
sophisticated monetary authorities go on for years
accepting ever more worthless paper instead of demanding
gold...But the time has come at last when people,
including even foreign central bankers, no longer want to hold
ore and more and ever more worthless currencies.
...Confidence in a currency can erode rapidly once it becomes
inconvertible, for only convertibility enables it to maintain its
store of value function indefinitely...Without convertibility,
history shows that a currency will ultimately become worthless
and disappear."
Federal Reserve – John Exter

In lay terms, there was a time that you could convert silver or
gold coins into a paper dollar, representing the exact same value
of the coin exchanged. If ever necessary, the holder of that
paper or note could exchange that paper for a silver or gold coin.
For example, a ten dollar gold piece could be exchanged for a
ten dollar U.S. Treasury Note. Conversely, that ten dollar
treasury note could be exchanged at any time for a ten dollar
gold piece. Today however, that is no longer the case.
As time passed, convertibility had been suspended, and holders
could no longer redeem gold or silver at least for face value of
what the note is worth. Further, banks no longer give out gold

as an exchange of currency. The reason is that gold is a life-line. The ruling elite would take any measures possible to make sure you do not have it. When it is too late, then your quest for gold will be too late, and unobtainable. No political power has ever defeated gold, especially by having a head-on war with it. Surely though, many people will be without gold and silver when the market collapse comes, leaving them at the mercy of the state. They will be nothing more than a welfare of the state, and in due time request the government to aid them in their troubles. The only choice they will most likely have is everlasting servitude or attendance in internment camps; closed military bases set up like prisons; or the now existing open fields with fences and barbed wire, where you will be left to die. It may sound unrealistic, but their already exists pre-designed open fields or what can be considered concentration camps throughout the U.S. There are some in Pennsylvania, Virginia and California that I know of. The reason the term open fields is used, because unlike concentration camps, these pre-designed areas do not have commissaries, barracks or latrines. They are just open fields whereby tents will be set up for sleep within the confined area. This should give you an indication as to why it is important to possess the precious metals for all basic necessities for survival.

History speaks for itself. Hitler and Stalin conducted a war on gold. Why? The answer was because they wanted to achieve a true authoritarian society. This means all sovereignty, which gold can create, would have to be condensed and placed into the hands of the authoritative powers. This would take away practically all of the spending power of the people.

Money has been Debauched

The constitution authorized congress to coin gold and silver, the only power that was granted by the founding fathers to circulate as money within the states. The right and responsibility to provide for the congress to coin the metal was reserved unto the people. Once the metal was coined, it was given back to the people debt free to circulate as money. Had everyone abided by the use and true value of coins, we would have honest money today and debt would not exist. However, the framers of the constitution anticipated that in times of extreme crisis such as war, and for a short period, the government might need more money than the people could immediately provide. This allowed congress for emergency purposes, to borrow money on the credit of the US. Emergency purposes only, and not for the purpose of abuse.

It would be wise to consider protecting yourself and your immediate family. Fiat money (paper money) is already overvalued, and in times of a stock market crash, it will be rendered worthless: no one will be willing to sell you products or services for that cash. Further, you need to recognize the fact that products that maintain the necessities of life will be hard to come by. This would become a total disruption in your personal life and that of your family. If you can't eat, you can't sleep. An unhealthy mind, body and spirit will follow.

As to non-gold or silver coins, once again, they are copper-clad based and are nothing more than worthless slugs. You will eventually have a hard time using them. Maybe not in the immediate future, but as time passes, it will no longer be accepted here in the U.S., and will continue not to be accepted around the world. Gold is the last resort for inflation and gold is by no means worthless. It can truly be used as collateral anywhere in the world.

I do not recommend that gold and silver be used immediately following a crisis. The first line of defense should be the use of the more recently non-precious metal minted coins from the Treasury; this means the newer quarters, nickels, dimes and pennies. For quarters and dimes, this means anything post-1964.

For those coins, they are now copper-clad based. Remember, your cash and copper clad coins will mostly likely be the least of the remaining currency that you will have to spend. In a short period of time, that so-called legal tender will have been fully devalued, that is until the new legal tender already minted and stored by the government underground in barrels is introduced. Remember, the government does not try prevent problems such as these, but they create contingency plans.

This country has basically been operating without a source of true currency since 1933. In fact, the United States is already bankrupt. President Roosevelt declared so by Executive Orders 6073, 6102,6111, and also by EO 6260 on March 9, 1933 whereby they all fell under the auspices of the "Trading With the Enemy Act of the 65th Congress, on Oct. 6, 1917. Such was also codified at 12 U.S.C.A. 95a, which gave the President unprecedented powers and control under a "State of Emergency." On June 5, 1933, Congress confirmed the bankruptcy through the "Joint Resolution to Suspend The Gold Standard And Abrogate The Gold Clause. This was HJR 192, 73rd Congress, 1st session. Thereafter, the U.S. declared bankruptcy again in 1953 and has not recovered since.
Then, through another EO issued by President Johnson in 1968, silver backing was removed from our currency. This was the

final step of debauching the currency and totally made the country insolvent. The Federal Reserve issues currency no longer redeemable for silver. Furthermore, it does not matter to them anyway, because the Federal Reserve Bank is not a government institution, but a private corporation.

Paper Money and a Crisis

When the market does crash, and if there happens to be some remote chance that minute value is still in your paper dollar, then use it up while you can in order to buy real tangible assets. Almost anything that may appear by many to have a measurable value for bartering, should be obtained in order to pay any immediate pending debts.   The advice of paying off all debts such as mortgage payments, utilities, taxes, loans, etc. before or after the crash is not really realistic for most people. Therefore, I do not recommend this as a critical action, but if you can take care of all of your expenses, then do so before the impending panic, Y2K problem or the financial collapse actually takes full affect.

It has been stressed that the value of paper money will not last long immediately after a crash, therefore it would be in your best interest to rid yourself of it as soon as possible. Your money may last for a month or two, and therefore, that is about how much you should have on hand. One month of small dollar denominations will probably be sufficient. Remember, a one or two month supply is recommended since there is a remote chance of value still remaining in the paper dollar.

Keep your money out of the financial institutions. I am talking about the banks and credit unions. In any major crises that demands that people withdraw money from banks to survive and/ or satisfy their daily needs, this will make it very difficult for you to obtain your money from an institution that has locked their doors to the public. You do not want to find yourself scrambling for cash during a market crash; knowing that your checks and credit cards will be worthless. Keeping your money out of the bank enables you to avoid the force to forfeit your assets.

The government will most likely execute Executive Orders and some of them will be taking over any and all failed financial institutions. A new monetary unit will immediately implemented, however it will only be more paper. Once the new bills are distributed adequately, hyper-inflation will soon be due to set in. This will assure the negative effect upon paper money and copper-clad coinage.

The Black Market

The Black Market (underground economy) will be in peak operation, and in order to get some of the things you request or desire, you will have to probably resort to this market in some form or another. If you choose not to use the Black Market, then you will be welcomed to be a part of the government and their controlled rationing.

Hopefully by now, you will have already purchased your gold and silver coins well before the impending panic or after a market collapse. If not, prepare to pay a much higher price for your coins, especially in the Black Market if gold is once again banned, as opposed to what you would have paid before a market collapse. During good times and bad, the Black Market always survives. It will thrive during such a disastrous time period, and almost anything and everything a person will want or need is available; with better bargains obtained when using precious metals to pay for the goods or services.

The importance of gold has once again been recognized, and with proper investment in gold and silver, you will be able to weather the storm of a crisis much longer than the individual that does not have any. This would make them the have-nots and a ward of the state; placing in jeopardy their own lives into a New World Order unknown to them. If you cannot get coins above ground during the crises, you may have to at some time or another, go to the Black Market.

As to real money, silver should be your first line of defense. Real money is most effective when all other monetary units you are accustomed to using are no longer of value. Junk silver and not numismatic or collectible silver is recommended. Junk silver is silver that has been circulated in the economy, which will consist of pre-1964 quarters and half - dollars. You should if not already, buy these coins at least five hundred or so in number at a time, if you can afford it. If anything, you should have at least $500.00 in silver per family member. Adjust this amount according to your budget. This metal can be used in the above ground economy and the Black Market if you need to use it.

Your second line of defense should be the use of gold. This line is used for obtaining items or making payments that value more than the costs for simple bartering of bread or coffee. To start, use 1/10 ounce gold coinage to buy tangible assets, and work your way up with more valuable gold for payments such as taxes or for a house or a mortgage.

To be safe, stay with U.S. gold coins, whereby you risk less chances of confiscation by the government during the monetary crisis. Confiscation of U.S. minted coins would bring about confidence issues regarding currency. The people must have confidence in U.S. money if the government wants to keep order. Of course the government can change up and do what FDR did when he banned gold in the 1930's.

FDR- Just One of the Good Old Boys

On the Roosevelt side of the family tree, the ties with big banking date back to the 1780s when FDR's great grandfather founded the Bank of New York. Over the years since that then, many other members to the Roosevelt clan-- men like James I. Roosevelt, Clinton Roosevelt, Teddy Roosevelt and George E. Roosevelt -- had been heavily involved in politics and high finance.

"Gold always has been and always will be the irresistible power. Handled by expert hands, it always will be the most useful lever for those who possess it, and the object of envy for those who do not."
"Funeral Oration of Rabbi Reichorn."

In order to refresh your memory, with FDR's New Deal (an attempted New Order), the last of the gold from the U.S. Treasury was minted in 1933. President Franklin Delano Roosevelt announced a 4 day bank holiday and an embargo (ban) on gold. He essentially told the public that gold was no good and 1) that he was confiscating it, and 2) gave a reward to anyone who told on another person known to be possessing or hoarding it. FDR collected 15% of the gold minted in 1933, however the question should come to your mind as to what ever happened to the other 85% of the gold minted? Did people just throw it away because the government told the people that gold was no good? Did people forget to hand it in? Since when does the government tell people that something is no good and then collect it back instead of telling them to just throw it away? Are the people that stupid?

"With gold we can buy the most rebellious consciences, can fix the rate of all values, the current price of all products, can subsidize all State loans, and thereafter hold the states at our mercy."

Funeral Oration of Rabbi Reichorn.

What Signs to Look For

Yes, I do speak of a market crash, but one should look at the following signs that may lead to an increase in value of both gold and silver. I believe that in March of 1999, you will start to see significant turbulence in the stock market. In April or early May, a market crash may be inevitable. Remember, the first fiscal financial quarter begins in April, particularly April 1, for many states and branches of the federal government. If their computers cannot calculate into the following April of 2000 because of Y2K, many state and Federal agencies will encounter difficulties funding branches and agencies of government; branches and agencies that many funds, bonds and stocks depend on. A panic will then be created.

The following represent extreme activities that could also create such a panic or crash:

1. An increase in prices or inflation.
2. The devaluation of the current monetary unit (the dollar) in your country.
3. An Increase in Bank Failures.
4. Increase in the price of other commodities.
5. An increase in the demand for gold in the industrial and investment sector.
6. Stock market crash.

7. A Large scale war.

People Without Much Money

A lot of people will tell me that they have no money. Well, I've come to the realization there are many people without it, and they may have no choice when it is time to pay the piper. It would be best to try to come up with something; for something is better than nothing. Some people may have a vice for alcohol, drugs or entertainment, and there are many and varied vices. Take that same bit of money that you might have taken for x-amount of packs of cigarettes or whatever and put some of it toward silver if you can't afford gold. Silver has a property and monetary value.

I had an interesting conversation about gold, conversing with a man at a Charlotte, North Carolina airport. He said to me, it's impossible that the paper called fiat money can become valueless, because all of his money is tied up in the market he was taught to believe in: not that that has any bearing on his investments, right? I brought back the claim to say that he has been enslaved through the power of a constant barrage of belief in the fiat monetary system, and that he can see nothing else. Think about how many people think the same way, or believe that the government will never let a market collapse happen. To many, the thought of a New World Order is nothing more than a fantasy for conspiratorial individuals. If so, then you should ask yourself why did President George Bush mention it so many times.

No money in the bank? You don't know what to do? You're destitute? If you do not believe or understand what is being said here, then you must depend on your Uncle Sam. Behold the Pale Horse! They'll come in and say, we can't help you if you have no money in the bank, but we can surely give you a loan or menial job. Basically, they will be enslaving you to the government for the rest of your life; and you become nothing more than an indentured servant, serf or slave. If you don't mind, no problem then.

You say that won't happen? Let the stock markets collapse the way they will, and when they do, all those people with their 401ks, their IRAs, Roth IRAs, SIRA's will have nothing but a silly look on their face. Or for those with other types of pension plans, that are related to the company you work for, you will also find that due to the stock market crash your money will be worth nothing. Once it's worth nothing, the only thing the company you are vested in can say is, we're sorry but that's how the market goes; and you're an indentured servant to them for the rest of your life. There is no out! There is no entrepreneurship! There is no so-called independence!

A small note: one company that is an example of having knowledge of what is going on in this world, is a midtown Manhattan Swiss Bank that gave their employees in NY a watch as a 1998 Christmas bonus. In Switzerland, they gave all of their employees small bars of gold. Here, in the U.S., such a gift would create a lot of problems for that bank.

"No State shall enter into any treaty, alliance, or confederation; grant letters of marque and reprisal; coin money; emit letters of credit; make anything but gold and silver coin a tender in payment of debts; pass any bill of attainder, ex post facto law, or law impairing the obligation of contracts, or grant any title of nobility."
The United States Constitution *(Article I, Section 10)*

Emergency used to Seize Gold

On April 5, 1933, FDR issued this Executive Order:

"All persons are required to deliver on or before May 1, 1933

all gold coins, gold bullion, and gold certificates now owned by them to a Federal Reserve Bank, branch or agency, or to any member bank of the Federal Reserve System."

It was during the great depression of the 1930's that congress declared an emergency existed and seized all the people's peacetime constitutional money. The mints were closed, no longer coining the people's metal into money. An emergency currency was created to bring the country out of the depression.

"You are aware that the gold standard has been the ruin of the states which adopted it, for it has not been able to satisfy the demands for money, the more so that we have removed gold from circulation as far as possible."
Protocol 20

The gold standard was abandoned, and without it, the country continues to plummet deeper into financial chaos.

"The abandonment of the gold standard made it possible for the welfare statists (government bureaucrats) to use the banking system as an unlimited expansion for credit. In the absence of the gold standard, there is no way to protect savings from confiscation through inflation... Deficit spending is simply a

scheme for the "hidden" confiscation of wealth... Gold stands in the way of this insidious process.
"Chairman of Federal Reserve Board, Alan Greenspan"

Who Should be Buying Coins?

Everyone that would like to save their investments. No matter what profession you may happen to be in, you are not exempt! Whether you are a stock broker, underwriter, electrician or elevator operator if your earnings are vested in a 401K plan, IRA, CD, Keogh, mutual funds, bonds or stocks just to name a few, or any paper you need to invest in gold and silver coinage. I do not wish to be the one to make the recommendation that you place all of your invested earnings into coinage, or even a specific percentage, but in writing this book, hopefully you will have a new understanding of banks and the stock market manipulation. You should be able to make a wise decision on your own. Once you have made a wise decision and invested in coinage, you will not regret it. Times ahead promise to be quite disturbing. Remember the definition of the "Age of the Aquarius?"

Whether you are old, young, wealthy, poor, black, white, yellow red or blue, it does not matter; if you have some form of savings, this applies to you. Now is the time to protect what you have. This is not a racial war, but soon to be a war of the classes, and there will no longer be a middle class if the ruling elite can help it.

Anyone and everyone that would like their investments protected from a pending stock market collapse should take heed. Long before the revision of this book I have warned about the volatility of the market. It will soon take a turn for the worst and whether you are prepared or not your surroundings will drastically be affected. For people who actively participate in the stock market or those abreast of financial news are aware of the constant fluctuations in the market and still pay no attention to it. What more information do they need?

Maybe you cannot understand what belief is all about, meaning that the so-called informed believe a market crash could never happen again. If not in the month of April, then by August 22, 1999 when the Global Positioning Satellite shuts down they will believe. This satellite works in conjunction with the Atomic Clock and synchronizes many computer networks around the world; including telecommunication networks. The stock market cannot function without it.

What Should A Coin Buyer Look For?

Silver needs to purchased as your first line of defense. Silver can be used for purchase of basic necessities and used when others offer to barter with you. This can be wisely done by buying circulated silver; silver that has been passed from hand to hand.

Gold is your second line of defense, and can be used to buy property, pay taxes, car notes or pay for more high priced items. This is to be used for smaller priced items when low on first line of defense. You must take the gold to a coin dealer in order to break it down to an amount in silver for the lower – priced items. All this can be explained in further detail at my seminars and in my survival guide.

Both circulated and uncirculated are important when it comes to purchasing both gold and silver. Uncirculated is more valuable in most cases than circulated. You need to know what to look for. If you have questions, contact your coin dealer or me U.S. mail or e mail.

Types of Gold

Bullion gold are coins that are sold by weight and not their gold value. Therefore, if you are a conservative investor, this is surely one means of protecting yourself. You are buying gold and paying for its weight in ounces; ounce for ounce with the market value. A bullion coin is the South African Krugerrand or the American Eagle containing one ounce of pure gold. The price varies according to the price of gold in the market. I recommend the American Eagle.

Numismatic coins include gold coins but these coins are in demand by collectors and have numismatic premium which can be substantial. An analogy would be, an antique dealer putting a price on a rare antique. An example of a coin with numismatic value: The $20 St. Gaudens (or Liberty) U.S. $20 coin has almost one ounce of gold (90% gold, exact weight .9677 ounces) plus 10% copper (weight = 33.436 grams) but has considerable numismatic value.

Buy a Safe

"I know of no safe repository of the ultimate power of society but the people. And if we think they are not enlightened enough, the remedy is not to take power from them, but to inform them

by education. "

Thomas Jefferson

You will need to keep your coins in special casings and in a safe.
A safe that is reputable in name, and can withstand a tremendous
amount of heat in case of fire; at least twelve hundred degrees
Fahrenheit. Remember, you get what you pay for. This is not to
say that the safe that you purchase be the top of the line, but I
am saying that it should not be a low end priced safe either.
Your safe dealer should be very informative in helping you select
the proper kind you need for the proper purposes.

Local safe dealers are usually offer the best insurance. When I
say insurance, I am not speaking of policy insurance, but I am
speaking of a dealer that can deliver it to your premises and bolt
it down. Mail order companies cannot always do the same, but if
they can contract a person to bolt it down, then there is no
problem. The safe does not have to be bolted down if you plan
to be mobile with it in the near future; just make sure it is heavy
enough. With local dealers, if you ever experience problems
with the safe, you can always approach your local dealer to
rectify the problem.

I prefer non-electronic combination safes; turning the dial does not require me to have a battery in the time of an emergency. Nothing is foolproof. You can buy the most expensive safe in the world, however, all a thief needs is time. The object is to make it as difficult as possible for them to obtain such time. You must learn to think ahead of them if you are looking to preserve the valuables you need for survival.

I mentioned investing in a safe for the specific purpose of protecting your wealth. I do not recommend that you place your coinage in a safe deposit box. If the bank closes, and closes for a long period of time, you will not have access to your money. A thief likes nothing more than watching his victims exit a bank. Are you going to make yourself a victim?

If you happen to need more advice on safes, and would like someone who has been in the business for more than 25 years to help you in choosing a safe in the New York Metropolitan area or set up proper contacts with your safe dealer in another state, then call Bob of Mega Safe at 1800 851 2555. They are located at 12 East 46th Street in New York City. His shop also specializes in bullet–proof clothing and very high tech surveillance for your home. Let him know where you obtained this information and I am sure he will know exactly how to tailor to your needs.

The Psychology of it All

No one should know that you are collecting coins. You will become an initial target if people know. When it all comes down to D-Day, people will become desperate, and you will be the first person on the list they visit. Thieves know no boundaries. Learn to keep your mouth shut, for otherwise you risk all you have saved.

If possible, bury this safe on your property if you can, something I talk about in depth in my seminars. Dig a hole on your property and have it deep and wide enough for storage of other valuables. One method to use in order to avoid anyone knowing exactly what you are doing, place a shed over it. The trap door will be placed in the shed.

If you are in an urban environment, one must be more creative. I know that apartments are small. Public storage may be an alternative. A Public Storage facility that has security people working around the clock will be helpful. Remember, no one will know what you will be hiding in there; and make sure that it is bolted down as well as too heavy for them to outright lift and walk away. Let us not forget an alarm system to ward them off

and to alert guards at the storage area. Those that live in an
urban environment should use this method in what may appear to
be extenuating circumstances that prohibit them to place the safe
in their apartment.

Reputable Coin Dealers

These are the only type of people you should be buying from.
Reputation is as important as if you were seeking out an attorney
or a doctor. It is up to you to investigate for yourself and use
the advice of those that know of reputable dealers.

Reputation is key, that is why they have been in business so long.
Once they get a bad reputation, they may as well close shop:
business is over. Pay close attention when I say reputation is
key. Now, from time to time, some dealers make mistakes in the
value of the coins they sell, but not too often. They are human,
and humans make mistakes. Rest - assured that they will be
more than willing to rectify a mistake, and show you that it was
not intentional. Moreover, that the mistake is not a gross
negligence mistake, usually a minor one.

Your dealer should be one of experience. If you have any questions, they are there to answer them. Of course you must know what questions to ask. Make sure that they are a member of a professional organization. Here you will be able to find out for yourself whether or not they are in good standing in one of the most important organizations. This organization is the American Numismatic Association. If they are not a member of this organization, I would move on to the next dealer that is, and find out what their status is.

I should note the fact that membership in this organization is personal, therefore, a broker that is not reputable will be exposed, even if they are hiding behind a company membership. This will make it difficult for a company to go out of business and then start up again with a new membership. Call this association for a great reference. If they are not a part of the association, I would just like to say be careful. This association gives you the ability to use arbitration and/or mediation if you happen to be in conflict with any transactions that prove unsatisfactory. This serves as great protection. Remember, the dealer's reputation is on the line.

Businesses that have been around for at least 10 years or more are safe bets. You know that they are not going anywhere. You can find them in your local neighborhood where you can develop a personal relationship with them as if they were your personal jeweler. If you do not wish to deal locally, which is perfectly fine, then purchase a copy of one of the popular magazines such as Coin Age or Coin World. They contain reputable dealers who advertise in their magazine. They even tell you how long they have been in business.

When To Buy Coins

The sense of urgency cannot be expressed enough, you need to start buying now! If you do not, you will get first hand experience of the Herd Instinct when everyone catches on and tries to buy coinage, and prepare for the New World Order all at once. How many more stories and scenarios do you need? If I haven't provided you with enough already, then I suggest you pray for a miracle on the day this all comes to fruition, or just accept what is already planned for you.

You the reader knows well enough whether the markets are stable or volatile. Presently, the herd is looking the other way, and I am giving much of the information that you will need to be prepared. When the herd becomes informed, and you can bet your last dollar that they will, it will be too late. They will be paying high prices for everything; meaning gold and necessities such as water and food.

Timing is critical. Buy low and sell high is always the motto, but if you wait, you know the deal. Do not hesitate, for if you do, you will pay the price. You do not have to jump into this head first, because you may still have time to evaluate all of your options in buying all the things that you will need to survive this coming chaos.

Again: Why Should You Buy?

In a nutshell! The market crash within the near future. You know that nothing lasts forever. Take off your rose-colored glasses and realize that history repeats itself. Preparation is the key to success. There are some countries that don't even accept paper money. Gold and silver will be a necessity to barter. Things will become chaotic. However, gold, silver and other precious metals thrive on confusion, disorder and instability.

Here is a brief summary about precious metals. As to the characteristics of money, true money, precious metals and/or tangibles are:

1. Easily definable.
2. Very difficult to denominate or devalue.
3. Scarce.
4. Divisible.
5. Measurable
6. Value of the metal is high due to its content and in relation to its volume and weight.
7. Easily recognized.
8. Portable

How to Purchase Your Coins

If you are a first time buyer: I recommend starting with bullion coins until you have a comfortable understanding of the numismatic market. When you begin to purchase, you may charge the coins, but a paper trail of what you bought will be made; something to note just in case the government decides to ban and confiscate gold as FDR did back in 1934-34. You can pay by check or money order, and I recommend money order or check. This enables you to track your own purchases. Of course cash is always best, but this decision is up to you. All forms of payment are legal.

Look for registered and insured mail when your coins are delivered to you. The dealer should send them to you in this fashion, just in case anything may happen to them; such as being delivered to the wrong address. Sending coins registered and insured mail is standard procedure. Upon purchase, it is your job to take physical delivery of the coins by having the dealer send the coins out immediately upon their availability to them. You do not want to leave your coins in possession of a dealer.

Start buying coin magazines to make yourself familiar with what you are getting into. If you are still hesitant, then start attending coin shows and ask around about how many years the dealer you are considering has been in the business. I suggest only one dealer in this book because I know him well and his knowledge of everything I have written about. I am a coin dealer, and have been in the business of collecting coins for years. Andy Gause's dealership is S.D.L. Coins. Dial 1 800 468-2646. The address is P.O. Box 198, Hawthorne, NJ, 07507. If you mention this book or my name, he has provided special packages that I deem very valuable for the beginning collector to the advanced collector. Be sure to ask about his gold and silver bucket special as well as prices on $20.00 gold pieces; they are very hot items.

Snail mail or E mail me with any of your questions, and I will answer as many as I can handle. The E mail address is destech@pcrealm.net. Start buying in small amounts until you feel comfortable enough to gradually increase your purchases. During each purchase, look for a guarantee. If the dealer does not offer one, then choose another one. SDL also offers a 30 day money back guarantee. No questions asked.

Choose a dealer that is willing to educate you about buying coins. The dealer should be able to understand your objective and then help you plan and buy accordingly. For instance, a dealer should explain what the value is in having a graded coin and why an independent grader is necessary. Surely, one should question a person who grades a coin themselves and places a value on the coin. The question is, can the dealer/grader be objective? It is risky for them to do that and remember, their reputation is on the line.

CHAPTER EIGHT

YOUR HEALTH IS KEY

According to Webster's Dictionary, the definition of health is the condition of being of sound in mind; body or spirit. I believe that you need all three together to achieve total health. One cannot do without the other. In preparation for Y2K, 5/5/2000 and a One World Government, you need to have your health together if you want to survive the chaos. Everyone should keep in good health, but of course, such is not the case. However, without good health, you can't do anything you wish to do or enjoy anything you may want to do because you are too busy laying on your back wishing to get better.

Good health is the key factor in motivation. To achieve, you must be willing to take on any challenges that may come your way. Basically, without it, you will be close to useless in protecting yourself and family. This means in money, love, or happiness. Too many people happen to take it for granted. That is why so many people die an early death, succumb to unwarranted ailments and the like.

I believe that it is very important that you get to know your self and prepare yourself for all of the above events. I have written a book called <u>Finding Your Perfect Soulmate or Business Partner,</u> and here the actual science of Numerology is used to find out more about a persons' positive and negative characteristics. No opinion are expressed. All you need to know is a birth date of a person. Numbers do not lie.

The word Health in numerology represents number nine. The number nine represents totality or completion; such as in the date 1999. For example:

There are nine planets in the solar system.

There are nine radiation belts in the solar system.

It takes nine months for a woman to have a baby.

There are 360 degrees in a circle (3+6=9).

There are 180 degrees in half a circle (1+8=9).

There are nine letters in the month of September.

September is the ninth month.

The same thing can be done for each number counting from numbers one through the number nine.

As for the year of 1999, notice how many number nines are in this year. This is a year of completion; simply making a path for the new. If you reverse the nines, you will kind of get the idea. For your safety, and possibly a peace of mind, do not make any special arrangements on the dates of September 9, 1999 or September 18, 1999. I believe you need no further explanation.

I recommend my Perfect Soulmate book and then my materials on numbers and health for a better understanding of yourself. Once you have that, then you have obtained a part of the keys to your own success.

The importance of good health cannot be expressed enough, and since it is difficult to perform any function without it, it is important to build your Mind, Body and Spirit. In general, the mind represents all of the faculties necessary to clearly think and reason. The body represents the physical faculties that allow the body to achieve feats of strength. The spirit represents the spirit that keeps all of your energy flowing in a positive or negative state.

There is a significant relevance of numbers and foods. In brief, once you become familiar with foods associated with each of the numbers one through nine, your health will improve dramatically. Basically it is up to you to understand your purpose in life, and maintain your good health as handed down by the creator. The object is not to abuse what you have been blessed with. Therefore, one should soon begin to know some of the basics: to keep yourself in good health.

There are foods to avoid with each number. Some of the major foods to avoid are pork; fluoridated water; red meat; shell fish and canned foods if possible. You must learn to concentrate on the consumption of nutritious foods during the critical moments. This can be done by starting with the consumption of foods within your immediate environment.

Health Maintenance is key, and here are some things to consider: All the foods that you eat and activities you conduct, should fortify the mind, body and spirit. For example, proper preparation of foods and ingredients to prevent any ailments that stem from uncooked foods. Exercise to condition the mind, body and spirit to withstand all challenges that lie ahead.

Martial Arts – This is an exercise that actually exercises all three, and make no mistakes about it that it does in fact work. It will help you improve in all that you wish to do.

Chess – This game may be taken lightly by many as just a game, but this is a game to be taken seriously. It represents a heavy thought process that one must develop; equations for winning; use of strategy once used by ancient Egyptians; provides a martial artist with keys of development and movement and conditioning of mind with concentration just to name a few.

Reading (selective reading) – No longer should one have time to read fiction, but read things that are relevant to survival and educating the mind for development of knowledge. This would be done in order to possibly, one day, become more in tune with the universe and the knowledge given for one to possess.

Meditation – The same as prayer whereby a person is supposed to still the mind, and let the

Creator provide you with the answers necessary for fulfillment in life. This is for people who are religious or not.

Prayer – Give thanks to the Creator for all the achievements one has made in life.

Scheduling an exercise routine will create the discipline you need to get started, and remain in a desired condition.

Be realistic when you set up a routine for yourself.

Create a schedule for yourself, and do not stray from it. You must crawl before you can work. Conduct basic body exercises and gradually increase your routine to maximize your efforts.

Importance of breathing – It is truly important to breathe correctly if you want your mental, spiritual and physical faculties to improve. Breathing actually changes your body chemistry for the positive. Continue taking time out to conduct deep breathing exercises throughout the day and the change within yourself will immediately become apparent.

Basic Spiritual Exercises – Read or create positive affirmations each and every day, if you truly would like to accomplish a task. You must see that task in your mind and make positive affirmations with words that mention the task.

All of the important facets mentioned above have been mentioned to give you just a brief synopsis of preparing for the year 2000. It also applies to daily life, and therefore there is no time to waste in starting to look after your health now. If more detailed information is desired, you may contact my company in order to learn more about numbers and health.

CHAPTER NINE

SURVIVAL SKILLS

"Come out of her (Babylon) Lest you partake of her sins and receive her plagues."
Revelation 18:4

Survival is the ability to maintain one's own life in times of crisis. Needless to say, not much convincing should be necessary to convince a reader of the fact that preparation is needed for the aftermath. You have come to understand that people will definitely be without basic necessities and facilities that they were once accustomed. Most people will not be exempt from this event, and in this chapter, I will provide you with many tips on how to plan properly. Remember, this is a no nonsense guide or what some may call a radical approach to bringing you into an organized state of mind.

Learn to work with your neighbors. No one, and I mean no one will be able to survive this catastrophe alone. The number two in

Numerology as in the year 2000 represents, cooperation, communication, tact and diplomacy. In other words, you must get to know your neighbor now and not to wait until D-Day. If you have enemies as neighbors, now is time to see if you can rectify differences. They may even respect you more if you make an attempt and try to calmly educate them on the Y2K problem. If they are not interested in what you have to say, don't worry, they will eventually come around and become friends, or possibly die.

Numbers do not lie, and the creator designed the number two to be the number of challenge during the year of initiation of a New World Order; which will make disastrous effects upon people. See my book Finding Your Perfect Soulmate or Business Partner for an explanation of the numbers.

***Here are some of the important necessities one should consider for survival*:**

Bottled water:

Water is more important than any other liquid or substance on earth. At least a 90 day supply along with water filters should be sufficient initially. It may sound unrealistic for some, but start storing now. If you wait too long, rest assured that bottled water will be scarce or outright unavailable. Further, do not keep your water in bio-degradable containers. They will eventually deteriorate and you will lose the water that you so preciously stored. Use water bottles, pumps and filters specifically designed for storage purposes.

Water Purification:

Water purification devices and tablets are necessary to maintain your life. Water I must repeat is essential, and there is no guarantee that when the chaos begins or ends, that water will be fit to drink; at least in your environment. Be health conscious in all of your activities, especially when it comes to the water that you will be drinking and cleansing with. Nothing can be worse than ingesting bad water into your body. You will be on your back faster than you know what hit you.

Boiling water that you obtain is a must. If you do not have access to a water purification device, at least make sure that you have a stock of water purification tablets, bleach or iodine. Someone else may have a water purification device and your tablets will be for emergency back up. Not only is good water beneficial to you, but to others. Both the water purifier and water purification tablets will be good for barter.

Underground Storage

You will certainly need a place to keep your food, firearms and coinage in a safe and easily accessible location; such as an underground storage. That is, if you have access to such a place. If not, you will have to make due with what you have. Underground storage keeps all materials cool and dry from exposure to the harmful elements above ground. Friends and neighbors will not know that you even have a place, unless you tell them. Therefore, I suggest that you don't! This is for the safety of you, your family and your valuables that you placed underground.

You know what happens when people get desperate, and you know that you cannot feed or protect the entire world; or part of it. Visit your storage site outside the view of onlookers, and make sure that it is securely locked and bolted. Some may consider an alarm system and/or (not my recommendation) a booby trap. If you do not have a storage outlet, then you should consider building one. Remember, we are talking survival of the fittest!

Food Storage

Food Supplies, freeze dried and dehydrated foods are the types of foods you should consider storing. Non - canned preferred, but it is still okay. These are of course things that can be used as another barter item. Short and long term food storage is another form of insurance for you and your family. Survival truly means nothing if you do not have anything to eat. Here are just some of the foods discussed to protect you in a society that is extremely vulnerable to events and conditions that are difficult to control. A food supply company that I recommend is Mountain House Foods. They are a company located out in Utah. Dial 1 800 866 4876 for further information and ordering. Tell them that I sent you, and they will present you with unique discount packages.

We will first start with what are called Military Rations. Military Rations are an effective way for many people to prepare for emergency food needs. Such foods are for short term and mobile use. Many people may find themselves without shelter once things first begin to happen. This could stem from fire, flooding or nuclear plant meltdown threats. In any event, one must be ready to bring food with them on their journey to a safe haven.

These foods may not be the healthiest of foods; and in fact many are fiberless. However, they do have nutritional value that will sustain you. Military rations should be consumed within 21 days from its date of manufacture; that is, if it is stored at room temperature. The shelf - life period is fluctuates depending upon the temperature of the storage facility. Look to see if the date on the package is the manufacture or inspection date. The inspection date can be anywhere up to three years later than the stamped date. You want to minimize your mistakes. Life is nothing to make mistakes with.

Some rations, depending on what they are and where they come from can last a very long time. If the temperature can be kept at 70 degrees or less in the proper environment, then shelf life can increase to approximately 8 to 10 years. What a difference! Ask the manufacturer if you choose this route. Store your foods right, and they will be ready to eat. Water is seldom needed. Just open the product and you will be set to go.

Remember these are Military Rations and are for mobile use. This type of food resource is recommended if you will be consistently mobile.

Canned Foods

I do not recommend them as a first alternative, but they will do. Whether you are mobile or not, they are extremely heavy and only retain 50 – 60% of their nutritional value. The reason for this, is that during their manufacturing process, companies use a heat sealing process. This process in effect actually sterilizes the foods in the can. Therefore, you will be lucky to get at least half the nutritional value.

Dehydrated and freeze dried foods are the best for easy storage, but cans can be stacked neatly. They are both very nutritious and retain a high percentage of their nutrition because of the way that they are packaged and are very lightweight. The drawback of dehydrated and freeze dried foods are however, that they need water to be edible. If not, these foods will be no good to you. Make sure that you keep these foods off the ground and on shelves or wood pallets when storing them.

Supply

If you anticipate storage of food, a one month supply would be a whole lot better than nothing at all. Finding food in bad times would be extremely difficult, especially in light of the nonexistent food reserves in this country. The best method of preserving fruits is freeze drying. As for fruits, they retain a whole appearance since using this method leaves their composite makeup intact. Many of these products have exceptional flavor because they are processed when ripe or ready to be harvested.

This is accomplished by flash freezing the food and then sublimating it (in other words removing the moisture at low temperature and low vacuum). A freeze dried product would have roughly a 2% moisture content. The end-product would leave about 90% of its nutrient content intact. The ultra light weight, the nutrition and the increased variety would be the major benefits.

The best method of preserving meats is freeze drying also. Long term storage of meats such as chicken, beef, turkey and shrimp are possible with the freeze drying process allows the fat to be kept to a minimum; ensuring long shelf life at 70 degrees Fahrenheit or less.

The shelf life of freeze-dried products would be in excess of 5 years, however, they should be rotated within that 5 year period of storage. A few companies offer freeze-dried items, dehydrated items and staples in a combination food system. With the proper mix of products, you end up with a large variety of foods that are familiar, very nutritious, lightweight foods which last for long periods of time without the need for refrigeration. The main thing to remember is that prudent people prepare for all possible situations.

At the very least, get started on it. Remember, it is better to buy one hundred days early rather than one day too late. All the freeze-dried and dehydrated food manufacturers combined can handle only 5,000 clients at a time. This is a very finite resource.

Before you buy somewhere else on a promise of faster shipping, ask them if they will guarantee shipment delivery time, give it to you in writing, and even pay you a per-day-late penalty if they don't get it to you on time. You will truly find out how sincere these food distributors are.

This is all about Insurance

Food insurance that is. Whether it is how to navigate with a compass, find safe water, start fires, or build emergency shelters, you need to sharpen those skills. Many of these aspects of survival only require common sense to apply such skills.

If the Y2K problem does in fact become a serious factor as I believe, then in order to go about your daily regimen and buy food as if nothing ever happened, then you must continue believe that everything else will work perfectly as it does today. The things that need to operate perfectly are: your bank; your job; and your health. We could even make the list go on if you think that's all? Hopefully you will receive the correct paycheck, your supermarket will be well stocked; the local delivery trucks and their warehouses are operable; the manufacturer's shippers and the plant itself have no interruptions; the farmers and their harvesting equipment can produce; and the weather is not to bad to travel in. Remember, this problem will start in the dead of winter.

If there is a break in this chain, then it will only take a few days before you actually start going hungry; not to mention your family. Choose a permanent place for storage and stop wasting time. A permanent place is necessary because you will indeed find it very difficult to move one hundred ten gallon grain storage barrels or water barrels. You will have already fixed fences around your property, provided fuel generators powered by diesel fuel, solar or wind. Your storage of firewood, the weight of a wood or coal burning stove, tools need to be considered; and the list goes on.

Protect Your Surroundings

Today you may be one of the unnoticed, however, if you are a well prepared individual or family when such catastrophic events occur, then you will become a target. A target to those who were rich and had it all, and by those who never had anything at all. People will become hungry, greedy, desperate and on the hunt for what you have, and what others wish they had to survive.

If you live in an urban environment, you should consider scouting out locations wherein you can secure yourself and/or family. However, you must make it appear that your secured area has nothing to offer to outsiders. In other words, your area needs to appear invisible. There should be no signs of food, weapons or gold storage. When people start scrambling, they tend to look anywhere and everywhere their eyes and senses take them. Pretend you have nothing, and hopefully they will pass you by. If they don't, then you must be prepared to handle the situation as you see fit. In looking for a place, remember that you will be looking for a great location and if you consider it great, others will also. You will not be the only one in the search for a better living.

Evaluate your surroundings. You may not have everything necessary to consider yourself prepared. Therefore, locate warehouses owned by industries that would be important to you such as: agriculture, medical, hygiene and water storage just to name a few. If you do not have the money to give them, hopefully you will have something to trade with the owners of these facilities.

If you are in a suburban or rural and own a house, then make sure that you have the ability to drill a well in your house. Not necessarily around your house, which is in sight of possible scavengers, but inside of your house. There would be no better place than in your basement. You do not have to drill it at the moment, but be sure that you have the capability to do so when the time is near or when the time comes. Hand drill and hand pump systems cost around $2,500 and are designed to go at least 100 feet deep. Do not forget however, that it is very difficult to dig in the winter; meaning that the ground may be frozen when you decide to drill. Therefore, do this ahead of time.

It would be great if you could gather everything and manage all of it at the same time, but what is the likelihood of that? That is unless you truly have the space like a farm. It will definitely be important to have food, non-hybrid seeds, a generator, fuel storage tanks, heating elements, livestock, weapons and so forth. These things you will need wherever you are; and this is why the space is needed.

If you are located or will be in a metropolitan area for a while, you may have to work harder than those in areas that have a lesser population. Things you need to scout out in advance would be:

1. Where you can get easy access to a farming ground for food and possible storage for your valuables. This may be a bartering route if you become friendly with your local farmer. If you need your own farm land, then gather people in your apartment building, complex, co-op or whatever and use vacant lots and ball fields for farming. Houses that are built around courtyards can even be converted to green houses for plant life. Many plants cannot survive winter months, and a greenhouse would be perfect.

    Map out areas like the military does, where industries and warehouses are located, and what is in them that can be useful to you and your neighbors. Identify all stores like a Home Depot where you can go get basic supplies to build anything you need. People who are desperate or rioters will not be likely to loot lumber, fertilizer, clothes, greenhouse materials, solar batteries, short wave radios and other immediate non-apparent materials.

3. Make yourself appear invisible. Take time to think through how to make your area appear abandoned and burned over. It is important to go unnoticed by others for at least a month or more. This way, you can keep what you may have longer than if you were a target by scavengers.

4. Think through all other forms of preparation that anyone else would take to survive.

5. Settle differences among your enemies. Whatever the differences, I am sure they can be rectified in some form. It is easier to hate and get things accomplished, as opposed to loving a person and getting things accomplished.

This is a short list of what you may need immediately after Y2K causes disruptions.

- Medical care and Hygiene products.
- Digging tools
- Search lights
- Fuel
- Tent

David E. Smith

- Generators (China Diesel Imports at 1800 341 7027)
- Hard copies of all financials
- Check your computer system to see if it is Y2K ready.
- Build a computer network in your own house.
- Buy weapons, particularly a handgun for urban areas.

Caught between a rock and a hard place? The recommendation is to take your money out of the bank at least seven or eight months in advance. However, even though I wish that all people would do this, this would not be beneficial to you as an individual or a family. That is unless the United States adopts a policy of gold as a monetary standard instead of fiat paper.

So, if too many people withdraw their money from the bank at the same period of time, you will find a "A Run on the Bank," consequently affecting your savings and other financial treasures. Say if there was a "Run on the Bank" of both Citibank and Chase, two of the largest banks in the world, such a run would ripple outwards to other banks, mutual funds, pension funds, and a myriad of other financial institutions. It would definitely set the stage for a US financial collapse of the U.S. debt structure. If this were to happen, then the debt pyramid would crumble while leaving gold and silver or in other words, liquid assets intact.

CHAPTER TEN

5/5/2000

Enough has been said. If you believe that you are up to par with the Y2K issue and are prepared, then I suggest you also consider preparation for 5/5/2000. The Age of Aquarius is not a period of time to take lightly.

On May 5, 2000, the Sun, Mercury, Venus, Mars, Jupiter, and Saturn will be aligned with the Earth and her Moon. On that day, there will be an ice buildup at the South Pole will upset the Earth's axis. This will send trillions of tons of ice and water sweeping over the surface of our planet.

This is an extremely important event whereby it is safe to say, that you will probably not hear enough about it or the truth about it in the media any time soon. If you do, will you be prepared? I am not fully adept with knowledge on this topic, but after reading the book 5/5/2000 by Richard Noone, I have read enough to relate my opinion that this is a cataclysmic and/or catastrophic event that involves the restructuring of the Earth's surface. I am talking about a total shift of all land masses through massive tidal waves, earthquakes, volcanic activity, extreme temperature changes, change in length of time for daylight and night time.

Author Richard Noone's diligent, thorough and extensive investigation and study, has revealed some of the mysteries of the Great Pyramid. The Great Pyramid has left the world with a mathematical message of warning displayed within the great structure by the survivors of a catastrophic event that happened years ago.

This author had spent more than twenty years researching his theories and analyzing the information handed through the writings on the walls in the great structures. This is an event that has been recorded and pin – pointed to happen more than six thousand years ago. Noone received numerous acclaims and even the Georgia Grand Master 's Award for his discovery of Masonic Influence in Ancient Egypt and his work has been featured on major national media.

History has proven that over time, through the remains of lost civilizations preserved in museums, that evidence of entire forests fossilized instantly, and animals quick-frozen and preserved for thousands of years prove that a sudden, momentous change in the Earth's surface occurred in the past.

All this is mentioned, not to scare you into thinking that the end of the world is near, but to be conscious as an individual or people that you must be prepared, using the Creator – given talents you have been blessed with.

CHAPTER ELEVEN

THE MASTER AGENDA

What the Truth Brings Forth

An attack upon me as an author and as a person is sure to come since I have included the Protocols of the Learned Elders of Zion by Victor Marsden. I include this material that indicates Jewish influence: not to accuse all Jews, but to show you the role played by the illuminati to disguise their evil plan. The world Jews I believe, were possibly used to throw readers off and to blame a particular group of individuals. However, there are too many people involved in this entire conspiracy to be just one group of people. The ones who will attack me with the words anti-Semite will be those who have not read extensively on their own history; have succumb to the brainwashing about their true history and refuse to accept any scholarly work; and Jewish members of the conspiracy who are so skillful and crafty at denouncing their role in this plan, that with their money and power involved, people do not see their evil intentions. This is not about the evilness of

Jews, but the evilness of a small group of individuals who will stop at nothing to bring civilizations to their knees. Evil has no color, ethnic or religious boundaries.

Surely the anti-defamation league will be one of the many groups of attack, however if you truly knew who finances them and why it is in their interest to create a distraction from the research I bring forth, then you will pay them no mind. Why them, because they are agents of the Elite groups that keep tabs on anybody or organizations that the elite perceive as a threat to a One-World government. Therefore, when they speak, the media who is controlled by the conspirators, gives them enough air-time to denounce any honest scholarship regarding Jews and agents of other international bankers. They are some of the many groups who suppress scholars, as well as elite universities and the media. Just take a look at who is in charge of these various groups and notice that they too are either Trilateralists or on the Council on Foreign Relations.

From Rothschild to Warburg, both international bankers should in fact be loathed by Jews and anyone else who understand how these individuals and their empire have robbed them for years and their families, and are still doing so. Furthermore, not to mention that these same Jews, helped finance Adolph Hitler; a man who had a mother that was Jewish. Understand something

here. Money is of course the root of all evil and these were two
individuals that happened to be Jewish, were involved in what
was a war that money was the major issue. Hitler was not some
"beer-hall junkie" (the exact words of my 7th grade history
teacher) who supposedly came out of no where and was allowed
to lead a tremendously powerful army to destroy countries and
lives in Europe. Does that even sound logical to you? One man
alone cannot achieve such a feat.

Everyone in an industrialized nation was affected and not just
Jews. The reader should realize that these international bankers
sole interest were placing a government, a government indebted
to them, in deeper debt. The more debt, the more control over a
nation. The higher the debt, the greater the interest. There is no
greater means than war to drive a nation into greater debt.

Further, they finance both sides of the fighting factions. The
international banker doesn't have any enemies, and their only
friend is money. More Money! Both sides needed weapons,
intelligence and mercenaries. Both sides have to pay for all of
the above. The international banker even had control of who
would win the war before it even started. Cut off the supplies on
one side, and eventually the other side will win. Ah, but wait!
The winning side must pay more. I am speaking of urban
renewal. Cities and towns must be rebuilt and services must be

provided. Who would have such money to finance these projects after a war. You guessed it, international bankers! This is a game that has been played for years and nothing has changed.

Take a look at both the Republicans and Democrats who argue themselves silly over a created issue. Usually an issue is handed down by the elite to the media to both parties, who later jump up with a thesis and antithesis. Finally after pointless arguing, they come up with a synthesis, usually meaning an agreement. If an agreement is not reached, a vote is conducted or the issue is suspended. Regardless, a decision made upon vote is a decision towards a One World government. As to a suspended issue, the elite have already decided its fate before handed down; whether the issue is agreed upon or not.

Many people over time have pointed to the Jews as truly power hungry individuals that focus on world domination. No, it is not just the Jews involved in this forthcoming atrocity, but once again, all races, religions and ethnicities are involved in this conspiracy.

It was Colonel House that went on to note that for the conspiracy to be successful, it needs to place "itself into the primaries, in order that no candidate might be nominated whose views were not in accord with theirs." This should alarm you to the point to realize that major elections, which in the past and presently, have gone practically unquestioned. Many, are nothing more than a mere electronically controlled charade or magic show for the masses to participate. It is their voting rights that have disappeared.

Clinton Roosevelt was the Illuminist philosopher who wrote <u>The Science of Government, Founded on Natural Law</u>. In his book, Roosevelt outlined the Illuminati's plans for the regimentation of mankind under those who, like himself, were the enlightened ones. He revealed their plans to emasculate and then destroy the Constitution which he likened to a "leaky vessel" which was "hastily put together when we left the British flag." Many observers recognize this amazing document as the basic blueprint for what later became known as FDR's "New Deal" or what could be seen as a proposed New World Order.

Below is a document that can be considered the blueprint or Master Agenda for the systematic destruction of our National Sovereignty, U.S. Constitution and Civilization. This document has been published in many forms and has been circulated among the Illuminati since the late 1700's. This document is part of a Luciferian Conspiracy and should not be directed as a hatred towards or from Jews. It is a document disguised by the Illuminati to portray that it was written by Jews. This document was planned by evil conspirators that wish to remain anonymous.

In reading this document, you can compare it with history and the present. You will, after careful reading and comprehension, understand that what is being said is already taking place.

In this public domain document, two words would frequently recur. These two words were "Goyim" and "Agentur." The first word, is a word that means "human cattle," and is used in a demeaning manner to indicate all peoples of all races, creed or nationality that are not members of the selected class called the Illuminati (those considered the power and intellectual elite). The word "Agentur" represents the entire group of agents made use of by the Illuminati. In other words, they are "experts," advisers," and "specialists" to those who represent influential power in the government. Any reference to the word "Jew" should be replaced with "Illuminati" and "Goyims" with "cattle." I have already made the substitutions; depicting the true words of the document.

THE PROTOCOLS OF THE MEETINGS OF THE LEARNED ELDERS OF ZION

PROTOCOL No. 1

....Putting aside fine phrases we shall speak of the significance of each thought: by comparisons and deductions we shall throw light upon surrounding facts.

What I am about to set forth, then, is our system from the two points of view, that of ourselves and that of the [GENERAL MASSES] [HUMAN CATTLE]. (i.e., non-[illuminati]).

It must be noted that men with bad instincts are more in number than the good, and therefore the best results in governing them are attained by violence and terrorization, and not by academic discussions. Every man aims at power, everyone would like to become a dictator if only he could, and rare indeed are the men who would not be willing to sacrifice the welfare of all for the sake of securing their own welfare.

What has restrained the beasts of prey who are called men? What has served for their guidance hitherto?

In the beginnings of the structure of society, they were subjected to brutal and blind force; after words - to Law, which is the same force, only disguised. I draw the conclusion that by the law of nature right lies in force.

Political freedom is an idea but not a fact. This idea one must know how to apply whenever it appears necessary with this bait of an idea to attract the masses of the people to one's party for the purpose of crushing another who is in authority. This task is rendered easier of the opponent has himself been infected with the idea of freedom, SO-CALLED LIBERALISM, and, for the sake of an idea, is willing to yield some of his power. It is precisely here that the triumph of our theory appears; the slackened reins of government are immediately, by the law of life, caught up and gathered together by a new hand, because the blind might of the nation cannot for one single day exist without guidance, and the new authority merely fits into the place of the old already weakened by liberalism.

In our day the power which has replaced that of the rulers who were liberal is the power of Gold. Time was when Faith ruled. The idea of freedom is impossible of realization because no one knows how to use it with moderation. It is enough to hand over a people to self-government for a certain length of time for that people to be turned into a disorganized mob. From that moment on we get internecine strife which soon develops into battles between classes, in the midst of which States burn down and their importance is reduced to that of a heap of ashes.

Whether a State exhausts itself in its own convulsions, whether its internal discord brings it under the power of external foes - in any case it can be accounted irretrievable lost: IT IS IN OUR POWER. The despotism of Capital, which is entirely in our hands, reaches out to it a straw that the State, willy-nilly, must take hold of: if not - it goes to the bottom.

Should anyone of a liberal mind say that such reflections as the above are immoral, I would put the following questions: If every State has two foes and if in regard to the external foe it is allowed and not considered immoral to use every manner and art of conflict, as for example to keep the enemy in ignorance of plans of attack and defense, to attack him by night or in superior numbers, then in what way can the same means in regard to a worse foe, the destroyer of the structure of society and the commonweal, be called immoral and not permissible?

Is it possible for any sound logical mind to hope with any

success to guide crowds by the aid of reasonable counsels and arguments, when any objection or contradiction, senseless though it may be, can be made and when such objection may find more favor with the people, whose powers of reasoning are superficial? Men in masses and the men of the masses, being guided solely by petty passions, paltry beliefs, traditions and sentimental theorems, fall a prey to party dissension, which hinders any kind of agreement even on the basis of a perfectly reasonable argument. Every resolution of a crowd depends upon a chance or packed majority, which, in its ignorance of political secrets, puts forth some ridiculous resolution that lays in the administration a seed of anarchy.

The political has nothing in common with the moral. The ruler who is governed by the moral is not a skilled politician, and is therefore unstable on his throne. He who wishes to rule must have recourse both to cunning and to make-believe. Great national qualities, like frankness and honesty, are vices in politics, for they bring down rulers from their thrones more effectively and more certainly than the most powerful enemy. Such qualities must be the attributes of the kingdoms of the [GENERAL MASSES] [HUMAN CATTLE], but we must in no wise be guided by them.

Our right lies in force. The word "right" is an abstract

thought and proved by nothing. The word means no more than: Give me what I want in order that thereby I may have a proof that I am stronger than you.

Where does right begin? Where does it end?

In any State in which there is a bad organization of authority, an impersonality of laws and of the rulers who have lost their personality amid the flood of rights ever multiplying out of liberalism, I find a new right - to attack by the right of the strong, and to scatter to the winds all existing forces of order and regulation, to reconstruct all institutions and to become the sovereign lord of those who have left to us the rights of their power by laying them down voluntarily in their liberalism.

Our power in the present tottering condition of all forms of power will be more invincible than any other, because it will remain invisible until the moment when it has gained such strength that no cunning can any longer undermine it.

Out of the temporary evil we are now compelled to commit will emerge the good of an unshakable rule, which will restore the regular course of the machinery of the national life, brought to naught by liberalism. The result justifies the means.

Let us, however, in our plans, direct our attention not so much to what is good and moral as to what is necessary and useful.

Before us is a plan in which is laid down strategically the line from which we cannot deviate without running the risk of seeing the labor of many centuries brought to naught.

In order to elaborate satisfactory forms of action it is necessary to have regard to the rascality, the slackness, the instability of the mob, its lack of capacity to understand and respect the conditions of its own life, or its own welfare. It must be understood that the might of a mob is blind, senseless and un-reasoning force ever at the mercy of a suggestion from any side. The blind cannot lead the blind without bringing them into the abyss; consequently, members of the mob, upstarts from the people even though they should be as a genius for wisdom, yet having no understanding of the political, cannot come forward as leaders of the mob without bringing the whole nation to ruin.

Only one trained from childhood for independent rule can have understanding of the words that can be made up of the political alphabet.

A people left to itself, i.e., to upstarts from its midst,

brings itself to ruin by party dissentions excited by the pursuit of power and honors and the disorders arising therefrom. Is it possible for the masses of the people calmly and without petty jealousies to form judgment, to deal with the affairs of the country, which cannot be mixed up with personal interest? Can they defend themselves from an external foe? It is unthinkable; for a plan broken up into as many parts as there are heads in the mob, loses all homogeneity, and thereby becomes unintelligible and impossible of execution.

It is only with a despotic ruler that plans can be elaborated extensively and clearly in such a way as to distribute the whole properly among the several parts of the machinery of the State: from this the conclusion is inevitable that a satisfactory form of government for any country is one that concentrates in the hands of one responsible person. Without an absolute despotism there can be no existence for civilization which is carried on not by the masses but by their guide, whosoever that person may be. The mob is savage, and displays its savagery at every opportunity. The moment the mob seizes freedom in its hands it quickly turns to anarchy, which in itself is the highest degree of savagery.

Behold the alcoholic animals, bemused with drink, the

right to an immoderate use of which comes along with freedom. It is not for us and ours to walk that road. The peoples of the [GENERAL MASSES] [HUMAN CATTLE] are bemused with alcoholic liquors; their youth has grown stupid on classicism and from early immorality, into which it has been inducted by our special [AGENT]s - by tutors, lackeys, governesses in the houses of the wealthy, by clerks and others, by our women in the places of dissipation frequented by the [GENERAL MASSES] [HUMAN CATTLE]. In the number of these last I count also the so-called "society ladies," voluntary followers of the others in corruption and luxury.

Our countersign is - Force and Make-believe. Only force conquers in political affairs, especially if it be concealed in the talents essential to statesmen. Violence must be the principle, and cunning and make-believe the rule for governments which do not want to lay down their crowns at the feet of [AGENT]s of some new power. This evil is the one and only means to attain the end, the good. Therefore we must not stop at bribery, deceit and treachery when they should serve towards the attainment of our end. In politics one must know how to seize the property of others without hesitation if by it we secure submission and sovereignty.

Our State, marching along the path of peaceful conquest,

has the right to replace the horrors of war by less noticeable and more satisfactory sentences of death, necessary to maintain the terror which tends to produce blind submission. Just but merciless severity is the greatest factor of strength in the State: not only for the sake of gain but also in the name of duty, for the sake of victory, we must keep to the programme of violence and make-believe. The doctrine of squaring accounts is precisely as strong as the means of which it makes use. Therefore it is not so much by the means themselves as by the doctrine of severity that we shall triumph and bring all governments into subjection to our super-government. It is enough for them to know that we are too merciless for all disobedience to cease.

Far back in ancient times we were the first to cry among the masses of the people the words "Liberty, Equality, Fraternity," words many times repeated since these days by stupid poll-parrots who, from all sides around, flew down upon these baits and with them carried away the well-being of the world, true freedom of the individual, formerly so well guarded against the pressure of the mob. The would-be wise men of the [GENERAL MASSES] [HUMAN CATTLE], the intellectuals, could not make anything out of the uttered words in their abstractedness; did not see that in nature there is no equality, cannot be freedom: that Nature herself has established inequality of minds, of characters, and capacities, just as immutably as she has established subordination to her laws: never stopped to think that the mob is a blind thing, that upstarts elected from among it to bear rule are, in regard to the political, the same blind men as the mob itself, that the adept, though he be a fool, can yet rule, whereas the non-adept, even if he were a genius, understands nothing in the political - to all those things the [GENERAL MASSES] [HUMAN CATTLE] paid no regard; yet all the time it was based upon these things that dynastic rule rested: the father passed on to the son a knowledge of the course of political affairs in such wise that none should know it but members of the dynasty and none could betray it to the governed. As time went on, the meaning of the dynastic transference of the true position of affairs in the political was lost, and this aided the success of our cause.

In all corners of the earth the words "Liberty, Equality, Fraternity," brought to our ranks, thanks to our blind [AGENT]s, whole legions who bore our banners with enthusiasm. And all the time these words were canker-worms at work boring into the well-being of the [GENERAL MASSES] [HUMAN CATTLE], putting an end everywhere to peace, quiet, solidarity and destroying all the foundations of the WORKING CLASS States. As you will see later, this helped us to our triumph: it gave us the possibility, among other things, of getting into our hands the master card - the destruction of the privileges, or in other words of the very existence of the aristocracy of the [GENERAL MASSES] [HUMAN CATTLE], that class which was the only defense peoples and countries had against us. On the ruins of the eternal and genealogical aristocracy of the [GENERAL MASSES] [HUMAN CATTLE] we have set up the aristocracy of our educated class headed by the aristocracy of money. The qualifications for this aristocracy we have established in wealth, which is dependent upon us, and in knowledge, for which our learned elders provide the motive force.

Our triumph has been rendered easier by the fact that in our relations with the men, whom we wanted, we have always worked upon the most sensitive chords of the human mind, upon the cash account, upon the cupidity, upon the insatiability for material needs of man; and each one of these human weaknesses, taken alone, is sufficient to paralyze initiative, for it hands over the will of men to the disposition of him who has bought their activities.

The abstraction of freedom has enabled us to persuade the mob in all countries that their government is nothing but the steward of the people who are the owners of the country, and that the steward may be replaced like a worn-out glove.

It is this possibility of replacing the representatives of the people which has placed at our disposal, and, as it were, given us the power of appointment.

PROTOCOL No. 2

It is indispensable for our purpose that wars, so far as possible, should not result in territorial gains: war will thus be brought on to the economic ground, where the nations will not fail to perceive in the assistance we give the strength of our predominance, and this state of things will put both sides at the mercy of our international [AGENT]S; which possesses millions of eyes ever on the watch and unhampered by any limitations whatsoever. Our international rights will then wipe out national rights, in the proper sense of right, and will rule the nations precisely as the civil law of States rules the relations of their subjects among themselves.

The administrators, whom we shall choose from among the public, with strict regard to their capacities for servile obedience, will not be persons trained in the arts of government, and will therefore easily become pawns in our game in the hands of men of learning and genius who will be their advisers, specialists bred and reared from early childhood to rule the affairs of the whole world. As is well known to you, these specialists of ours have been drawing to fit them for rule the information they need from our political plans from the lessons of history, from observations made of the events of every moment as it passes. The [GENERAL MASSES] [HUMAN CATTLE] are not guided by practical use of unprejudiced historical observation, but by theoretical routine without any critical regard for consequent results. We need not, therefore, take any account of them - let them amuse themselves until the hour strikes, or live on hopes of new forms of enterprising pastime, or on the memories of all they have enjoyed. For them let that play the principal part which we have persuaded them to accept as the dictates of science (theory). It is with this object in view that we are constantly, by means of our press, arousing a blind confidence in these theories. The intellectuals of the [GENERAL MASSES] [HUMAN CATTLE] will puff themselves up with their knowledges and without any logical verification of them will put into effect all the information available from science, which our [AGENT]S specialists have cunningly pieced together for the purpose of educating their minds in the direction we want.

Do not suppose for a moment that these statements are empty words: think carefully of the successes we arranged for Darwinism, Marxism, Nietzsche-ism. To us [illuminati], at any rate, it should be plain to see what a disintegrating importance these directives have had upon the minds of the [GENERAL MASSES] [HUMAN CATTLE].

It is indispensable for us to take account of the thoughts, characters, tendencies of the nations in order to avoid making slips in the political and in the direction of administrative affairs. The triumph of our system of which the component parts of the machinery may be variously disposed according to the temperament of the peoples met on our way, will fail of success if the practical application of it be not based upon a summing up of the lessons of the past in the light of the present.

In the hands of the States of to-day there is a great force that creates the movement of thought in the people, and that is the Press. The part played by the Press is to keep pointing our requirements supposed to be indispensable, to give voice to the complaints of the people, to express and to create discontent. It is in the Press that the triumph of freedom of speech finds its incarnation. But the [GENERAL MASSES] [HUMAN CATTLE] States have not known how to make use of this force;

and it has fallen into our hands. Through the Press we have gained the power to influence while remaining ourselves in the shade; thanks to the Press we have got the GOLD in our hands, notwithstanding that we have had to gather it out of the oceans of blood and tears. But it has paid us, though we have sacrificed many of our people. Each victim on our side is worth in the sight of God a thousand [GENERAL MASSES] [HUMAN CATTLE].

PROTOCOL No. 3

To-day I may tell you that our goal is now only a few steps off. There remains a small space to cross and the whole long path we have trodden is ready now to close its cycle of the Symbolic Snake, by which we symbolize our people. When this ring closes, all the States of Europe will be locked in its coil as in a powerful vice.

The constitution scales of these days will shortly break down, for we have established them with a certain lack of accurate balance in order that they may oscillate incessantly until they wear through the pivot on which they turn. The [GENERAL MASSES] [HUMAN CATTLE] are under the impression that they have welded them sufficiently strong and they have all along kept on expecting that the scales would come into equilibrium. But the pivots - the kings on their thrones - are hemmed in by their representatives, who play the fool, distraught with their own uncontrolled and irresponsible power. This power they owe to the terror which has been breathed into the palaces. As they have no means of getting at their people, into their very midst, the kings on their thrones are no longer able to come to terms with them and so strengthen themselves against seekers after power. We have made a gulf between the far-seeing Sovereign Power and the blind force of the people so that both have lost all meaning, for like the blind man and his stick, both are powerless apart.

In order to incite seekers after power to a misuse of power we have set all forces in opposition one to another, breaking up their liberal tendencies towards independence. To this end we have stirred up every form of enterprise, we have armed all parties, we have set up authority as a target for every ambition. Of States we have made gladiatorial arenas where a lot of confused issues contend .... A little more, and disorders and bankruptcy will be universal ....

Babblers, inexhaustible, have turned into oratorical contests the sittings of Parliament and Administrative Boards.

Bold journalists and unscrupulous pamphleteers daily fall upon executive officials. Abuses of power will put the final touch in preparing all institutions for their overthrow and everything will fly skyward under the blows of the maddened mob.

All people are chained down to heavy toil by poverty more firmly than ever. They were chained by slavery and serfdom; from these, one way and another, they might free themselves. These could be settled with, but from want they will never get away. We have included in the constitution such rights as to the masses appear fictitious and not actual rights. All these so-called "Peoples Rights" can exist only in idea, an idea which can never be realized in practical life. What is it to the proletariat laborer, bowed double over his heavy toil, crushed by his lot in life, if talkers get the right to babble, if journalists get the right to scribble any nonsense side by side with good stuff, once the proletariat has no other profit out of the constitution save only those pitiful crumbs which we fling them from our table in return for their voting in favor of what we dictate, in favor of the men we place in power, the servants of our [AGENT]S ... Republican rights for a poor man are no more than a bitter piece of irony, for the necessity he is under of toiling almost all day gives him no present use of them, but the other hand robs him of all guarantee of regular and certain earnings by making him dependent on strikes by his comrades or lockouts by his masters.

The people, under our guidance, have annihilated the aristocracy, who were their one and only defense and foster-mother for the sake of their own advantage which is inseparably bound up with the well-being of the people. Nowadays, with the destruction of the aristocracy, the people have fallen into the grips of merciless money-grinding scoundrels who have laid a pitiless and cruel yoke upon the necks of the workers.

We appear on the scene as alleged saviours of the worker from this oppression when we propose to him to enter the ranks of our fighting forces - Socialists, Anarchists, Communists - to whom we always give support in accordance with an alleged brotherly rule (of the solidarity of all humanity) of our SOCIAL MASONRY. The aristocracy, which enjoyed by law the labor of the workers, was interested in seeing that the workers were well fed, healthy, and strong. We are interested in just the opposite - in the diminution, the KILLING OUT OF THE [GENERAL MASSES] [HUMAN CATTLE]. Our power is in the chronic shortness of food and physical weakness of the worker because by all that this implies he is made the slave of our will, and he will not find in his own authorities either strength or energy to set against our will. Hunger creates the right of capital to rule the worker more surely than it was given to the aristocracy by the legal authority of kings.

By want and the envy and hatred which it engenders we shall move the mobs and with their hands we shall wipe out all those who hinder us on our way.

WHEN THE HOUR STRIKES FOR OUR SOVEREIGN LORD OF ALL THE WORLD TO BE CROWNED IT IS THESE SAME HANDS WHICH WILL SWEEP AWAY EVERYTHING THAT MIGHT BE A HINDRANCE THERETO.

The [GENERAL MASSES] [HUMAN CATTLE] have lost the habit of thinking unless prompted by the suggestions of our specialists. Therefore they do not see the urgent necessity of what we, when our kingdom comes, shall adopt at once, namely this, that IT IS ESSENTIAL TO TEACH IN NATIONAL SCHOOLS ONE SIMPLE, TRUE PIECE OF KNOWLEDGE, THE BASIS OF ALL KNOWLEDGE - THE KNOWLEDGE OF THE STRUCTURE OF HUMAN LIFE, OF SOCIAL EXISTENCE, WHICH REQUIRES DIVISION OF LABOR, AND, CONSEQUENTLY, THE DIVISION OF MEN INTO CLASSES AND CONDITIONS. It is essential for all to know that OWING TO DIFFERENCE IN THE OBJECTS OF HUMAN ACTIVITY THERE CANNOT BE ANY EQUALITY, that he, who by any act of his compromises a whole class, cannot be equally responsible before the law with him who affects no one but only his own honor. The true knowledge of the structure of society, into the secrets of which we do not admit the [GENERAL MASSES] [HUMAN CATTLE], would demonstrate to all men that the positions and work must be kept within a certain circle, that they may not become a source of human suffering, arising from an education which does not correspond with the work which individuals are called upon to do. After a thorough study of this knowledge, the peoples will voluntarily submit to authority and accept such position as is appointed them in the State. In the present state of knowledge and the direction we have given to its development of the people, blindly believing things in print - cherishes - thanks to promptings intended to mislead and to its own ignorance - a blind hatred towards all conditions which it considers above itself, for it has no understanding of the meaning of class and condition.

[THIS HATRED WILL BE STILL FURTHER MAGNIFIED BY THE EFFECTS OF AN ECONOMIC CRISIS, WHICH WILL STOP DEALING ON THE EXCHANGES AND BRING INDUSTRY TO A STANDSTILL. WE SHALL CREATE BY ALL THE SECRET SUBTERRANEAN METHODS OPEN TO US AND WITH THE AID OF GOLD, WHICH IS ALL IN OUR HANDS, A UNIVERSAL ECONOMIC CRISIS WHEREBY WE SHALL THROW UPON THE STREETS WHOLE MOBS OF WORKERS SIMULTANEOUSLY IN ALL THE COUNTRIES OF EUROPE. THESE MOBS WILL RUSH DELIGHTEDLY TO SHED THE BLOOD OF THOSE WHOM, IN THE SIMPLICITY OF THEIR IGNORANCE, THEY HAVE ENVIED FROM THEIR CRADLES, AND WHOSE PROPERTY THEY WILL THEN BE ABLE TO LOOT.]

"OURS" THEY WILL NOT TOUCH, BECAUSE THE MOMENT OF ATTACK WILL BE KNOWN TO US AND WE SHALL TAKE MEASURES TO PROTECT OUR OWN.

We have demonstrated that progress will bring all the [GENERAL MASSES] [HUMAN CATTLE] to the sovereignty of reason. Our despotism will be precisely that; for it will know how, by wise severities, to pacificate all unrest, to cauterize liberalism out of all institutions.

When the populace has seen that all sorts of concessions and indulgences are yielded it, in the same name of freedom it has imagined itself to be sovereign lord and has stormed its way to power, but, naturally like every other blind man, it has come upon a host of stumbling blocks. IT HAS RUSHED TO FIND A GUIDE, IT HAS NEVER HAD THE SENSE TO RETURN TO THE FORMER STATE and it has laid down its plenipotentiary powers at OUR feet. Remember the French Revolution, to which it was we who gave the name of "Great": the secrets of its preparations are well known to us for it was wholly the work of our hands.

Ever since that time we have been leading the peoples from one disenchantment to another, so that in the end they should turn also from us in favor of that KING-DESPOT OF THE BLOOD OF ZION, WHOM WE ARE PREPARING FOR THE WORLD.

At the present day we are, as an international force, invincible, because if attacked by some we are supported by other States. It is the bottomless rascality of the [GENERAL

MASSES] [HUMAN CATTLE] peoples, who crawl on their bellies to force, but are merciless towards weakness, unsparing to faults and indulgent to crimes, unwilling to bear the contradictions of a free social system but patient unto martyrdom under the violence of a bold despotism - it is those qualities which are aiding us to independence. From the premier- dictators of the present day, the [GENERAL MASSES] [HUMAN CATTLE] peoples suffer patiently and bear such abuses as for the least of them they would have beheaded twenty kings.

What is the explanation of this phenomenon, this curious inconsequence of the masses of the peoples in their attitude towards what would appear to be events of the same order?

It is explained by the fact that these dictators whisper to the peoples through their [AGENT]s that through these abuses they are inflicting injury on the States with the highest purpose - to secure the welfare of the peoples, the international brotherhood of them all, their solidarity and equality of rights. Naturally they do not tell the peoples that this unification must be accomplished only under our sovereign rule.

And thus the people condemn the upright and acquit the guilty, persuaded ever more and more that it can do whatsoever it wishes. Thanks to this state of things, the people are destroying every kind of stability and creating disorders at every step.

The word "freedom" brings out the communities of men to fight against every kind of force, against every kind of authority even against God and the laws of nature. For this reason we, when we come into our kingdom, shall have to erase this word from the lexicon of life as implying a principle of brute force which turns mobs into bloodthirsty beasts.

These beasts, it is true, fall asleep again every time when they have drunk their fill of blood, and at such time can easily be riveted into their chains. But if they be not given blood they will not sleep and continue to struggle.

PROTOCOL No. 4

Every republic passes through several stages. The first of these is comprised in the early days of mad raging by the blind mob, tossed hither and thither, right and left: the second is demagogy from which is born anarchy, and that leads inevitably to despotism - not any longer legal and overt, and therefore responsible despotism, but to unseen and secretly hidden, yet nevertheless sensibly felt despotism in the hands of some secret organization or other, whose acts are the more unscrupulous inasmuch as it works behind a screen, behind the backs of all sorts of [AGENT]s, the changing of whom not only does not injuriously affect but actually aids the secret force by saving it, thanks to continual changes, from the necessity of expanding its resources on the rewarding of long services.

Who and what is in a position to overthrow an invisible force? And this is precisely what our force is. GENTILE masonry blindly serves as a screen for us and our objects, but the plan of action of our force, even its very abiding-place, remains for the whole people an unknown mystery.

[THE DESTRUCTION IN THE FAITH IN GOD]

But even freedom might be harmless and have its place in the State economy without injury to the well-being of the peoples if it rested upon the foundation of faith in God, upon the brotherhood of humanity, unconnected with the conception of equality, which is negatived by the very laws of creation, for they have established subordination. With such a faith as this a people might be governed by a wardship of parishes, and would walk contentedly and humbly under the guiding hand of its spiritual pastor submitting to the dispositions of God upon earth. This is the reason why IT IS INDISPENSABLE FOR US TO UNDERMINE ALL FAITH, TO TEAR OUT OF THE MIND OF THE "[GENERAL MASSES] [HUMAN CATTLE]" THE VERY PRINCIPLE OF GOD-HEAD AND THE SPIRIT, AND TO PUT IN ITS PLACE ARITHMETICAL CALCULATIONS AND MATERIAL NEEDS.

In order to give the [GENERAL MASSES] [HUMAN CATTLE] no time to think and take note, their minds must be diverted towards industry and trade. Thus, all the nations will be swallowed up in the pursuit of gain and in the race for it will not take note of their common foe. But again, in order that freedom may once for all disintegrate and ruin the communities of the [GENERAL MASSES] [HUMAN CATTLE], we must put industry on a speculative basis: the result of this will be that what is withdrawn from the land by industry will slip through the hands and pass into speculation, that is, to our classes.

The intensified struggle for superiority and shocks delivered to economic life will create, nay, have already created, disenchanted, cold and heartless communities. Such communities will foster a strong aversion towards the higher political and towards religion. Their only guide is gain, that is Gold, which they will erect into a veritable cult, for the sake of those material delights which it can give. Then will the hour strike when, not for the sake of attaining the good, not even to win wealth, but solely out of hatred towards the privileged, the lower classes of the [GENERAL MASSES] [HUMAN CATTLE] will follow our lead against our rivals for power, the intellectuals of the [GENERAL MASSES] [HUMAN CATTLE].

PROTOCOL No. 5

What form of administrative rule can be given to communities in which corruption has penetrated everywhere, communities where riches are attained only by the clever surprise tactics of semi-swindling tricks; where loseness reigns: where morality is maintained by penal measures and harsh laws but not by voluntarily accepted principles: where the feelings towards faith and country are obligated by cosmopolitan convictions? What form of rule is to be given to these communities if not that despotism which I shall describe to you later? We shall create an intensified centralization of government in order to grip in our hands all the forces of the community. We shall regulate mechanically all the actions of the political life of our subjects by new laws. These laws will withdraw one by one all the indulgences and liberties which have been permitted by the

[GENERAL MASSES] [HUMAN CATTLE], and our kingdom will be distinguished by a despotism of such magnificent proportions as to be at any moment and in every place in a position to wipe out any [GENERAL MASSES] [HUMAN CATTLE] who oppose us by deed or word.

We shall be told that such a despotism as I speak of is not consistent with the progress of these days, but I will prove to you that it is.

In the times when the peoples looked upon kings on their thrones as on a pure manifestation of the will of God, they submitted without a murmur to the despotic power of kings: but from the day when we insinuated into their minds the conception of their own rights they began to regard the occupants of thrones as mere ordinary mortals. The holy unction of the Lord's Anointed has fallen from the heads of kings in the eyes of the people, and when we also robbed them of their faith in God the might of power was flung upon the streets into the place of public proprietorship and was seized by us.

[THE MASSES WILL NOT BE TOLD THE TRUTH]

Moreover, the art of directing masses and individuals by

means of cleverly manipulated theory and verbiage, by regulations of life in common and all sorts of other quirks, in all which the [GENERAL MASSES] [HUMAN CATTLE] understand nothing, belongs likewise to the specialists of our administrative brain. Reared on analysis, observation, on delicacies of fine calculation, in this species of skill we have no rivals, any more than we have either in the drawing up of plans of political actions and solidarity. In this respect the Jesuits alone might have compared with us, but we have contrived to discredit them in the eyes of the unthinking mob as an overt organization, while we ourselves all the while have kept our secret organization in the shade. However, it is probably all the same to the world who is its sovereign lord, whether the head of Catholicism or our despot of the blood of Zion! But to us, the Chosen People, it is very far from being a matter of indifference.

FOR A TIME PERHAPS WE MIGHT BE SUCCESSFULLY DEALT WITH BY A COALITION OF THE "[GENERAL MASSES] [HUMAN CATTLE]" OF ALL THE WORLD: but from this danger we are secured by the discord existing among them whose roots are so deeply seated that they can never now be plucked up. We have set one against another the personal and national reckonings of the [GENERAL MASSES] [HUMAN CATTLE], religious and race hatreds, which we have fostered into a huge growth in the course of the past twenty centuries. This is the reason why there is not one State which would anywhere receive support if it were to raise its arm, for every one of them must bear in mind that any agreement against us would be unprofitable to itself. We are too strong - there is no evading our power. THE NATIONS CANNOT COME TO EVEN AN INCONSIDERABLE PRIVATE AGREEMENT WITHOUT OUR SECRETLY HAVING A HAND IN IT.

PER ME REGES REGNANT. "It is through me that Kings reign." And it was said by the prophets that we were chosen by God Himself to rule over the whole earth. God has endowed us with genius that we may be equal to our task. Were genius in the opposite camp it would still struggle against us, but even so, a newcomer is no match for the old-established settler: the struggle would be merciless between us, such a fight as the world has never seen. Aye, and the genius on their side would have arrived too late. All the wheels of the machinery of all States go by the force of the engine, which is in our hands, and that engine of the machinery of States is - Gold. The science of political economy invented by our learned elders has for long past been giving royal prestige to capital.

[THE NEED FOR TOTAL CONTROL OF INDUSTRY]

Capital, if it is to co-operate untrammeled, must be free to establish a monopoly of industry and trade: this is already being put in execution by an unseen hand in all quarters of the world. This freedom will give political force to those engaged in industry, and that will help to oppress the people. Nowadays it is more important to disarm the peoples than to lead them into war: more important to use for our advantage the passions which have burst into flames than to quench their fire: more important to eradicate them. THE PRINCIPLE OBJECT OF OUR DIRECTORATE CONSISTS IN THIS: TO DEBILITATE THE PUBLIC MIND BY CRITICISM; TO LEAD IT AWAY FROM SERIOUS REFLECTIONS CALCULATED TO AROUSE RESISTANCE; TO DISTRACT THE FORCES OF THE MIND TOWARDS A SHAM FIGHT OF EMPTY ELOQUENCE.

In all ages the people of the world, equally with individuals, have accepted words for deeds, for THEY ARE CONTENT WITH A SHOW and rarely pause to note, in the public arena, whether promises are followed by performance. Therefore we shall establish show institutions which will give eloquent proof of their benefit to progress.

We shall assume to ourselves the liberal physiognomy of all parties, of all directions, and we shall give that physiognomy a VOICE IN ORATORS WHO WILL SPEAK SO MUCH THAT THEY WILL EXHAUST THE PATIENCE OF THEIR HEARERS AND PRODUCE AN ABHORRENCE OF ORATORY.

IN ORDER TO PUT PUBLIC OPINION INTO OUR HANDS WE MUST BRING IT INTO A STATE OF BEWILDERMENT BY GIVING EXPRESSION FROM ALL SIDES TO SO MANY CONTRADICTORY OPINIONS AND FOR SUCH LENGTH OF TIME AS WILL SUFFICE TO MAKE THE "[GENERAL MASSES] [HUMAN CATTLE]" LOSE THEIR HEADS IN THE LABYRINTH AND COME TO SEE THAT THE BEST THING IS TO HAVE NO OPINION OF ANY KIND IN MATTERS POLITICAL, which it is not given to the public to understand, because they are understood only by him who guides the public. This is the first secret.

The second secret requisite for the success of our government is comprised in the following: To multiply to such an extent national failings, habits, passions, conditions of civil life, that it will be impossible for anyone to know where he is in the resulting chaos, so that the people in consequence will fail to understand one another. This measure will also serve us in another way, namely, to sow discord in all parties, to dislocate all collective forces which are still unwilling to submit to us, and to discourage any kind of personal initiative which might in any degree hinder our affair. THERE IS NOTHING MORE DANGEROUS THAN PERSONAL INITIATIVE: if it has genius behind it, such initiative can do more than can be done by millions of people among whom we have sown discord. We must so direct the education of the [GENERAL MASSES] [HUMAN CATTLE] communities that whenever they come upon a matter requiring initiative they may drop their hands in despairing impotence. The strain which results from freedom of action saps the forces when it meets with the freedom of another. From this collision arise grave moral shocks, disenchantments, failures. BY ALL THESE MEANS WE SHALL SO WEAR DOWN THE "[GENERAL MASSES] [HUMAN CATTLE]" THAT THEY WILL BE COMPELLED TO OFFER US INTERNATIONAL POWER OF A NATURE THAT BY ITS POSITION WILL ENABLE US WITHOUT ANY VIOLENCE GRADUALLY TO ABSORB ALL THE STATE FORCES OF THE WORLD AND TO FORM A SUPER-GOVERNMENT.

In place of the rulers of to-day we shall set up a bogey which will be called the Super-Government Administration. Its hands will reach out in all directions like nippers and its organization will be of such colossal dimensions that it cannot fail to subdue all the nations of the world.

PROTOCOL No. 6

We shall soon begin to establish huge monopolies, reservoirs of colossal riches, upon which even, large fortunes of the [GENERAL MASSES] [HUMAN CATTLE] will depend to such an extent that they will go to the bottom together with the credit of the States on the day after the political smash ...

You gentlemen here present who are economists, just strike an estimate of the significance of this combination! ...

In every possible way we must develop the significance of our Super-Government by representing it as the Protector and Benefactor of all those who voluntarily submit to us.

The aristocracy of the [GENERAL MASSES] [HUMAN CATTLE] as a political force, is dead - We need not take it into account; but as landed proprietors they can still be harmful to us from the fact that they are self-sufficing in the resources upon which they live. It is essential therefore for us at whatever cost to deprive them of their land. This object will be best attained by increasing the burdens upon landed property - in loading lands with debts. These measures will check land- holding and keep it in a state of humble and un-conditional submission.

The aristocrats of the [GENERAL MASSES] [HUMAN CATTLE], being hereditarily incapable of contenting themselves with little, will rapidly burn up and fizzle out.

At the same time we must intensively patronize trade and industry, but, first and foremost, speculation, the part played by which is to provide a counterpoise to industry: the absence of speculative industry will multiply capital in private hands and will serve to restore agriculture by freeing the land from indebtedness to the land banks. What we want is that industry should drain off from the land both labor and capital and by means of speculation transfer into our hands all the money of the world, and thereby throw all the [GENERAL MASSES] [HUMAN CATTLE] into the ranks of the proletariat. Then the [GENERAL MASSES] [HUMAN CATTLE] will bow down before us, if for no other reason but to get the right to exist.

To complete the ruin of the industry of the [GENERAL MASSES] [HUMAN CATTLE] we shall bring to the assistance of speculation the luxury which we have developed among the [GENERAL MASSES] [HUMAN CATTLE], that greedy demand for luxury which is swallowing up everything. WE SHALL RAISE THE RATE OF WAGES WHICH, HOWEVER, WILL NOT BRING ANY ADVANTAGE TO THE WORKERS, FOR, AT THE SAME TIME, WE SHALL PRODUCE A RISE IN PRICES OF THE FIRST NECESSARIES OF LIFE, ALLEGING THAT IT ARISES FROM THE DECLINE OF AGRICULTURE AND [CATTLE]-BREEDING: WE SHALL FURTHER UNDERMINE ARTFULLY AND DEEPLY SOURCES OF PRODUCTION, BY ACCUSTOMING THE WORKERS TO ANARCHY AND TO DRUNKENNESS AND SIDE BY SIDE THEREWITH TAKING ALL MEASURE TO EXTIRPATE FROM THE FACE OF THE EARTH ALL THE EDUCATED FORCES OF THE "[GENERAL MASSES] [HUMAN CATTLE]."

IN ORDER THAT THE TRUE MEANING OF THINGS MAY NOT STRIKE THE "[GENERAL MASSES] [HUMAN CATTLE]" BEFORE THE PROPER TIME WE SHALL MASK IT UNDER AN ALLEGED ARDENT DESIRE TO SERVE THE WORKING CLASSES AND THE GREAT PRINCIPLES OF POLITICAL ECONOMY ABOUT WHICH OUR ECONOMIC THEORIES ARE CARRYING ON AN ENERGETIC PROPAGANDA.

PROTOCOL No. 7

The intensification of armaments, the increase of police forces - are all essential for the completion of the aforementioned plans. What we have to get at is that there should be in all the States of the world, besides ourselves, only the masses of the proletariat, a few millionaires devoted to our interests, police and soldiers.

Throughout all Europe, and by means of relations with Europe, in other continents also, we must create ferments, discords and hostility. Therein we gain a double advantage. In the first place we keep in check all countries, for they will know that we have the power whenever we like to create disorders or to restore order. All these countries are accustomed to see in us an indispensable force of coercion. In the second place, by our intrigues we shall tangle up all the threads which we have stretched into the cabinets of all States by means of the political, by economic treaties, or loan obligations. In order to succeed in this we must use great cunning and penetration during negotiations and agreements, but, as regards what is called the "official language," we shall keep to the opposite tactics and assume the mask of honesty and complacency. In this way the peoples and governments of the [GENERAL MASSES]

[HUMAN CATTLE], whom we have taught to look only at the outside whatever we present to their notice, will still continue to accept us as the benefactors and saviours of the human race.

We must be in a position to respond to every act of opposition by war with the neighbors of that country which dares to oppose us: but if these neighbors should also venture to stand collectively together against us, then we must offer resistance by a universal war.

The principal factor of success in the political is the secrecy of its undertakings: the word should not agree with the deeds of the diplomat.

We must compel the governments of the [GENERAL MASSES] [HUMAN CATTLE] to take action in the direction favored by our widely conceived plan, already approaching the desired consummation, by what we shall represent as public opinion, secretly promoted by us through the means of that so-called "Great Power" - THE PRESS, WHICH, WITH A FEW EXCEPTIONS THAT MAY BE DISREGARDED, IS ALREADY ENTIRELY IN OUR HANDS.

PROTOCOL No. 8

We must arm ourselves with all the weapons which our opponents might employ against us. We must search out in the very finest shades of expression and the knotty points of the lexicon of law justification for those cases where we shall have to pronounce judgments that might appear abnormally audacious and unjust, for it is important that these resolutions should be set forth in expressions that shall seem to be the most exalted moral principles cast into legal form. Our directorate must surround itself with all these forces of civilization among which it will have to work.

It will surround itself with publicists, practical jurists, administrators, diplomats and, finally, with persons prepared by a special super-educational training IN OUR SPECIAL SCHOOLS. These persons will have consonance of all the secrets of the social structure, they will know all the languages that can be made up by political alphabets and words; they will be made acquainted with the whole underside of human nature, with all its sensitive chords on which they will have to play. These chords are the cast of mind of the [GENERAL MASSES] [HUMAN CATTLE], their tendencies, short-comings, vices and qualities, the particularities of classes and conditions. Needless to say that the talented assistants of authority, of whom I speak,

will be taken not from among the [GENERAL MASSES] [HUMAN CATTLE], who are accustomed to perform their administrative work without giving themselves the trouble to think what
its aim is, and never consider what it is needed for. The administrators of the [GENERAL MASSES] [HUMAN CATTLE] sign papers without reading them, and they serve either for mercenary reasons or from ambition.

We shall surround our government with a whole world of economists. That is the reason why economic sciences form the principal subject of the teaching given to the [illuminati]. Around us again will be a whole constellation of bankers, industrialists, capitalists and - THE MAIN THING -MILLIONAIRES, BECAUSE IN SUBSTANCE EVERYTHING WILL BE SETTLED BY THE QUESTION OF FIGURES.

For a time, until there will no longer be any risk in entrusting responsible posts in our State to our brother- [illuminati], we shall put them in the hands of persons whose past and reputation are such that between them and the people lies an abyss, persons who, in case of disobedience to our instructions, must face criminal charges or disappear - this in order to make them defend our interests to their last gasp.

PROTOCOL No. 9

In applying our principles let attention be paid to the character of the people in whose country you live and act; a general, identical application of them, until such time as the people shall have been re-educated to our pattern, cannot have success. But by approaching their application cautiously you will see that not a decade will pass before the most stubborn character will change and we shall add a new people to the ranks of those already subdued by us.

The words of the liberal, which are in effect the words of our masonic watchword, namely, "Liberty, Equality, Fraternity," will, when we come into our kingdom, be changed by us into words no longer of a watchword, but only an expression of idealism, namely, into "The right of liberty, the duty of equality, the ideal of brotherhood." That is how we shall put it, - and so we shall catch the bull by the horns ... DE FACTO we have already wiped out every kind of rule except our own, although DE JURE there still remain a good many of them. Nowadays, if any States raise a protest against us it is only PRO FORMA at our discretion and by our direction, for THEIR ANTI-SEMITISM IS INDISPENSABLE TO US FOR THE

MANAGEMENT OF OUR LESSER BRETHREN. I will not enter into further explanations, for this matter has formed the subject of repeated discussions amongst us.

For us there are not checks to limit the range of our activity. Our Super-Government subsists in extra-legal conditions which are described in the accepted terminology by the energetic and forcible word - Dictatorship. I am in a position to tell you with a clear conscience that at the proper time we, the law-givers, shall execute judgment and sentence, we shall slay and we shall spare, we, as head of all our troops, are mounted on the steed of the leader. We rule by force of will, because in our hands are the fragments of a once powerful party, now vanquished by us. AND THE WEAPONS IN OUR HANDS ARE LIMITLESS AMBITIONS, BURNING GREEDINESS, MERCILESS VENGEANCE, HATREDS AND MALICE.

IT IS FROM US THAT THE ALL-ENGULFING TERROR PROCEEDS. WE HAVE IN OUR SERVICE PERSONS OF ALL OPINIONS, OF ALL DOCTRINES, RESTORATING MONARCHISTS, DEMAGOGUES, SOCIALISTS, COMMUNISTS, AND UTOPIAN DREAMERS OF EVERY KIND. We have harnessed them all to the task: EACH ONE OF THEM ON HIS OWN ACCOUNT IS BORING AWAY AT

THE LAST REMNANTS OF AUTHORITY, IS STRIVING
TO OVERTHROW ALL ESTABLISHED FORM OF ORDER.
By these acts all States are in torture; they exhort to tranquility,
are ready to sacrifice everything for peace: BUT WE WILL
NOT GIVE THEM PEACE UNTIL THEY OPENLY
ACKNOWLEDGE OUR INTERNATIONAL SUPER-
GOVERNMENT, AND WITH SUBMISSIVENESS.

The people have raised a howl about the necessity of
settling the question of Socialism by way of an international
agreement. DIVISION INTO FRACTIONAL PARTIES HAS
GIVEN THEM INTO OUR HANDS, FOR, IN ORDER TO
CARRY ON A CONTESTED STRUGGLE ONE MUST
HAVE MONEY, AND THE MONEY IS ALL IN OUR
HANDS.

We might have reason to apprehend a union between the
"clear-sighted" force of the [GENERAL MASSES] [HUMAN
CATTLE] kings on their thrones and the "blind" force of the
[GENERAL MASSES] [HUMAN CATTLE] mobs, but we have
taken all the needful measure against any such possibility:
between the one and the other force we have erected a bulwark
in the shape of a mutual terror between them. In this way the
blind force of the people remains our support and we, and we

only, shall provide them with a leader and, of course, direct them along the road that leads to our goal.

In order that the hand of the blind mob may not free itself from our guiding hand, we must every now and then enter into close communion with it, if not actually in person, at any rate through some of the most trusty of our brethren. When we are acknowledged as the only authority we shall discuss with the people personally on the market, places, and we shall instruct them on questions of the political in such wise as may turn them in the direction that suits us.

Who is going to verify what is taught in the village schools? But what an envoy of the government or a king on his throne himself may say cannot but become immediately known to the whole State, for it will be spread abroad by the voice of the people.

In order to annihilate the institutions of the [GENERAL MASSES] [HUMAN CATTLE] before it is time we have touched them with craft and delicacy, and have taken hold of the ends of the springs which move their mechanism. These springs lay in a strict but just sense of order; we have replaced them by the chaotic license of liberalism. We have got our hands into the administration of the law, into the conduct of elections, into the press, into liberty of the person, BUT PRINCIPALLY INTO EDUCATION AND TRAINING AS BEING THE CORNERSTONES OF A FREE EXISTENCE.

WE HAVE FOOLED, BEMUSED AND CORRUPTED THE YOUTH OF THE "[GENERAL MASSES] [HUMAN CATTLE]" BY REARING THEM IN PRINCIPLES AND THEORIES WHICH ARE KNOWN TO US TO BE FALSE ALTHOUGH IT IS THAT THEY HAVE BEEN INCULCATED.

Above the existing laws without substantially altering them, and by merely twisting them into contradictions of interpretations, we have erected something grandiose in the way of results. These results found expression in the fact that the INTERPRETATIONS MASKED THE LAW: afterwards they entirely hid them from the eyes of the governments owing to the impossibility of making anything out of the tangled web of legislation. This is the origin of the theory of course of arbitration.

You may say that the [GENERAL MASSES] [HUMAN CATTLE] will rise upon us, arms in hand, if they guess what is going on before the time comes; but in the West we have against this a manoeuvre of such appalling terror that the very stoutest hearts quail - the undergrounds, metropolitans, those subterranean corridors which, before the time comes, will be driven under all the capitals and from whence those capitals will be blown into the air with all their organizations and archives.

PROTOCOL No. 10

To-day I begin with a repetition of what I said before, and I BEG YOU TO BEAR IN MIND THAT GOVERNMENTS AND PEOPLE ARE CONTENT IN THE POLITICAL WITH OUTSIDE APPEARANCES. And how, indeed, are the [GENERAL MASSES] [HUMAN CATTLE] to perceive the underlying meaning of things when their representatives give the best of their energies to enjoying themselves? For our policy it is of the greatest importance to take cognizance of this detail; it will be of assistance to us when we come to consider the division of authority of property, of the dwelling, of taxation, of the reflex force of the laws. All these questions are such as ought not to be touched upon directly and openly before the people. In cases where it is indispensable to touch upon them they must not be categorically named, it must merely be declared without detailed exposition that the principles of contemporary law are acknowledged by us. The reason of keeping silence in this respect is that by not naming a principle we leave ourselves freedom of action to drop this or that out of it without attracting notice; if they were all categorically named they would all appear to have been already given.

The mob cherishes a special affection and respect for the geniuses of political power and accepts all their deeds of violence with the admiring response: "rascally, well, yes, it is rascally, but it's clever! ... a trick, if you like, but how craftily played, how magnificently done, what impudent audacity!" ...

We count upon attracting all nations to the task of erecting the new fundamental structure, the project for which has been drawn up by us. This is why, before everything, it is indispensable for us to arm ourselves and to store up in ourselves that absolutely reckless audacity and irresistible might of the spirit which in the person of our active workers will break down all hindrances on our way.

WHEN WE HAVE ACCOMPLISHED OUR COUP D'ETAT WE SHALL SAY THEN TO THE VARIOUS PEOPLES: "EVERYTHING HAS GONE TERRIBLY BADLY, ALL HAVE BEEN WORN OUT WITH

SUFFERING. WE ARE DESTROYING THE CAUSES OF YOUR TORMENT - NATIONALITIES, FRONTIERS, DIFFERENCES OF COINAGES. YOU ARE AT LIBERTY, OF COURSE, TO PRONOUNCE SENTENCE UPON US, BUT CAN IT POSSIBLY BE A JUST ONE IF IT IS CONFIRMED BY YOU BEFORE YOU MAKE ANY TRIAL OF WHAT WE ARE OFFERING YOU." ... THEN WILL THE MOB EXALT US AND BEAR US UP IN THEIR HANDS IN A UNANIMOUS TRIUMPH OF HOPES AND EXPECTATIONS. VOTING, WHICH WE HAVE MADE THE INSTRUMENT WHICH WILL SET US ON THE THRONE OF THE WORLD BY TEACHING EVEN THE VERY SMALLEST UNITS OF MEMBERS OF THE HUMAN RACE TO VOTE BY MEANS OF MEETINGS AND AGREEMENTS BY GROUPS, WILL THEN HAVE SERVED ITS PURPOSES AND WILL PLAY ITS PART THEN FOR THE LAST TIME BY A UNANIMITY OF DESIRE TO MAKE CLOSE ACQUAINTANCE WITH US BEFORE CONDEMNING US.

TO SECURE THIS WE MUST HAVE EVERYBODY VOTE WITHOUT DISTINCTION OF CLASSES AND QUALIFICATIONS, in order to establish an absolute majority, which cannot be got from the educated propertied classes. In this way, by inculcating in all a sense of self-importance, we shall destroy among the [GENERAL MASSES] [HUMAN CATTLE] the importance of the family and its educational value and remove the possibility of individual minds splitting off, for the mob, handled by us, will not let them come to the front nor even give them a hearing; it is accustomed to listen to us only who pay it for obedience and attention. In this way we shall create a blind, mighty force which will never be in a position to move in any direction without the guidance of our [AGENT]s set at its head by us as leaders of the mob. The people will submit to this regime because it will know that upon these leaders will depend its earnings, gratifications and the receipt of all kinds of benefits.

A scheme of government should come ready made from one brain, because it will never be clinched firmly if it is allowed to be split into fractional parts in the minds of many. It is allowable, therefore, for us to have cognizance of the scheme of action but not to discuss it lest we disturb its artfulness, the interdependence of its component parts, the practical force of the secret meaning of each clause. To discuss and make alterations in a labor of this kind by means of numerous votings is to impress upon it the stamp of all ratiocinations and misunderstandings which have failed to penetrate the depth and nexus of its plottings. We want our schemes to be forcible and suitably concocted. Therefore WE OUGHT NOT TO FLING THE WORK OF GENIUS OF OUR GUIDE to the fangs of the mob or even of a select company.

These schemes will not turn existing institutions upside down just yet. They will only effect changes in their economy and consequently in the whole combined movement of their progress, which will thus be directed along the paths laid down in our schemes.

Under various names there exists in all countries approximately one and the same thing. Representation, Ministry, Senate, State Council, Legislative and Executive Corps. I need not explain to you the mechanism of the relation of these institutions to one another, because you are aware of all that; only take note of the fact that each of the above-named institutions corresponds to some important function of the State, and I would beg you to remark that the word "important" I apply not to the institution but to the function, consequently it is not the institutions which are important but their functions. These institutions have divided up among themselves all the functions of government - administrative, legislative, executive, wherefore they have come to operate as do the organs in the human body. If we injure one part in the machinery of State, the State falls sick, like a human body, and ... will die.

When we introduced into the State organism the poison of Liberalism its whole political complexion underwent a change. States have been seized with a mortal illness - blood poisoning. All that remains is to await the end of their death agony.

Liberalism produced Constitutional States, which took the place of what was the only safeguard of the [GENERAL MASSES] [HUMAN CATTLE], namely, Despotism; and A CONSTITUTION, AS YOU WELL KNOW, IS NOTHING ELSE BUT A SCHOOL OF DISCORDS, misunderstandings, quarrels, disagreements, fruitless party agitations, party whims - in a word, a school of everything that serves to destroy the personality of State activity. THE TRIBUNE OF THE "TALKERICS" HAS, NO LESS EFFECTIVELY THAN THE PRESS, CONDEMNED THE RULERS TO INACTIVITY AND IMPOTENCE, and thereby rendered them useless and superfluous, for which reason indeed they have been in many countries deposed. THEN IT WAS THAT THE ERA OF REPUBLICS BECOME POSSIBLE OF REALIZATION; AND THEN IT WAS THAT WE REPLACED THE RULER BY A CARICATURE OF A GOVERNMENT - BY A PRESIDENT, TAKEN FROM THE MOB, FROM THE MIDST OF OUR

PUPPET CREATURES, OR SLAVES. This was the foundation of the mine which we have laid under the [GENERAL MASSES] [HUMAN CATTLE] people, I should rather say, under the [GNERAL MASSES] [HUMAN CATTLE] peoples.

[WE DETERMINE WHO THE OFFICIALS OF THE MASSES WILL BE]

In the near future we shall establish the responsibility of presidents.

By that time we shall be in a position to disregard forms in carrying through matters for which our impersonal puppet will be responsible. What do we care if the ranks of those striving for power should be thinned, if there should arise a deadlock from the impossibility of finding presidents, a deadlock which will finally disorganize the country?

In order that our scheme may produce this result we shall arrange elections in favor of such presidents as have in their past some dark, undiscovered stain, some "Panama" or other - then they will be trustworthy [AGENT]s for the accomplishment of our plans out of fear of revelations and from the natural desire of everyone who has attained power, namely, the retention of the privileges, advantages and honor connected with the office of president. The chamber of deputies will provide cover for, will protect, will elect presidents, but we shall take from it the right to propose new, or make changes in existing laws, for this right will be given by us to the responsible president, a puppet in our hands. Naturally, the authority of the presidents will then become a target for every possible form of attack, but we shall provide him with a means of self-defense in the right of an appeal to the people, for the decision of the people over the heads of their representatives, that is to say, an appeal to that some blind slave of ours - the majority of the mob. Independently of this we shall invest the president with the right of declaring a state of war. We shall justify this last right on the ground that the president as chief of the whole army of the country must have it at his disposal, in case of need for the defense of the new republican constitution, the right to defend which will belong to him as the responsible representative of this constitution.

It is easy to understand them in these conditions the key of the shrine will lie in our hands, and no one outside ourselves will any longer direct the force of legislation.

Besides this we shall, with the introduction of the new republican constitution, take from the Chamber the right of interpolation on government measures, on the pretext of preserving political secrecy, and, further, we shall by the new constitution reduce the number of representatives to a minimum, thereby proportionately reducing political passions and the passion for politics. If, however, they should, which is hardly to be expected, burst into flame, even in this minimum, we shall nullify them by a stirring appeal and a reference to the majority of the whole people ... Upon the president will depend the appointment of presidents and vice-presidents of the Chamber and the Senate. Instead of constant sessions of Parliaments we shall reduce their sittings to a few months. Moreover, the president, as chief of the executive power, will have the right to summon and dissolve Parliament, and, in the latter case, to prolong the time for the appointment of a new parliamentary assembly. But in order that the consequences of all these acts which in substance are illegal, should not, prematurely for our plans, upon the responsibility established by use of the president, WE SHALL INSTIGATE MINISTERS AND OTHER OFFICIALS OF THE HIGHER ADMINISTRATION ABOUT THE PRESIDENT TO EVADE HIS DISPOSITIONS BY TAKING MEASURES OF THEIR OWN, for doing which they will be made the scapegoats in his place ... This part we especially recommend to be given to be played by the Senate, the Council of State, or the Council of Ministers, but not to an individual official.

The president will, at our discretion, interpret the sense of such of the existing laws as admit of various interpretation; he will further annul them when we indicate to him the necessity to do so, besides this, he will have the right to propose temporary laws, and even new departures in the government constitutional working, the pretext both for the one and the other being the requirements for the supreme welfare of the State.

By such measure we shall obtain the power of destroying little by little, step by step, all that at the outset when we enter on our rights, we are compelled to introduce into the constitutions of States to prepare for the transition to an imperceptible abolition of every kind of constitution, and then the time is come to turn every form of government into OUR DESPOTISM.

The recognition of our despot may also come before the destruction of the constitution; the moment for this recognition will come when the peoples, utterly wearied by the irregularities and incompetence - a matter which we shall arrange for - of their rulers, will clamor: "Away with them and give us one king over all the earth who will unite us and annihilate the causes of disorders - frontiers, nationalities, religions, State debts - who will give us peace and quiet which we cannot find under our rulers and representatives."

But you yourselves perfectly well know that TO PRODUCE THE POSSIBILITY OF THE EXPRESSION OF SUCH WISHES BY ALL THE NATIONS IT IS INDISPENSABLE TO TROUBLE IN ALL COUNTRIES THE PEOPLE'S RELATIONS WITH THEIR GOVERNMENTS SO AS TO UTTERLY EXHAUST HUMANITY WITH DISSENSION, HATRED, STRUGGLE, ENVY AND EVEN BY THE USE OF TORTURE, BY STARVATION, BY THE INOCULATION OF DISEASES, BY WANT, SO THAT THE "[GENERAL MASSES] [HUMAN CATTLE]" SEE NO OTHER ISSUE THAN TO TAKE REFUGE IN OUR COMPLETE SOVEREIGNTY IN MONEY AND IN ALL ELSE.

But if we give the nations of the world a breathing space the moment we long for is hardly likely ever to arrive.

PROTOCOL No. 11

The State Council has been, as it were, the emphatic expression of the authority of the ruler: it will be, as the "show" part of the Legislative Corps, what may be called the editorial committee of the laws and decrees of the ruler.

This, then, is the program of the new constitution. We shall make Law, Right and Justice (1) in the guise of proposals to the Legislative Corps, (2) by decrees of the president under the guise of general regulations, of orders of the Senate and of resolutions of the State Council in the guise of ministerial orders, (3) and in case a suitable occasion should arise - in the form of a revolution in the State.

Having established approximately the MODUS AGENDI we will occupy ourselves with details of those combinations by which we have still to complete the revolution in the course of the machinery of State in the direction already indicated. By these combinations I mean the freedom of the Press, the right of association, freedom of conscience, the voting principle, and many another that must disappear for ever from the memory of man, or undergo a radical alteration the day after the promulgation of the new constitution. It is only at the moment that we shall be able at once to announce all our orders, for, afterwards, every noticeable alteration will be dangerous, for the following reasons: if this alteration be brought in with harsh severity and in a sense of severity and limitations, it may lead to a feeling of despair caused by fear of new alterations in the same direction; if, on the other hand, it be brought in a sense of further indulgences it will be said that we have recognized our own wrong-doing and this will destroy the prestige of the infallibility of our authority, or else it will be said that we have become alarmed and are compelled to show a yielding disposition, for which we shall get no thanks because it will be supposed to be compulsory ... Both the one and the other are injurious to the prestige of the new constitution. What we want is that from the first moment of its promulgation, while the peoples of the world are still stunned by the accomplished fact of the revolution, still in a condition of terror and uncertainty, they should recognize once for all that we are so strong, so inexpugnable, so super-abundantly filled with power, that in no case shall we take any account of them, and so far from paying any attention to their opinions or wishes, we are ready and able to crush with irresistible power all expression or manifestation thereof at every moment and in every place, that we have seized at once everything we wanted and shall in no case divide our power with them ... Then in fear and trembling they will close their eyes to everything, and be content to await what will be the end of it all.

The [GENERAL MASSES] [HUMAN CATTLE] are a flock of sheep, and we are their wolves. And you know what happens when the wolves get hold of the flock? ....

There is another reason also why they will close their eyes: for we shall keep promising them to give back all the liberties we have taken away as soon as we have quelled the enemies of peace and tamed all parties....

It is not worth to say anything about how long a time they will be kept waiting for this return of their liberties ....

For what purpose then have we invented this whole policy and insinuated it into the minds of the WORKING CLASS without giving them any chance to examine its underlying meaning? For what, indeed, if not in order to obtain in a roundabout way what is for our scattered tribe unattainable by the direct road? It is this which has served as the basis for our organization of SECRET MASONRY WHICH IS NOT KNOWN TO, AND AIMS WHICH ARE NOT EVEN SO MUCH AS SUSPECTED BY, THESE "WORKING CLASS" [CATTLE], ATTRACTED BY US INTO THE "SHOW" ARMY OF MASONIC LODGES IN ORDER TO THROW DUST IN THE EYES OF THEIR FELLOWS.

God has granted to us, His Chosen People, the gift of the dispersion, and in this which appears in all eyes to be our weakness, has come forth all our strength, which has now brought us to the threshold of sovereignty over all the world.

There now remains not much more for us to build up upon the foundation we have laid.

PROTOCOL No. 12

The word "freedom," which can be interpreted in various ways, is defined by us as follows:

Freedom is the right to do what which the law allows. This interpretation of the word will at the proper time be of service to us, because all freedom will thus be in our hands, since the laws will abolish or create only that which is desirable for us according to the aforesaid program.

We shall deal with the press in the following way: what is the part played by the press to-day? It serves to excite and inflame those passions which are needed for our purpose or else it serves selfish ends of parties. It is often vapid, unjust, mendacious, and the majority of the public have not the slightest idea what ends the press really serves. We shall saddle and bridle it with a tight curb: we shall do the same also with all productions of the printing press, for where would be the sense of getting rid of the attacks of the press if we remain targets for pamphlets and books? The produce of publicity, which nowadays is a source of heavy expense owing to the necessity of censoring it, will be turned by us into a very lucrative source of income to our State: we shall law on it a special stamp tax and require deposits of caution-money before permitting the establishment of any organ of the press or of printing offices; these will then have to guarantee our government against any kind of attack on the part of the press. For any attempt to attack us, if such still be possible, we shall inflict fines without mercy. Such measures as stamp tax, deposit of caution-money and fines secured by these deposits, will bring in a huge income to the government. It is true that party organs might not spare money for the sake of publicity, but these we shall shut up at the second attack upon us. No one shall with impunity lay a finger on the aureole of our government infallibility. The pretext for stopping any publication will be the alleged plea that it is agitating the public mind without occasion or justification. I BEG YOU TO NOTE THAT AMONG THOSE MAKING ATTACKS UPON US WILL ALSO BE ORGANS ESTABLISHED BY US, BUT THEY WILL ATTACK EXCLUSIVELY POINTS THAT WE HAVE PRE-DETERMINED TO ALTER.

[WE WILL HAVE TOTAL CONTROL OF THE PRESS]

NOT A SINGLE ANNOUNCEMENT WILL REACH THE PUBLIC WITHOUT OUR CONTROL. Even now this is already being attained by us inasmuch as all news items are received by a few agencies, in whose offices they are focused from all parts of the world. These agencies will then be already entirely ours and will give publicity only to what we dictate to them.

If already now we have contrived to possess ourselves of the minds of the [GENERAL MASSES] [HUMAN CATTLE] communities to such an extent the they all come near looking upon the events of the world through the colored glasses of those spectacles we are setting astride their noses; if already now there is not a single State where there exist for us any barriers to admittance into what [GENERAL MASSES] [HUMAN CATTLE] stupidity calls State secrets: what will our positions be then, when we shall be acknowledged supreme lords of the world in the person of our king of all the world ....

Let us turn again to the FUTURE OF THE PRINTING PRESS. Every one desirous of being a publisher, librarian, or printer, will be obliged to provide himself with the diploma instituted therefore, which, in case of any fault, will be

immediately impounded. With such measures THE
INSTRUMENT OF THOUGHT WILL BECOME AN
EDUCATIVE MEANS ON THE HANDS OF OUR
GOVERNMENT, WHICH WILL NO LONGER ALLOW THE
MASS OF THE NATION TO BE LED ASTRAY IN BY-
WAYS AND FANTASIES ABOUT THE BLESSINGS OF
PROGRESS. Is there any one of us who does not know that
these phantom blessings are the direct roads to foolish
imaginings which give birth to anarchical relations of men among
themselves and towards authority, because progress, or rather
the idea of progress, has introduced the conception of every kind
of emancipation, but has failed to establish its limits .... All the
so-called liberals are anarchists, if not in fact, at any rate in
thought. Every one of them in hunting after phantoms of
freedom, and falling exclusively into license, that is, into the
anarchy of protest for the sake of protest ....

[THE MASSES WILL BE LED TO BELIEVE THAT THERE
IS A FREE PRESS]

We turn to the periodical press. We shall impose on it, as
on all printed matter, stamp taxes per sheet and deposits of
caution- money, and books of less than 30 sheets will pay
double. We shall reckon them as pamphlets in order, on the one

hand, to reduce the number of magazines, which are the worst form of printed poison, and, on the other, in order that this measure may force writers into such lengthy productions that they will be little read, especially as they will be costly. At the same time what we shall publish ourselves to influence mental development in the direction laid down for our profit will be cheap and will be read voraciously. The tax will bring vapid literary ambitions within bounds and the liability to penalties will make literary men dependent upon us. And if there should be any found who are desirous of writing against us, they will not find any person eager to print their productions in print the publisher or printer will have to apply to the authorities for permission to do so. Thus w shall know beforehand of all tricks preparing against us and shall nullify them by getting ahead with explanations on the subject treated of.

Literature and journalism are two of the most important educative forces, and therefore our government will become proprietor of the majority of the journals. This will neutralize the injurious influence of the privately-owned press and will put us in possession of a tremendous influence upon the public mind .... If we give permits for ten journals, we shall ourselves found thirty, and so on in the same proportion. This, however, must in no wise be suspected by the public. For which reason all journals published by us will be of the most opposite, in appearance, tendencies and opinions, thereby creating confidence in us and bringing over to us quite unsuspicious opponents, who will thus fall into our trap and be rendered harmless.

In the front rank will stand organs of an official character. They will always stand guard over our interests, and therefore their influence will be comparatively insignificant.

In the second rank will be the semi-official organs, whose part it will be to attack the tepid and indifferent.

In the third rank we shall set up our own, to all appearance, off position, which, in at least one of its organs, will present what looks like the very antipodes to us. Our real opponents at heart will accept this simulated opposition as their own and will show us their cards.

All our newspapers will be of all possible complexions - aristocratic, republican, revolutionary, even anarchical - for so long, of course, as the constitution exists .... Like the Indian idol "Vishnu" they will have a hundred hands, and every one of them will have a finger on any one of the public opinions as required. When a pulse quickens these hands will lead opinion in the direction of our aims, for an excited patient loses all power of judgment and easily yields to suggestion. Those fools who will think they are repeating the opinion of a newspaper of their own camp will be repeating our opinion or any opinion that seems desirable for us. In the vain belief that they are following the organ of their party they will, in fact, follow the flag which we hang out for them.

In order to direct our newspaper militia in this sense we must take special and minute care in organizing this matter. Under the title of central department of the press we shall institute literary gatherings at which our [AGENT]s will without attracting attention issue the orders and watchwords of the day. By discussing and controverting, but always superficially, without touching the essence of the matter, our organs will carry on a sham fight fusillade with the official newspapers solely for the purpose of giving occasion for us to express ourselves more fully than could well be done from the outset in official announcements, whenever, of course, that is to our advantage.

THESE ATTACKS UPON US WILL ALSO SERVE ANOTHER PURPOSE, NAMELY, THAT OUR SUBJECTS WILL BE CONVINCED TO THE EXISTENCE OF FULL FREEDOM OF SPEECH AND SO GIVE OUR [AGENT]S AN

266 *David E. Smith*

OCCASION TO AFFIRM THAT ALL ORGANS WHICH
OPPOSE US ARE EMPTY BABBLERS, since they are
incapable of finding any substantial objections to our orders.

Methods of organization like these, imperceptible to the
public eye but absolutely sure, are the best calculated to succeed
in bringing the attention and the confidence of the public to the
side of our government. Thanks to such methods we shall be in a
position as from time to time may be required, to excite or to
tranquilize the public mind on political questions, to persuade or
to confuse, printing now truth, now lies, facts or their
contradictions, according as they may be well or ill received,
always very cautiously feeling our ground before stepping upon
it .... WE SHALL HAVE A SURE TRIUMPH OVER OUR
OPPONENTS SINCE THEY WILL NOT HAVE AT THEIR
DISPOSITION ORGANS OF THE PRESS IN WHICH THEY
CAN GIVE FULL AND FINAL EXPRESSION TO THEIR
VIEWS owing to the aforesaid methods of dealing with the
press. We shall not even need to refute them except very
superficially.

Trial shots like these, fired by us in the third rank of our
press, in case of need, will be energetically refuted by us in our
semi-official organs.

Even nowadays, already, to take only the French press, there are forms which reveal Masonic solidarity in acting on the watchword: all organs of the press are bound together by professional secrecy; like the augurs of old, not one of their numbers will give away the secret of his sources of information unless it be resolved to make announcement of them. Not one journalist will venture to betray this secret, for not one of them is ever admitted to practice literature unless his whole past has some disgraceful sore or other .... These sores would be immediately revealed. So long as they remain the secret of a few the prestige of the journalist attacks the majority of the country - the mob follow after him with enthusiasm.

Our calculations are especially extended to the provinces. It is indispensable for us to inflame there those hopes and impulses with which we could at any moment fall upon the capital, and we shall represent to the capitals that these expressions are the independent hopes and impulses of the provinces. Naturally, the source of them will be always one and the same - ours. WHAT WE NEED IS THAT, UNTIL SUCH TIME AS WE ARE IN THE PLENITUDE POWER, THE CAPITALS SHOULD FIND THEMSELVES STIFLED BY THE PROVINCIAL OPINION OF THE NATIONS, I.E., OF A MAJORITY ARRANGED BY OUR [AGENT]S. What we need is that at the psychological moment the capitals should not be in a position to discuss an accomplished fact for the simple reason, if for no other, that it has been accepted by the public opinion of a majority in the provinces.

WHEN WE ARE IN THE PERIOD OF THE NEW REGIME TRANSITIONAL TO THAT OF OUR ASSUMPTION OF FULL SOVEREIGNTY WE MUST NOT ADMIT ANY REVELATION BY THE PRESS OF ANY FORM OF PUBLIC DISHONESTY; IT IS NECESSARY THAT THE NEW REGIME SHOULD BE THOUGHT TO HAVE SO PERFECTLY CONTENDED EVERYBODY THAT EVEN CRIMINALITY HAS DISAPPEARED ... Cases of the manifestation of criminality should remain known only to their victims and to chance witnesses - no more.

PROTOCOL No. 13

The need for daily forces the [GENERAL MASSES] [HUMAN CATTLE] to keep silence and be our humble servants. [AGENT]s taken on to our press from among the [GENERAL MASSES] [HUMAN CATTLE] will at our orders discuss anything which it is inconvenient for us to issue directly in official documents, and we meanwhile, quietly amid the din of the discussion so raised, shall simply take and carry through such measures as we wish and then offer them to the public as an accomplished fact. No one will dare to demand the abrogation of a matter once settled, all the more so as it will be represented as an improvement ... And immediately the press will distract the current of thought towards, new questions. Into the discussions of these new questions will throw themselves those of the brainless dispensers of fortunes who are not able even now to understand that they have not the remotest conception about the matters which they undertake to discuss. Questions of the political are unattainable for any save those who have guide it already for many ages, the creators.

From all this you will see that in seeming the opinion of the mob we are only facilitating the working of our machinery, and you may remark that it is not for actions but for words issued by us on this or that question that we seem to seek approval. We are constantly making public declaration that we are guided in all our undertakings by the hope, joined to the conviction, that we are serving the common wealth.

In order to distract people who may be too troublesome from discussions of questions of the political we are now putting forward what we allege to be new questions of the political, namely, questions of industry. In this sphere let them discuss themselves silly! The masses are agreed to remain inactive, to take a rest from what they suppose to be political only on condition of being found new employments, in which we are prescribing them something that looks like the same political object. In order that the masses themselves may not guess what they are about WE FURTHER DISTRACT THEM WITH AMUSEMENTS, GAMES, PASTIMES, PASSIONS, PEOPLE'S PALACES .... SOON WE SHALL BEGIN THROUGH THE PRESS TO PROPOSE COMPETITIONS IN ART, IN SPORT IN ALL KINDS: these interests will finally distract their minds from questions in which we should find ourselves compelled to oppose them. Growing more and more dis- accustomed to reflect and form any opinions of their own, people will begin to talk in the same tone as we because we alone shall be offering them new directions for thought ... of course through such persons as will not be suspected of solidarity with us.

The part played by the liberals, utopian dreamers, will be finally played out when our government is acknowledged. Till such time they will continue to do us good service. Therefore we shall continue to direct their minds to all sorts of vain conceptions of fantastic theories, new and apparently progressive: for have we not with complete success turned the brainless heads of the [GENERAL MASSES] [HUMAN CATTLE] with progress, till there is not among the [GENERAL MASSES] [HUMAN CATTLE] one mind able to perceive that under this word lies a departure from truth in all cases where it is not a question of material inventions, like a fallacious idea, serves to obscure truth so that none may know it except us, the Chosen of God, its guardians.

When, we come into our kingdom our orators will expound great problems which have turned humanity upside down in order to bring it at the end under our beneficent rule.

Who will ever suspect then that ALL THESE PEOPLES WERE STAGE-MANAGED BY US ACCORDING TO A POLITICAL PLAN WHICH NO ONE HAS SO MUCH AS GUESSED AT IN THE COURSE OF MANY CENTURIES?

PROTOCOL No. 14

When we come into our kingdom it will be undesirable for us that there should exist any other religion than ours of the One God with whom our destiny is bound up by our position as the Chosen People and through whom our same destiny is united with the destinies of the world. We must therefore sweep away all other forms of belief. If this gives birth to the atheists whom we see to-day, it will not, being only a transitional stage, interfere with our views, but will serve as a warning for those generations which will hearken to our preaching of the religion of Moses, that, by its stable and thoroughly elaborated system has brought all the peoples of the world into subjection to us.

Therein we shall emphasize its mystical right, on which, as we shall say, all its educative power is based.... Then at every possible opportunity we shall publish articles in which we shall make comparisons between our beneficent rule and those of past ages. The blessing of tranquillity, though it be a tranquillity forcibly brought about by centuries of agitation, will throw into higher relief the benefits to which we shall point. The errors of the [GENERAL MASSES] [HUMAN CATTLE] governments will be depicted by us in the most vivid hues. We shall implant such an abhorrence of them that the peoples will prefer tranquillity in a state of serfdom to those rights of vaunted freedom which have tortured humanity and exhausted the very sources of human existence, sources which have been exploited by a mob of rascally adventurers who know not what they do .... USELESS CHANGES OF FORMS OF GOVERNMENT TO WHICH WE INSTIGATED THE "[GENERAL MASSES]

[HUMAN CATTLE]" WHEN WE WERE UNDERMINING THEIR STATE STRUCTURES, WILL HAVE SO WEARIED THE PEOPLES BY THAT TIME THAT THEY WILL PREFER TO SUFFER ANYTHING UNDER US RATHER THAN RUN THE RISK OF ENDURING AGAIN ALL THE AGITATIONS AND MISERIES THEY HAVE GONE THROUGH.

At the same time we shall not omit to emphasize the historical mistakes of the WORKING CLASS governments which have tormented humanity for so many centuries by their lack of understanding of everything that constitutes the true good of humanity in their chase after fantastic schemes of social blessings, and have never noticed that these schemes kept on producing a worse and never a better state of the universal relations which are the basis of human life ....

The whole force of our principles and methods will lie in the fact that we shall present them and expound them as a splendid contrast to the dead and decomposed old order of things in social life.

Our philosophers will discuss all the shortcomings of the various beliefs of the "[GENERAL MASSES] [HUMAN

CATTLE]," BUT NO ONE WILL EVER BRING UNDER DISCUSSION OUR FAITH FROM ITS TRUE POINT OF VIEW SINCE THIS WILL BE FULLY LEARNED BY NONE SAVE OURS WHO WILL NEVER DARE TO BETRAY ITS SECRETS.

IN COUNTRIES KNOWN AS PROGRESSIVE AND ENLIGHTENED WE HAVE CREATED A SENSELESS, FILTHY, ABOMINABLE LITERATURE. For some time after our entrance to power we shall continue to encourage its existence in order to provide a telling relief by contrast to the speeches, party program, which will be distributed from exalted quarters of ours .... Our wise men, trained to become leaders of the [GENERAL MASSES] [HUMAN CATTLE], will compose speeches, projects, memoirs, articles, which will be used by us to influence the minds of the [GENERAL MASSES] [HUMAN CATTLE], directing them towards such understanding and forms of knowledge as have been determined by us.

PROTOCOL No. 15

When we at last definitely come into our kingdom by the aid of COUPS D'ETAT prepared everywhere for one and the same day, after definitely acknowledged (and not a little time will pass before that comes about, perhaps even a whole century) we shall make it our task to see that against us such things as plots shall no longer exist. With this purpose we shall slay without mercy all who take arms (in hand) to oppose our coming into our kingdom. Every kind of new institution of anything like a secret society will also be punished with death; those of them which are now in existence, are known to us, serve us and have served us, we shall disband and send into exile to continents far removed from Europe. IN THIS WAY WE SHALL PROCEED WITH THOSE "WORKING CLASS" MASONS WHO KNOW TOO MUCH; such of these as we may for some reason spare will be kept in constant fear of exile. We shall promulgate a law making all former members of secret societies liable to exile from Europe as the center of rule.

Resolutions of our government will be final, without appeal.

In the WORKING CLASS societies, in which we have planted and deeply rooted discord and Protestantism, the only possible way of restoring order is to employ merciless measures that prove the direct force of authority: no regard must be paid to the victims who fall, they suffer for the well-being of the future. The attainment of that well-being, even at the expense of sacrifices, is the duty of any kind of government that acknowledges as justification for its existence not only its privileges but its obligations. The principal guarantee of stability of rule is to confirm the aureole of power, and this aureole is attained only by such a majestic inflexibility of might as shall carry on its face the emblems of inviolability from mystical causes - from the choice of God. SUCH WAS, UNTIL RECENT TIMES, THE RUSSIAN AUTOCRACY, THE ONE AND ONLY SERIOUS FOE WE HAD IN THE WORLD, WITHOUT COUNTING THE PAPACY. Bear in mind the example when Italy, drenched with blood, never touched a hair of the head of Sulla who had poured forth that blood: Sulla enjoyed an apotheosis for his might in him, but his intrepid return to Italy ringed him round with inviolability. The people do not lay a finger on him who hypnotizes them by his daring and strength of mind.

Meantime, however, until we come into our kingdom, we shall act in the contrary way: we shall create and multiply free Masonic lodges in all the countries of the world, absorb into them all who may become or who are prominent in public activity, for these lodges we shall find our principal intelligence office and means of influence. All these lodges we shall bring under one central administration, known to us alone and to all others absolutely unknown, which will be composed of our learned elders. The lodges will have their representatives who will serve to screen the above-mentioned administration of MASONRY and from whom will issue the watchword and program. In these lodges we shall tie together the knot which binds together all revolutionary and liberal elements. Their composition will be made up of all strata of society. The most secret political plots will be known to us and fall under our guiding hands on the very day of their conception. AMONG THE MEMBERS OF THESE LODGES WILL BE ALMOST ALL THE [AGENT] OF INTERNATIONAL AND NATIONAL POLICE since their service is for us irreplaceable in the respect that the police is in a position not only to use its own particular measures with the insubordinate, but also to screen our activities and provide pretexts for discontents, ET CETERA.

The class of people who most willingly enter into secret societies are those who live by their wits, careerists, and in general people, mostly light-minded, with whom we shall have no difficulty in dealing and in using to wind up the mechanism of the machine devised by us. If this world grows agitated the meaning of that will be that we have had to stir up in order to break up its too great solidarity. BUT IF THERE SHOULD ARISE IN ITS MIDST A PLOT, THEN AT THE HEAD OF THAT PLOT

WILL BE NO OTHER THAN ONE OF OUR MOST TRUSTED SERVANTS. It is natural that we and no other should lead MASONIC activities, for we know whither we are leading, we know the final goal of every form of activity whereas the [GENERAL MASSES] [HUMAN CATTLE] have knowledge of nothing, not even of the immediate effect of action; they put before themselves, usually, the momentary reckoning of the satisfaction of their self- opinion in the accomplishment of their thought without even remarking that the very conception never belonged to their initiative but to our instigation of their thought ....

[THE MASSES CANNOT AND REFUSE TO THINK FOR THEMSELVES]

The [GENERAL MASSES] [HUMAN CATTLE] enter the lodges out of curiosity or in the hope by their means to get a nibble at the public pie, and some of them in order to obtain a hearing before the public for their impracticable and groundless fantasies: they thirst for the emotion of success and applause, of which we are remarkably generous. And the reason why we give them this success is to make use of the nigh conceit of themselves to which it gives birth, for that insensibly disposes them to assimilate our suggestions without being on their guard against them in the fullness of their confidence that it is their own infallibility which is giving utterance to their own thoughts and that it is impossible for them to borrow those of others .... You cannot imagine to what extent the wisest of the [GENERAL MASSES] [HUMAN CATTLE] can be brought to a state of unconscious naivete in the presence of this condition of high conceit of themselves, and at the same time how easy it is to take the heart out of them by the slightest ill-success, though it be nothing more than the stoppage of the applause they had, and to reduce them to a slavish submission for the sake of winning a renewal of success .... BY SO MUCH AS OURS DISREGARD SUCCESS IF ONLY THEY CAN CARRY THROUGH THEIR PLANS, BY SO MUCH THE "[GENERAL MASSES] [HUMAN CATTLE]" ARE WILLING TO SACRIFICE ANY PLANS ONLY TO HAVE SUCCESS. This psychology of theirs materially facilitates for us the task of setting them in the required direction. These tigers in appearance have the souls of sheep and the wind blows freely through their heads. We have set them on the hobby-horse of an idea about the absorption of individuality by the symbolic unit of COLLECTIVISM .... They have never yet and they never will have the sense to reflect that this hobby-horse is a manifest violation of the most important law of nature, which has established from the very creation of the world one unit unlike another and precisely for the purpose of instituting individuality....

If we have been able to bring them to such a pitch of stupid blindness is it not a proof, and an amazingly clear proof, of the degree to which the mind of the [GENERAL MASSES] [HUMAN CATTLE] is undeveloped in comparison with our mind? This it is, mainly, which guarantees our success.

THE MASSES ARE NOTHING MORE THAN [CATTLE] WITH HERD INSTINCTS

And how far-seeing were our learned elders in ancient times when they said that to attain a serious end it behooves not to stop at any means or to count the victims sacrificed for the sake of that end .... We have not counted the victims of the seed of the WORKING CLASS [cattle], though we have sacrificed many of our own, but for that we have now already given them such a position on the earth as they could not even have dreamed of. The comparatively small numbers of the victims from the number of ours have preserved our nationality from destruction.

Death is the inevitable end for all. It is better to bring that end nearer to those who hinder our affairs than to ourselves, to the founders of this affair. WE EXECUTE MASONS IN SUCH WISE THAT NONE SAVE THE BROTHERHOOD CAN EVER HAVE A SUSPICION OF IT, NOT EVEN THE VICTIMS THEMSELVES OF OUR DEATH SENTENCE, THEY ALL DIE WHEN REQUIRED AS IF FROM A NORMAL KIND OF ILLNESS ..... Knowing this, even the brotherhood in its turn dare not protest. By such methods we have plucked out of the midst of MASONRY the very root of protest against our disposition. While preaching liberalism to the WORKING CLASS we at the same time keep our own people and our [AGENT]s in a state of unquestioningly submission.

Under our influence the execution of the laws of the [GENERAL MASSES] [HUMAN CATTLE] has been reduced to a minimum. The prestige of the law has been exploded by the liberal interpretations introduced into this sphere. In the most important and fundamental affairs and questions, JUDGES DECIDE AS WE DICTATE TO THEM, see matters in the light wherewith we enfold them for the administration of the [GENERAL MASSES] [HUMAN CATTLE], of course, through persons who are our tools though we do not appear to have anything in common with them - by newspaper opinion or by other means .... Even senators and the higher administration accept our counsels. The purely brute mind of the [GENERAL MASSES] [HUMAN CATTLE] is incapable of use for analysis and observation, and still more for the foreseeing whither a certain manner of setting a question may tend.

In this difference in capacity for thought between the [GENERAL MASSES] [HUMAN CATTLE] and ourselves may be clearly discerned the seal of our position as the Chosen People and of our higher quality of humanness, in contradistinction to the brute mind of the [GENERAL MASSES] [HUMAN CATTLE]. Their eyes are open, but see nothing before them and do not invent. From this it is plain that nature herself has destined us to guide and rule the world.

When comes the time of our overt rule, the time to manifest its blessing, we shall remake all legislatures, all our laws will be brief, plain, stable, without any kind of interpretations, so that anyone will be in a position to know them perfectly. The main feature which will run right through them is submission to orders, and this principle will be carried to a grandiose height. Every abuse will then disappear in consequence of the responsibility of all down to the lowest unit before the higher authority of the representative of power. Abuses of power subordinate to this last instance will be so mercilessly punished that none will be found anxious to try experiments with their own powers. We shall follow up jealously every action of the administration on which depends the smooth running of the machinery of the State, for slackness in this produces slackness everywhere; not a single case of illegality or abuse of power will be left without exemplary punishment.

Concealment of guilt, connivance between those in the service of the administration - all this kind of evil will disappear after the very first examples of severe punishment. The aureole of our power demands suitable, that is, cruel, punishments for the slightest infringement, for the sake of gain, of its supreme prestige. The sufferer, though his punishment may exceed his fault, will count as a soldier falling on the administrative field of battle in the interest of authority, principle and law, which do not permit that any of those who hold the reins of the public coach should turn aside from the public highway to their own private paths. FOR EXAMPLES OUR JUDGES WILL KNOW THAT WHENEVER THEY FEEL DISPOSED TO PLUME THEMSELVES ON FOOLISH CLEMENCY THEY ARE VIOLATING THE LAW OF JUSTICE WHICH IS

INSTITUTED FOR THE EXEMPLARY EDIFICATION OF
MEN BY PENALTIES FOR LAPSES AND NOT FOR
DISPLAY OF THE SPIRITUAL QUALITIES OF THE
JUDGES .... Such qualities it is proper to show in private life,
but not in a public square which is the educationally basis of
human life.

Our legal staff will serve not beyond the age of 55, firstly
because old men more obstinately hold to prejudiced opinions,
and are less capable of submitting to new directions, and
secondly because this will give us the possibility by this measure
of securing elasticity in the changing of staff, which will thus the
more easily bend under our pressure: he who wishes to keep his
place will have to give blind obedience to deserve it. In general,
our judges will be elected by us only from among those who
thoroughly understand that the part they have to play is to punish
and apply laws and not to dream about the manifestations of
liberalism at the expense of the educational scheme of the State,
as the [GENERAL MASSES] [HUMAN CATTLE] in these
days imagine it to be .... This method of shuffling the staff will
serve also to explode any collective solidarity of those in the
same service and will bind all to the interests of the government
upon which their fate will depend. The young generation of
judges will be trained in certain views regarding the

inadmissibility of any abuses that might disturb the established order of our subjects among themselves.

In these days the judges of the [GENERAL MASSES] [HUMAN CATTLE] create indulgences to every kind of crimes, not having a just understanding of their office, because the rulers of the present age in appointing judges to office take no care to inculcate in them a sense of duty and consciousness of the matter which is demanded of them. As a brute beast lets out its young in search of prey, so do the [GENERAL MASSES] [HUMAN CATTLE] give to them for what purpose such place was created. This is the reason why their governments are being ruined by their own forces through the acts of their own administration.

Let us borrow from the example of the results of these actions yet another lesson for our government.

We shall root out liberalism from all the important strategic posts of our government on which depends the training of subordinates for our State structure. Such posts will fall exclusively to those who have been trained by us for administrative rule. To the possible objection that the retirement of old servants will cost the Treasury heavily, I reply, firstly, they will be provided with some private service in place of what they lose, and, secondly, I have to remark that all the money in the world will be concentrated in our hands, consequently it is not our government that has to fear expense.

Our absolutism will in all things be logically consecutive and therefore in each one of its decrees our supreme will be respected and unquestionably fulfilled: it will ignore all murmurs, all discontents of every kind and will destroy to the root every kind of manifestation of them in act by punishment of an exemplary character.

We shall abolish the right of cessation, which will be transferred exclusively to our disposal - to the cognizance of him who rules, for we must not allow the conception among the people of a thought that there could be such a thing as a decision that is not right of judges set up by us. If, however, anything like this should occur, we shall ourselves castrate the decision, but inflict therewith such exemplary punishment on the judge for lack of understanding of his duty and the purpose of his appointment as will prevent a repetition of such cases .... I repeat that it must be born in mind that we shall know every step of our administration which only needs to be closely watched for the people to be content with us, for it has the right to demand from a good government a good official.

OUR GOVERNMENT WILL HAVE THE APPEARANCE OF A PATRIARCHAL PATERNAL GUARDIANSHIP ON THE PART OF OUR RULER. Our own nation and our subjects will discern in his person a father caring for their every need, their every act, their every inter-relation as subjects one with another, as well as their relations to the ruler. They will then be so thoroughly imbued with the thought that it is impossible for them to dispense with this wardship and guidance, if they wish to live in peace and quiet, THAT THEY WILL ACKNOWLEDGE THE AUTOCRACY OF OUR RULER WITH A DEVOTION BORDERING ON "APOTHEOSIS," especially when they are convinced that those whom we set up do not put their own in place of authority, but only blindly execute his dictates. They will be rejoiced that we have regulated everything in their lives as is done by wise parents who desire to train children in the cause of duty and submission. For the peoples of the world in regard to the secrets of our polity are ever through the ages only children under age, precisely as are also their governments.

As you see, I found our despotism on right and duty: the right to compel the execution of duty is the direct obligation of a government which is a father for its subjects. It has the right of the strong that it may use it for the benefit of directing humanity towards that order which is defined by nature, namely, submission. Everything in the world is in a state of submission, if not to man, then to circumstances or its own inner character, in all cases, to what is stronger. And so shall we be this something stronger for the sake of good.

We are obliged without hesitation to sacrifice individuals, who commit a breach of established order, for in the exemplary punishment of evil lies a great educational problem.

When the King of Israel sets upon his sacred head the crown offered him by Europe he will become patriarch of the world. The indispensable victims offered by him in consequence of their suitability will never reach the number of victims offered in the course of centuries by the mania of magnificence, the emulation between the WORKING CLASS governments.

Our King will be in constant communion with the peoples, making to them from the tribune speeches which fame will in that same hour distribute over all the world.

PROTOCOL No. 16

In order to effect the destruction of all collective forces except ours we shall emasculate the first stage of collectivism - the UNIVERSITIES, by re-educating them in a new direction. THEIR OFFICIALS AND PROFESSORS WILL BE PREPARED FOR THEIR BUSINESS BY DETAILED SECRET PROGRAMS OF ACTION FROM WHICH THEY WILL NOT WITH IMMUNITY DIVERGE, NOT BY ONE IOTA. THEY WILL BE APPOINTED WITH ESPECIAL PRECAUTION, AND WILL BE SO PLACED AS TO BE WHOLLY DEPENDENT UPON THE GOVERNMENT.

We shall exclude from the course of instruction State Law as also all that concerns the political question. These subjects will be taught to a few dozen of persons chosen for their pre-eminent capacities from among the number of the initiated. THE UNIVERSITIES MUST NO LONGER SEND OUT FROM THEIR HALLS MILK SOPS CONCOCTING PLANS FOR A CONSTITUTION, LIKE A COMEDY OR A TRAGEDY, BUSYING THEMSELVES WITH QUESTIONS OF POLICY IN WHICH EVEN THEIR OWN FATHERS NEVER HAD ANY POWER OF THOUGHT.

The ill-guided acquaintance of a large number of persons with questions of polity creates utopian dreamers and bad subjects, as you can see for yourselves from the example of the universal education in this direction of the [GENERAL MASSES] [HUMAN CATTLE]. We must introduce into their education all those principles which have so brilliantly broken up their order. But when we are in power we shall remove every kind of disturbing subject from the course of education and shall make out of the youth obedient children of authority, loving him who rules as the support and hope of peace and quiet.

Classicism as also any form of study of ancient history, in which there are more bad than good examples, we shall replace with the study of the program of the future. We shall erase from the memory of men all facts of previous centuries which are undesirable to us, and leave only those which depict all the errors of the government of the [GENERAL MASSES] [HUMAN CATTLE]. The study of practical life, of the obligations of order, of the relations of people one to another, of avoiding bad and selfish examples, which spread the infection of evil, and similar questions of an educative nature, will stand in the forefront of the teaching program, which will be drawn up on a separate plan for each calling or state of life, in no wise generalizing the teaching. This treatment of the question has special importance.

Each state of life must be trained within strict limits corresponding to its destination and work in life. The OCCASIONAL GENIUS HAS ALWAYS MANAGED AND ALWAYS WILL MANAGE TO SLIP THROUGH INTO OTHER STATES OF LIFE, BUT IT IS THE MOST PERFECT FOLLY FOR THE SAKE OF THIS RARE OCCASIONAL GENIUS TO LET THROUGH INTO RANKS FOREIGN TO THEM THE UNTALENTED WHO THUS ROB OF THEIR PLACES WHO BELONG TO THOSE RANKS BY BIRTH OR EMPLOYMENT. YOU KNOW YOURSELVES IN WHAT ALL THIS HAS ENDED FOR THE "[GENERAL MASSES] [HUMAN CATTLE]" WHO ALLOWED THIS CRYING ABSURDITY.

In order that he who rules may be seated firmly in the hearts and minds of his subjects it is necessary for the time of his activity to instruct the whole nation in the schools and on the market places about this meaning and his acts and all his beneficent initiatives.

We shall abolish every kind of freedom of instruction. Learners of all ages have the right to assemble together with their parents in the educational establishments as it were in a

club: during these assemblies, on holidays, teachers will read
what will pass as free lectures on questions of human relations,
of the laws of examples, of the philosophy of new theories not
yet declared to the world. These theories will be raised by us to
the stage of a dogma of faith as a traditional stage towards our
faith. On the completion of this exposition of our program of
action in the present and the future I will read you the principles
of these theories.

In a word, knowing by the experience of many centuries
that people live and are guided by ideas, that these ideas are
imbibed by people only by the aid of education provided with
equal success for all ages of growth, but of course by varying
methods, we shall swallow up and confiscate to our own use the
last scintilla of independence of thought, which we have for long
past been directing towards subjects and ideas useful for us. The
system of bridling thought is already at work in the so-called
system of teaching by OBJECT LESSONS, the purpose of
which is to turn the [GENERAL MASSES] [HUMAN
CATTLE] into unthinking submissive brutes waiting for things
to be presented before their eyes in order to form an idea of them
.... In France, one of our best [AGENT]s, Bourgeois, has already
made public a new program of teaching by object lessons.

PROTOCOL No. 17

The practice of advocacy produces men cold, cruel, persistent, unprincipled, who in all cases take up an impersonal, purely legal standpoint. They have the inveterate habit to refer everything to its value for the defense and not to the public welfare of its results. They do not usually decline to undertake any defense whatever, they strive for an acquittal at all costs, caviling over every petty crux of jurisprudence and thereby they demoralize justice. For this reason we shall set this profession into narrow frames which will keep it inside this sphere of executive public service. Advocates, equally with judges, will be deprived of the right of communication with litigant; they well receive business only from the court and will study it by notes of report and documents, defending their clients after they have been interrogated in court on facts that have appeared. They will receive an honorarium without regard to the quality of the defense. This will render them mere reporters on law-business in the interest of justice and as counterpoise to the proctor who will be the reporter in the interests of prosecution; this will shorten business before the courts. In this way will be established a practice of honest unprejudiced defense conducted not from personal interest but by conviction. This will also, by the way, remove the present practice of corrupt bargain between advocation to agree only to let that side win which pays most.....

WE HAVE LONG PAST TAKEN CARE TO DISCREDIT THE PRIESTHOOD OF "[GENERAL MASSES] [HUMAN CATTLE]," and thereby to ruin their mission on earth which in these days might still be a great hindrance to us. Day by day its influence on the peoples of the world is falling lower. FREEDOM OF CONSCIENCE HAS BEEN DECLARED EVERYWHERE, SO THAT NOW ONLY YEARS DIVIDE US FROM THE MOMENT OF THE COMPLETE WRECKING OF THAT CHRISTIAN RELIGION: as to other religions we shall have still less difficulty in dealing with them, but it would be premature to speak of this now. We shall act clericalism and clericals into such narrow frames as to make their influence move in retrogressive proportion to its former progress.

When the time comes finally to destroy the papal court the finger of an invisible hand will point the nations towards this court. When, however, the nations fling themselves upon it, we shall come forward in the guise of its defenders as if to save excessive bloodshed. By this diversion we shall penetrate to its very bowels and be sure we shall never come out again until we have gnawed through the entire strength of this place.

THE KING OF THE [ILLUMINATI] WILL BE THE REAL POPE OF THE UNIVERSE, THE PATRIARCH OF THE INTERNATIONAL CHURCH.

But, IN THE MEANTIME, while we are re-educating youth in new traditional religions and afterwards in ours, WE SHALL NOT OVERTLY LAY A FINGER ON EXISTING CHURCHES, BUT WE SHALL FIGHT AGAINST THEM BY CRITICISM CALCULATED TO PRODUCE SCHISM....

In general, then, our contemporary press will continue to CONVICT State affairs, religions, incapacities of the [GENERAL MASSES] [HUMAN CATTLE], always using the most unprincipled expressions in order by every means to lower their prestige in the manner which can only be practiced by the genius of our gifted tribe....

Our kingdom will be an apologia of the divinity Vishnu, in whom is found its personification - in our hundred hands will be, one in each, the springs of the machinery of social life. We shall see everything without the aid of official police which, in that scope of its rights which we elaborated for the use of the [GENERAL MASSES] [HUMAN CATTLE], hinders governments from seeing. In our programs ONE-THIRD OF OUR SUBJECTS WILL KEEP THE REST UNDER OBSERVATION from a sense of duty, on the principle of volunteer service to the State. It will then be no disgrace to be a spy and informer, but a merit: unfounded denunciations, however, will be cruelly punished that there may be development of abuses of this right.

Our [AGENT]s will be taken from the higher as well as the lower ranks of society, from among the administrative class who spend their time in amusements, editors, printers and publishers, booksellers, clerks, and salesmen, workmen, coachmen, lackeys, et cetera. This body, having no rights and not being empowered to take any action on their own account, and consequently a police without any power, will only witness and report: verification of their reports and arrests will depend upon a responsible group of controllers of police affairs, while the actual act of arrest will be performed by the gendarmerie and the municipal police. Any person not denouncing anything seen or heard concerning questions of polity will also be charged with and made responsible for concealment, if it be proved that he is guilty of this crime.

JUST AS NOWADAYS OUR BRETHREN, ARE OBLIGED AT THEIR OWN RISK TO DENOUNCE TO THE KABAL APOSTATES OF THEIR OWN FAMILY or members who have been noticed doing anything in opposition to the KABAL, SO IN OUR KINGDOM OVER ALL THE WORLD IT WILL BE OBLIGATORY FOR ALL OUR SUBJECTS TO OBSERVE THE DUTY OF SERVICE TO THE STATE IN THIS DIRECTION.

Such an organization will extirpate abuses of authority, of force, of bribery, everything in fact which we by our counsels, by out theories of the superhuman rights of man, have introduced into the customs of the [GENERAL MASSES] [HUMAN CATTLE] .... But how else were we to procure that increase of causes predisposing to disorders in the midst of their administration? .... Among the number of those methods one of the most important is - [AGENT]s for the restoration of order, so placed as to have the opportunity in their disintegrating activity of developing and displaying their evil inclinations - obstinate self-conceit, irresponsible exercise of authority, and, first and foremost, venality.

PROTOCOL No. 18

When it becomes necessary for us to strengthen the strict measures of secret defense we shall arrange a simulation of disorders or some manifestation of discontents finding expression through the co- operation of good speakers. Round these speakers will assemble all who are sympathetic to his utterances. This will give us the pretext for domiciliary prerequisitions and surveillance on the part of our servants from among the number of the [GENERAL MASSES] [HUMAN CATTLE] police....

As the majority of conspirators act of love for the game, for the sake of talking, so, until they commit some overt act we shall not lay a finger on them but only introduce into their midst observation elements.... It must be remembered that the prestige of authority is lessened if it frequently discovers conspiracies against itself: this implies a presumption of consciousness of weakness, or, what is still worse, of injustice. You are aware that we have broken the prestige of the WORKING CLASS kings by frequent attempts upon their lives through our [AGENT]s, blind sheep of our flock, who are easily moved by a few liberal phrases to crimes provided only they be painted in political colors. WE HAVE COMPELLED THE RULERS TO ACKNOWLEDGE THEIR WEAKNESS IN ADVERTISING OVERT MEASURES OF SECRET DEFENSE AND THEREBY WE SHALL BRING THE PROMISE OF AUTHORITY TO DESTRUCTION.

Our ruler will be secretly protected only by the most insignificant guard, because we shall not admit so much as a thought that there could exist against him any sedition with which he is not strong enough to contend and is compelled to hide from it.

If we should admit this thought, as the [GENERAL MASSES] [HUMAN CATTLE] have done and are doing, we should IPSO FACTO be signing a death sentence, if not for our ruler, at any rate for his dynasty, at no distant date.

According to strictly enforced outward appearances our ruler will employ his power only for the advantage of the nation and in no wise for his own or dynastic profits. Therefore, with the observance of this decorum, his authority will be respected and guarded by the subjects themselves, it will receive an apotheosis in the admission that with it is bound up the well-being of every citizen of the State, for upon it will depend all order in the common life of the pack....

OVERT DEFENSE OF THE KIND ARGUES
WEAKNESS IN THE ORGANIZATION OF HIS STRENGTH.

Our ruler will always be among the people and be surrounded by a mob of apparently curious men and women, who will occupy the front ranks about him, to all appearance by chance, and will restrain the ranks of the rest out of respect as it will appear for good order. This will sow an example of restraint also in others. If a petitioner appears among the people trying to hand a petition and forcing his way through the ranks, the first ranks must receive the petition and before the eyes of the petitioner pass it to the ruler, so that all may know that what is handed in reaches its destination, that consequently, there exists a control of the ruler himself. The aureole of power requires for its existence that the people may be able to say: "If the king knew of this," or: "the king will hear it."

WITH THE ESTABLISHMENT OF OFFICIAL DEFENSE, THE MYSTICAL PRESTIGE OF AUTHORITY DISAPPEARS: given a certain audacity, and everyone counts himself master of it, the sedition- monger is conscious of his strength, and when occasion serves watches for the moment to make an attempt upon authority .... For the [GENERAL MASSES] [HUMAN CATTLE] we have been preaching something else, but by that very fact we are enabled to see what measures of overt defense have brought them to....

CRIMINALS WITH US WILL BE ARRESTED AT THE FIRST, more or less, well-grounded SUSPICION: it cannot be allowed that out of fear of a possible mistake an opportunity should be given of escape to persons suspected of a political lapse of crime, for in these matters we shall be literally merciless. If it is still possible, by stretching a point, to admit a reconsideration of the motive causes in simple crimes, there is no possibility of excuse for persons occupying themselves with questions in which nobody except the government can understand anything .... And it is not all governments that understand true policy.

PROTOCOL No. 19

If we do not permit any independent dabbling in the political we shall on the other hand encourage every kind of report or petition with proposals for the government to examine into all kinds of projects for the amelioration of the condition of the people; this will reveal to us the defects or else the fantasies of our subjects, to which we shall respond either by accomplishing them or by a wise rebuttment to prove the shortsightedness of one who judges wrongly.

Sedition-mongering is nothing more than the yapping of a lap- dog at an elephant. For a government well organized, not from the police but from the public point of view, the lap-dog yaps at the elephant in entire unconsciousness of its strength and importance. It needs no more than to take a good example to show the relative importance of both and the lap-dogs will cease to yap and will wag their tails the moment they set eyes on an elephant.

In order to destroy the prestige of heroism for political crime we shall send it for trial in the category of thieving, murder, and every kind of abominable and filthy crime. Public opinion will then confuse in its conception of this category of crime with the disgrace attaching to every other and will brand it with the same contempt.

We have done our best, and I hope we have succeeded to obtain that the [GENERAL MASSES] [HUMAN CATTLE] should not arrive at this means of contending with sedition. It was for this reason that through the Press and in speeches, indirectly - in cleverly compiled school- books on history, we have advertised the martyrdom alleged to have been accredited by sedition-mongers for the idea of the commonwealth. This advertisement has increased the contingent of liberals and has brought thousands of [GENERAL MASSES] [HUMAN

CATTLE] into the ranks of our livestock [cattle].

PROTOCOL No. 20

To-day we shall touch upon the financial program, which I put off to the end of my report as being the most difficult, the crowning and the decisive point of our plans. Before entering upon it I will remind you that I have already spoken before by way of a hint when I said that the sum total of our actions is settled by the question of figures.

When we come into our kingdom our autocratic government will avoid, from a principle of self-preservation, sensibly burdening the masses of the people with taxes, remembering that it plays the part of father and protector. But as State organization cost dear it is necessary nevertheless to obtain the funds required for it. It will, therefore, elaborate with particular precaution the question of equilibrium in this matter.

Our rule, in which the king will enjoy the legal fiction that everything in his State belongs to him (which may easily be translated into fact), will be enabled to resort to the lawful confiscation of all sums of every kind for the regulation of their circulation in the State. From this follows that taxation will best be covered by a progressive tax on property. In this manner the dues will be paid without straitening or ruining anybody in the form of a percentage of the amount of property. The rich must be aware that it is their duty to place a part of their superfluities at the disposal of the State since the State guarantees them security of possession of the rest of their property and the right of honest gains, I say honest, for the control over property will do away with robbery on a legal basis.

This social reform must come from above, for the time is ripe for it - it is indispensable as a pledge of peace.

The tax upon the poor man is a seed of revolution and works to the detriment of the State which is hunting after the trifling is missing the big. Quite apart from this, a tax on capitalists diminishes the growth of wealth in private hands in which we have in these days concentrated it as a counterpoise to the government strength of the [GENERAL MASSES] [HUMAN CATTLE] - their State finances.

A tax increasing in a percentage ratio to capital will give much larger revenue than the present individual or property tax, which is useful to us now for the sole reason that it excites trouble and discontent among the [GENERAL MASSES] [HUMAN CATTLE].

The force upon which our king will rest consists in the equilibrium and the guarantee of peace, for the sake of which things it is indispensable that the capitalists should yield up a portion of their incomes for the sake of the secure working of the machinery of the State. State needs must be paid by those who will not feel the burden and have enough to take from.

Such a measure will destroy the hatred of the poor man for the rich, in whom he will see a necessary financial support for the State, will see in him the organizer of peace and well-being since he will see that it is the rich man who is paying the necessary means to attain these things.

In order that payers of the educated classes should not too much distress themselves over the new payments they will have full accounts given them of the destination of those payments, with the exception of such sums as will be appropriated for the needs of the throne and the administrative institutions.

He who reigns will not have any properties of his own once all in the State represented his patrimony, or else the one would be in contradiction to the other; the fact of holding private means would destroy the right of property in the common possessions of all.

Relatives of him who reigns, his heirs excepted, who will be maintained by the resources of the State, must enter the ranks of servants of the State or must work to obtain the right to property; the privilege of royal blood must not serve for the spoiling of the treasury.

Purchase, receipt of money or inheritance will be subject to the payment of a stamp progressive tax. Any transfer of property, whether money or other, without evidence of payment of this tax which will be strictly registered by names, will render the former holder liable to pay interest on the tax from the moment of transfer of these sums up to the discovery of his evasion of declaration of the transfer. Transfer documents must be presented weekly at the local treasury office with notifications of the name, surname and permanent place of residence of the former and the new holder of the property. This transfer with register of names must begin from a definite sum which exceeds the ordinary expenses of buying and selling necessaries, and these will be subject to payment only by a stamp impost of a definite percentage of the unit.

Just strike an estimate of how many times such taxes as

these will cover the revenue of the [GENERAL MASSES] [HUMAN CATTLE] States.

ILLUMINISTS WILL CREATE DEPRESSIONS

The State exchequer will have to maintain a definite complement of reserve sums, and all that is collected above that complement must be returned into circulation. On these sums will be organized public works. The initiative in works of this kind, proceeding from State sources, will blind the working class firmly to the interests of the State and to those who reign. From these same sums also a part will be set aside as rewards of inventiveness and productiveness.

On no account should so much as a single unit above the definite and freely estimated sums be retained in the State Treasuries, for money exists to be circulated and any kind of stagnation of money acts ruinously on the running of the State machinery, for which it is the lubricant; a stagnation of the lubricant may stop the regular working of the mechanism.

The substitution of interest-bearing paper for a part of the token of exchange has produced exactly this stagnation. The consequences of this circumstance are already sufficiently noticeable.

A court of account will also be instituted by us, and in it
the ruler will find at any moment a full accounting for State
income and expenditure, with the exception of the current
monthly account, not yet made up, and that of the preceding
month, which will not yet have been delivered.

The one and only person who will have no interest in
robbing the State is its owner, the ruler. This is why his personal
control will remove the possibility of leakage of extravagances.

The representative function of the ruler at receptions for
the sake of etiquette, which absorbs so much invaluable time,
will be abolished in order that the ruler may have time for control
and consideration. His power will not then be split up into
fractional parts among time-serving favorites who surround the
throne for its pomp and splendor, and are interested only in their
own and not in the common interests of the State.

Economic crises have been produced by us for the
[GENERAL MASSES] [HUMAN CATTLE] by no other means
than the withdrawal of money from circulation. Huge capitals
have stagnated, withdrawing money from States, which were

constantly obliged to apply to those same stagnant capitals for loans. These loans burdened the finances of the State with the payment of interest and made them the bond slaves of these capitals .... The concentration of industry in the hands of capitalists out of the hands of small masters has drained away all the juices of the peoples and with them also the States....

The present issue of money in general does not correspond with the requirements per head, and cannot therefore satisfy all the needs of the workers. The issue of money ought to correspond with the growth of population and thereby children also must absolutely be reckoned as consumers of currency from the day of their birth. The revision of issue is a material question for the whole world.

YOU ARE AWARE THAT THE GOLD STANDARD HAS BEEN THE RUIN OF THE STATES WHICH ADOPTED IT, FOR IT HAS NOT BEEN ABLE TO SATISFY THE DEMANDS FOR MONEY, THE MORE SO THAT WE HAVE REMOVED GOLD FROM CIRCULATION AS FAR AS POSSIBLE.

With us the standard that must be introduced is the cost of working-man power, whether it be reckoned in paper or in wood. We shall make the issue of money in accordance with the normal requirements of each subject, adding to the quantity with every birth and subtracting with every death.

The accounts will be managed by each department in each circle.

In order that there may be no delays in the paying our of money for State needs the sums and terms of such payments will be fixed by decree of the ruler; this will do away with the protection by a ministry of one institution to the detriment of others.

The budgets of income and expenditure will be carried out side by side that they may not be obscured by distance one to another.

The reforms projected by us in the financial institutions and principles of the [GENERAL MASSES] [HUMAN CATTLE] will be clothed by us in such forms as will alarm nobody. We shall point out the necessity of reforms in consequence of the disorderly darkness into which the [GENERAL MASSES] [HUMAN CATTLE] by their irregularities have plunged the finances. The first irregularity, as we shall point out, consists in their beginning with drawing up a single budget which year after year grows owing to the following cause: this budget is dragged out to half the year, then they demand a budget to put things right, and this they expend in three months, after which they ask for a supplementary budget, and all this ends with a liquidation budget. But, as the budget of the following year is drawn up in accordance with the sum of the total addition, the annual departure from the normal reaches as much as 50 per cent in a year, and so the annual budget is trebled in ten years. Thanks to such methods, allowed by the carelessness of the WORKING CLASS States, their treasuries are empty. The period of loans supervenes, and that has swallowed up remainders and brought all the WORKING CLASS States to bankruptcy.

You understand perfectly that economic arrangements of this kind, which have been suggested to the [GENERAL MASSES] [HUMAN CATTLE] by us, cannot be carried on by us.

Every kind of loan proves infirmity in the State and a want of understanding of the rights of the State. Loans hang like a sword of Damocles over the heads of rulers, who, instead of taking from their subjects by a temporary tax, come begging with outstretched palm of our bankers. Foreign loans are leeches which there is no possibility of removing from the body of the State until they fall off of themselves or the State flings them off. But the WORKING CLASS States do not tear them off; they go on in persisting in putting more on to themselves so that they must inevitably perish, drained by voluntary blood-letting.

USING USURY TO CREATE INFINITE SERVITUDE

What also indeed is, in substance, a loan, especially a foreign loan? A loan is - an issue of government bills of exchange containing a percentage obligation commensurate to the sum of the loan capital. If the loan bears a charge of 5 per cent, then in twenty years the State vainly pays away in interest a sum equal to the loan borrowed, in forty years it is paying a double sum, in sixty - treble, and all the while the debt remains an unpaid debt.

From this calculation it is obvious that with any form of taxation per head the State is baling out the last coppers of the poor taxpayers in order to settle accounts with wealth foreigners, from whom it has borrowed money instead of collecting these coppers for its own needs without the additional interest.

So long as loans were internal the [GENERAL MASSES] [HUMAN CATTLE] only shuffled their money from the pockets of the poor to those of the rich, but when we bought up the necessary person in order to transfer loans into the external sphere, all the wealth of States flowed into our cash-boxes and all the [GENERAL MASSES] [HUMAN CATTLE] began to pay us the tribute of subjects.

If the superficiality of WORKING CLASS kings on their thrones in regard to State affairs and the venality of ministers or the want of understanding of financial matters on the part of other ruling persons have made their countries debtors to our treasuries to amounts quite impossible to pay it has not been accomplished without, on our part, heavy expenditure of trouble and money.

Stagnation of money will not be allowed by us and therefore there will be no State interest-bearing paper, except a one per- cent series, so that there will be no payment of interest to leeches that suck all the strength out of the State. The right to issue interest-bearing paper will be given exclusively to industrial companies who will find no difficulty in paying interest out of profits, whereas the State does not make interest on borrowed money like these companies, for the State borrows to spend and not to use in operations.

Industrial papers will be bought also by the government which from being as now a paper of tribute by loan operations will be transformed into a lender of money at a profit. This measure will stop the stagnation of money, parasitic profits and idleness, all of which were useful for us among the [GENERAL MASSES] [HUMAN CATTLE] so long as they were independent but are not desirable under our rule.

How clear is the undeveloped power of thought of the purely brute brains of the [GENERAL MASSES] [HUMAN CATTLE], as expressed in the fact that they have been borrowing from us with payment of interest without ever thinking that all the same these very moneys plus an addition for payment of interest must be got by them from their own State pockets in order to settle up with us. What could have been simpler than to take the money they wanted from their own people?

But it is a proof of the genius of our chosen mind that we have contrived to present the matter of loans to them in such a light that they have even seen in them an advantage for themselves.

Our accounts, which we shall present when the time comes, in the light of centuries of experience gained by experiments made by us on the WORKING CLASS States, will be distinguished by clearness and definiteness and will show at a glance to all men the advantage of our innovations. They will put an end to those abuses to which we owe our mastery over the [GENERAL MASSES] [HUMAN CATTLE], but which cannot be allowed in our kingdom.

We shall so hedge about our system of accounting that neither the ruler nor the most insignificant public servant will be in a position to divert even the smallest sum from its destination without detection or to direct it in another direction except that which will be once fixed in a definite plan of action

And without a definite plan it is impossible to rule. Marching along an undetermined road and with undetermined resources brings to ruin by the way heroes and demi-gods.

The WORKING CLASS rulers, whom we once upon a time advised should be distracted from State occupations by representative receptions, observances of etiquette, entertainment, were only screens for our rule. The accounts of favorite courtiers who replaced them in the sphere of affairs were drawn up for them by our [AGENT]s, and every time gave satisfaction to short-sighted minds by promises that in the future economics and improvements were foreseen .... Economics from what? From new taxes? - were questions that might have been but were not asked by those who read our accounts and projects.

You know to what they have been brought by this carelessness, to what pitch of financial disorder they have arrived, notwithstanding the astonishing industry of their peoples....

PROTOCOL No. 21

To what I reported to you at the last meeting I shall now add a detailed explanation of internal loans. Of foreign loans I shall say nothing more, because they have fed us with national moneys of the [GENERAL MASSES] [HUMAN CATTLE], but for our State there will be no foreigners, that is, nothing external.

We have taken advantage of the venality of administrators and slackness of rulers to get our moneys twice, thrice and more times over, by lending to the WORKING CLASS governments moneys which were not at all needed by

the States. Could anyone do the like in regard to us? ....
Therefore, I shall only deal with the details of internal loans.

States announce that such a loan is to be concluded and
open subscriptions for their own bills of exchange, that is, for
their interest-bearing paper. That they may be within the reach of
all the price is determined at from a hundred to a thousand; and a
discount is made for the earliest subscribers. Next day by
artificial means the price of them goes up, the alleged reason
being that everyone is rushing to buy them. In a few days the
treasury safes are as they say overflowing and there's more
money than they can do with (why then take it?). The
subscription, it is alleged, covers many times over the issue total
of the loan; in this lies the whole stage effect - look you, they
say, what confidence is shown in the government's bills of
exchange.

But when the comedy is played out there emerges the
fact that a debit and an exceedingly burdensome debit has been
created. For the payment of interest it becomes necessary to have
recourse to new loans, which do not swallow up but only add to
the capital debt. And when this credit is exhausted it becomes
necessary by new taxes to cover, not the loan, BUT ONLY THE
INTEREST ON IT. These taxes are a debit employed to cover a

Later comes the time for conversions, but they diminish the payment of interest without covering the debt, and besides they cannot be made without the consent of the lenders; on announcing a conversion a proposal is made to return the money to those who are not willing to convert their paper. If everybody expressed his unwillingness and demanded his money back, the government would be hooked on their own files and would be found insolvent and unable to pay the proposed sums. By good luck the subjects of the WORKING CLASS governments, knowing nothing about financial affairs, have always preferred losses on exchange and diminution of interest to the risk of new investments of their moneys, and have thereby many a time enabled these governments to throw off their shoulders a debit of several millions.

Nowadays, with external loans, these tricks cannot be played by the [GENERAL MASSES] [HUMAN CATTLE] for they know that we shall demand all our moneys back.

In this way in acknowledged bankruptcy will best prove to the various countries the absence of any means between the interest of the peoples and of those who rule them.

I beg you to concentrate your particular attention upon this point and upon the following: nowadays all internal loans are consolidated by so-called flying loans, that is, such as have terms of payment more or less near. These debts consist of moneys paid into the savings banks and reserve funds. If left for long at the disposition of a government these funds evaporate in the payment of interest on foreign loans, and are placed by the deposit of equivalent amount of RENTS.

And these last it is which patch up all the leaks in the State treasuries of the [GENERAL MASSES] [HUMAN CATTLE].

When we ascend the throne of the world all these financial and similar shifts, as being not in accord with our interests, will be swept away so as not to leave a trace, as also will be destroyed all money markets, since we shall not allow the prestige of our power to be shaken by fluctuations of prices set upon our values, which we shall announce by law at the price which represents their full worth without any possibility of lowering or raising.

We shall replace the money markets by grandiose government credit institutions, the object of which will be to fix the price of industrial values in accordance with government views. These institutions will be in a position to fling upon the market five hundred millions of industrial paper in one day, or to buy up for the same amount. In this way all industrial undertakings will come into dependence upon us. You may imagine for yourselves what immense power we shall thereby secure for ourselves....

PROTOCOL No. 22

In all that has so far been reported by me to you, I have endeavored to depict with care the secret of what is coming, of what is past, and of what is going on now, rushing into the flood of the great events coming already in the near future, the secret of our relations to the [GENERAL MASSES] [HUMAN CATTLE] and of financial operations. On this subject there remains still a little for me to add.

IN OUR HANDS IS THE GREATEST POWER OF OUR DAY - GOLD: IN TWO DAYS WE CAN PROCURE FROM OUR STOREHOUSES ANY QUANTITY WE MAY PLEASE.

Surely there is no need to seek further proof that our rule is predestined by God? Surely we shall not fail with such wealth to prove that all that evil which for so many centuries we have had to commit has served at the end of ends the cause of true well- being - the bringing of everything into order? Though it be even by the exercise of some violence, yet all the same it will be established. We shall contrive to prove that we are benefactors who have restored to the rent and mangled earth the true good and also freedom of the person, and therewith we shall enable it to be enjoyed in peace and quiet, with proper dignity of relations, on the condition, of course, of strict observance of the laws established by us. We shall make plain therewith that freedom does not consist in dissipation and in the right of unbridled license any more than the dignity and force of a man do not consist in the right of everyone to promulgate destructive principles in the nature of freedom of conscience, equality and a like, that freedom of the person in no wise consists in the right to agitate oneself and others by abominable speeches before disorderly mobs, and that true freedom consists in the inviolability of the person who honorably and strictly observes all the laws of life in common, that human dignity is wrapped up in consciousness of the rights and also of the absence of rights of each, and not wholly and solely in fantastic imaginings about the subject of one's EGO.

One authority will be glorious because it will be all-

powerful, will rule and guide, and not muddle along after leaders
and orators shrieking themselves hoarse with senseless words
which they call great principles and which are noting else, to
speak honestly, but utopian .... Our authority will be the crown
of order, and in that is included the whole happiness of man. The
aureole of this authority will inspire a mystical bowing of the
knee before it and a reverent fear before it of all the peoples.
True force makes no terms with any right, not even with that of
God: none dare come near to it so as to take so much as a span
from it away.

PROTOCOL No. 23

That the peoples may become accustomed to obedience it
is necessary to inculcate lessons of humility and therefore to
reduce the production of articles of luxury. By this we shall
improve morals which have been debased by emulation in the
sphere of luxury. We shall re-establish small master production
which will mean laying a mine under the private capital of
manufactures. This is indispensable also for the reason that
manufacturers on the grand scale often move, though not always
consciously, the thoughts of the masses in directions against the
government. A people of small masters knows nothing of
unemployment and this binds him closely with existing order, and

consequently with the firmness of authority. For us its part will have been played out the moment authority is transferred into our hands. Drunkenness also will be prohibited by law and punishable as a crime against humanness of man who is turned into a brute under the influence of alcohol.

Subjects, I repeat once more, give blind obedience only to the strong hand which is absolutely independent of them, for in it they feel the sword of defense and support against social scourges .... What do they want with an angelic spirit in a king? What they have to see in him is the personification of force and power.

The supreme lord who will replace all now existing ruler, dragging in their existence among societies demoralized by us, societies that have denied even the authority of God, from whose midst breads out on all sides the fire of anarchy, must first of all proceed to quench this all-devouring flame. Therefore he will be obliged to kill off those existing societies, though he should drench them with his own blood, that he may resurrect them again in the form of regularly organized troops fighting consciously with every kind of infection that may cover the body of the State with sores.

This Chosen One of God is chosen from above to demolish the senseless forces moved by instinct and not reason, by brutishness and humanness. These forces now triumph in manifestations of robbery and every kind of violence under the mask of principles of freedom and every kind of violence under the mask of principles of freedom and rights. They have overthrown all forms of social order to erect on the ruins of the throne of the King of the [illuminati]; but their part will be played out the moment he enters into his kingdom. Then it will be necessary to sweep them away from his path, on which must be left no knot, no splinter.

Then will it be possible for us to say to the peoples of the world: Give thanks to God and bow the knee before him who bears on his front the seal of the predestination of man, to which God himself has led his star that none other but Him might free us from all the before-mentioned forces and evils.

PROTOCOL No. 24

I pass now to the method of confirming the dynastic roots of King David to the last strata of the earth.

This confirmation will first and foremost be included in

that which to this day has rested the force of conservatism by our learned elders of the conduct of the affairs of the world, in the directing of the education of thought of all humanity.

Certain members of the seed of David will prepare the kings and their heirs, selecting not by right of heritage but by eminent capacities, inducting them into the most secret mysteries of the political, into schemes of government, but providing always that none may come to knowledge of the secrets. The object of this mode of action is that all may know that government cannot be entrusted to those who have not been inducted into the secret places of its art....

To these persons only will be taught the practical application of the aforenamed plans by comparison of the experiences of many centuries, all the observations on the politico-economic moves and social sciences - in a word, all the spirit of laws which have been unshakably established by nature herself for the regulation of the relations of humanity.

Direct heirs will often be set aside from ascending the throne if in their time of training they exhibit frivolity, softness and other qualities that are the ruin of authority, which render them incapable of governing and in themselves dangerous for kingly office.

Only those who are unconditionally capable for firm, even if it be to cruelty, direct rule will receive the reins of rule from our learned elders.

In case of falling sick with weakness of will or other form of incapacity. kings must by law hand over the reins of rule to new and capable hands.

The king's plan of action for the current moment, and all the more so for the future, will be unknown, even to those who are called his closest counselors.

Only the king and the three who stood sponsor for him will know what is coming.

In the person of the king who with unbending will is master of himself and of humanity all will discern as it were fate with its mysterious ways. None will know what the king wishes to attain by his dispositions, and therefore none will dare to stand across an unknown path.

It is understood that the brain reservoir of the king must

correspond in capacity to the plan of government it has to contain. It is for this reason that he will ascend the throne not otherwise than after examination of his mind by the aforesaid learned elders.

That the people may know and love their king, it is indispensable for him to converse in the market-places with his people. This ensures the necessary clinching of the two forces which are now divided one from another by us by the terror.

This terror was indispensable for us till the time comes for both these forces separately to fall under our influence.

The king of the [illuminati] must not be at the mercy of his passions, and especially of sensuality: on no side of his character must he give brute instincts power over his mind. Sensuality worse than all else disorganizes the capacities of the mind and clearness of views, distracting the thoughts to the worst and most brutal side of human activity. The prop of humanity in the person of the supreme lord of all the world of the holy seed of David must sacrifice to his people all personal inclinations. Our supreme lord must be of an exemplary irreproachable.

CHAPTER TWELVE

A PROPOSED CONSTITUTIONAL MODEL FOR THE NEWSTATES OF AMERICA

The following document has been prepared over a ten year period by the Center For Democratic Studies of Santa Barbara, California. The total cost incurred by United States Taxpayers was more than $25 Million Dollars.

With a declared National State of Emergency, Martial Law can be imposed. Under the granted powers given to the Federal Emergency Management Agency (FEMA), this is the Constitution that is likely to be implemented and enforced. The conspirators are confident of creating a One World Government, which includes plans to destroy our current Constitution. These conspirators have been quietly acquiring the necessary 34 states' approval to call up a Constitution Convention in an effort to implement a new constitution. (see New States of America from

"The Emerging Constitution", by Rexford G. Tugwell, 1974, Harper & Row). The Constitution has already been written, and has been largely promoted by a group called the "Committee on a Constitutional System." Presently, 19 of its 51-member board of directors are also members of the CFR.

"Such a significant shift in our Constitution is unlikely to come about except as a result of a crisis that is very grave indeed."
CFR, former Secretary of Treasury, C. Douglas Dillon

A financial crisis today would further their goals just as it did in 1929. The Y2K problem or even terrorism can initiate a crisis that could bring about Martial Law and the suspension of the United States Constitution. Below is the New Constitution. I suggest that you take your time in reading it in order to comprehend the powers it expresses and extinguishes from the United States Constitution.

PREAMBLE

So that we may join in common endeavors, welcome the future in good order, and create an adequate and self-repairing government - we, the people, do establish the Newstates of America, herein provided to be ours, and do ordain this Constitution whose supreme law it shall be until the time prescribed for it shall have run.

ARTICLE 1

Rights and Responsibilities
A. Rights

SECTION 1. Freedom of expression, of communication, of movement, of assembly, or of petition shall not be abridged except in declared emergency.

SECTION 2. Access to information possessed by governmental agencies shall not be denied except in interest of national security; but communications among officials necessary to decision making shall be privileged.

SECTION 3. Public communicators may decline to reveal sources of information, but shall be responsible for hurtful disclosures.

SECTION 4. The privacy of individuals shall be respected; searches and seizures shall be made only on judicial warrant; persons shall be pursued or questioned only for the prevention of crime or the apprehension of suspected criminals, and only according to rules established under law.

SECTION 5. There shall be no discrimination because of race, creed, color, origin, or sex. The Court of Rights and Responsibilities may determine whether selection for various occupations has been discriminatory.

SECTION 6. All persons shall have equal protection of the laws, and in all electoral procedures the vote of every eligible citizen shall count equally with others.

SECTION 7. It shall be public policy to promote discussion of public issues and to encourage peaceful public gatherings for this purpose. Permission to hold such gatherings shall not be denied, nor shall they be interrupted, except in declared emergency or on a showing of imminent danger to public order and on judicial warrant.

SECTION 8. The practice of religion shall be privileged; but no religion shall be imposed by some on others, and none shall have public support.

SECTION 9. Any citizen may purchase, sell, lease, hold, convey and inherit real and personal property, and shall benefit equally from all laws for security in such transactions.

SECTION 10. Those who cannot contribute to productivity shall be entitled to a share of the national product; but distribution shall be fair and the total may not exceed the amount for this purpose held in the National Sharing Fund.

SECTION 11. Education shall be provided at public expense for those who meet appropriate tests of eligibility.

SECTION 12. No person shall be deprived of life, liberty, or property without due process of law. No property shall be taken without compensation.

SECTION 13. Legislatures shall define crimes and conditions requiring restraint, but confinement shall not be for punishment; and when possible, there shall be preparation for return to freedom.

SECTION 14. No person shall be placed twice in jeopardy for the same offense.

SECTION 15.   Writs of habeas corpus shall not be suspended except in declared emergency.

SECTION 16. Accused persons shall be informed of charges against them, shall have a speedy trial, shall have reasonable bail, shall be allowed to confront witnesses or to call others, and shall not be compelled to testify against themselves; at the time of arrest they shall be informed of their right to be silent and to have counsel, provided, if necessary, at public expense; and courts shall consider the contention that prosecution may be under an invalid or unjust statue.

B. Responsibilities

SECTION 1. Each freedom of the citizen shall prescribe a corresponding responsibility not to diminish that of others: of speech, communication, assembly, and petition, to grant the same freedom to others; of religion, to respect that others; of privacy, not to invade that of others; of the holding and disposal of property, the obligation to extend the same privilege to others.

SECTION 2. Individuals and enterprises holding themselves out to serve the public shall serve all equally and without intention to misrepresent, conforming to such standards as may improve health and welfare.

SECTION 3. Protection of the law shall be repaid by assistance in its enforcement; this shall include respect for the procedures of justice, apprehension of lawbreakers, and testimony at trial.

SECTION 4. Each citizen shall participate in the processes of democracy, assisting in the selection of officials and in the monitoring of their conduct in office.

SECTION 5.Each shall render such services to the nation as may be uniformly required by law, objection by reason of conscience being adjudicated as hereinafter provided; and none shall expect or may receive special privileges unless they be for a public purpose defined by law.

SECTION 6. Each shall pay whatever share of governmental costs is consistent with fairness to all.

SECTION 7. Each shall refuse awards or titles from the nations or their representatives except as they be authorized by law.

SECTION 8. There shall be a responsibility to avoid violence and to keep the peace; for this reason the bearing of arms or the possession of lethal weapons shall be confined to the police, members of the armed forces, and those licensed under law.

SECTION 9. Each shall assist in preserving the endowments of nature and enlarging the inheritance of future generations.

SECTION 10. Those granted of the use of public lands, the air , or waters shall have a responsibility for using these resources so that, if irreplaceable, they are conserved and, if replaceable, they are put back as they were.

SECTION 11. Retired officers of the armed forces, of the senior civil service, and of the Senate shall regard their service as a permanent obligation and shall not engage in enterprise seeking profit from the government.

SECTION 12. The devising or controlling of devices for management or technology shall establish responsibility for resulting costs.

SECTION 13. All rights and responsibilities defined herein shall extend to such associations of citizens as may be authorized by law.

ARTICLE II

The Newstates

SECTION 1. There shall be Newstates, each comprising no less than 5 percent of the whole population. Existing states may continue and may have the status of Newstates if the Boundary Commission, hereinafter provided, shall so decide. The Commission shall be guided in it recommendations by the probability of accommodation to the conditions for effective government. States electing by referendum to continue if the Commission recommend otherwise shall nevertheless accept all Newstates obligations.

SECTION 2. The Newstates shall have constitutions formulated and adopted by processes hereinafter prescribed.

SECTION 3. They shall have Governors; legislatures, and planning administrative and judicial systems.

SECTION 4. Their political procedures shall be organized and supervised by electoral Overseers; but their elections shall not be in years of presidential election.

SECTION 5. The electoral apparatus of the Newstates of America shall be available to them, and they may be allotted funds under rules agreed to by the national Overseer; but expenditures may not be made by or for any candidate except they be approved by the Overseer; and requirements of residence in a voting district shall be no longer than thirty days.

SECTION 6. They may charter subsidiary governments, urban or rural, and may delegate to them powers appropriate to responsibilities.

SECTION 7. They may lay, or may delegate the laying of, taxes; but these shall conform to the restraints stated hereinafter for the Newstates of America.

SECTION 8. They may not tax exports, may not tax with intent to prevent imports, and may not impose any tax forbidden by laws of the Newstates of America; but the objects appropriate for taxation shall be clearly designated.

SECTION 9. Taxes on land may be at higher rates than those on its improvements.

SECTION 10. They shall be responsible for the administration of public services not reserved to the government of the Newstates of America, such activities being concerted with those of corresponding national agencies, where these exist, under arrangements common to all.

SECTION 11. The rights and responsibilities prescribed in this Constitution shall be effective in the Newstates and shall be suspended only in emergency when declared by Governors and not disapproved by the Senate of the Newstates of America.

SECTION 12. Police powers of the Newstates shall extend to

all matters not reserved to the Newstates of America; but preempted powers shall not be impaired.

SECTION 13. Newstates may not enter into any treaty, alliance, confederation, or agreement unless approved by the Boundary Commission hereinafter provided.

They may not coin money, provide for the payment of debts in any but legal tender, or make any charge for inter-Newstate services. They may not enact ex post facto laws or ones impairing the obligation of contracts.

SECTION 14. Newstates may not impose barriers to imports from other jurisdictions or impose any hindrance to citizens' freedom of movement.

SECTION 15. If governments of the Newstates fail to carry out fully their constitutional duties, their officials shall be warned and may be required by the Senate, on there recommendation of the Watchkeeper, to forfeit revenues from the Newstates of America.

ARTICLE. III

The Electoral Branch

SECTION 1. To arrange for participation by the electorate in the determination of policies and the selection of officials, there shall be an Electoral Branch.

SECTION 2. An Overseer of electoral procedures shall be chosen by majority of the Senate and may be removed by a two-thirds vote. It shall be the Overseer's duty to supervise the organization national and district parties, arrange for discussion among them, and provide for the nomination and election of candidates for public office. While in office the Overseer shall belong to no political organization; and after each presidential election shall offer to resign.

SECTION 3. A national party shall be one having had at least a 5 percent affiliation in the latest general election; but a new party shall be recognized when valid petitions have been signed by at least 2 percent of the voters in each of 30 percent of the districts drawn for the House of Representatives. Recognition shall be suspended upon failure to gain 5 percent of the votes at a second election, 10 percent at a third, or 15 percent at further election. District parties shall be recognized when at least 2 percent of the voters shall have signed petitions of affiliation; but recognition shall be withdrawn upon failure to attract the same percentages as are necessary for the continuance of national parties.

SECTION 4. Recognition by the Overseer shall bring parties within established regulations and entitle them to common privileges.

SECTION 5. The Overseer shall promulgate rules for party conduct and shall see that fair practices are maintained, and for this purpose shall appoint deputies in each district and shall supervise the choice, in district and national conventions, of party administrators. Regulations and appointments may be objected to by the Senate.

SECTION 6. The Overseer, with the administrator and other officials, shall:

a. Provide the means for discussion, in each party, of public issues, and for this purpose, ensure that members have adequate facilities for participation.

b. Arrange for discussion, in annual district meetings, of the President's views, of the findings of the Planning Branch, and such other information as may be pertinent for the enlightened political discussion.

c. Arrange, on the first Saturday in each month, for enrollment, valid for one year, of voters at convenient places.

SECTION 7. The Overseer shall also:

a. Assist the parties in nominating candidates for district members of the House of Representatives each three years; and for this purpose designate one hundred districts, each with a similar number of eligible voters, redrawing districts after each election. In these there shall be party conventions having no more than three hundred delegates, so distributed that representation of voters be approximately equal.

Candidates for delegate may become eligible by presenting

petitions signed by two hundred registered voters. They shall be elected by party members on the first Tuesday in March, those having the largest number of votes being chosen until the three hundred be complete. Ten alternates shall also be chosen by the same process.

District conventions shall be held on the first Tuesday in April. Delegates shall choose three candidates for membership in the House of Representatives, the three having the most votes becoming candidates.

b. Arrange for the election each three years of three members of the House of Representatives in each district from among the candidates chosen in party conventions, the three having the most votes to be elected.

SECTION 8. The Overseer shall also:

a. Arrange for national conventions to meet nine years after previous presidential elections, with an equal number of delegates from each district, the whole number not to exceed one thousand.

Candidates for delegates shall be eligible when petitions signed by five hundred registered voters have been filed. Those with the most votes, together with two alternates, being those next in number of votes, shall be chosen in each district.

b. Approve procedures in these conventions for choosing one hundred candidates to be members-at-large of the House of

Representatives, who terms shall be coterminous with that of the President. For this purpose delegates shall file one choice with convention officials. Voting on submissions shall proceed until one hundred achieve 10 percent, but not more than three candidates may be resident in any one district; if any district have more than three, those with the fewest votes shall be eliminated, others being added from the districts having less than three, until equality be reached. Of those added, those having the most votes shall be chosen first.

c. Arrange procedures for the consideration and approval of party objectives by the convention.

d. Formulate rules for the nomination in these conventions of candidates for President and Vice Presidents when the offices are to fall vacant, candidates for nomination to be recognized when petitions shall have been presented by one hundred or more delegates, pledged to continue support until candidates can no longer win or until they consent to withdraw. Presidents and Vice-Presidents, together with Representatives-at-large, shall submit to referendum after serving for three years, and if they are rejected, new conventions shall be held within one month and candidates shall be chosen as for vacant offices. Candidates for President and Vice-Presidents shall be nominated on attaining a majority.

e. Arrange for the election on the first Tuesday in June, in appropriate years, of new candidates for President and Vice-Presidents, and members -at-large of the House of Representatives, all being presented to the nation's voters as a ticket; if no ticket achieve a majority, the Overseer shall arrange another election, on the third Tuesday in June, between the two persons having the most votes; and if referendum so determine he shall provide similar arrangements for the nomination and election of candidates.

In this election, the one having the most votes shall prevail.

SECTION 9. The Overseer shall also:

a. Arrange for the convening of the national legislative houses on the fourth Tuesday of July.

b. Arrange for inauguration of the President and Vice-President and Vice-Presidents on the second Tuesday of August.

SECTION 10. All costs of electoral procedures shall be paid from public funds, and there shall be no private contributions to parties or candidates; no contributions or expenditures for meetings, conventions, or campaigns shall be made; and no candidate for office may make any personal expenditures unless authorized by a uniform rule of the Overseer; and persons or groups making expenditures, directly or indirectly, in support of prospective candidates shall report to the Overseer and shall conform to this regulations.

SECTION 11. Expenses of the Electoral Branch shall be met by the addition of one percent to the net annual taxable income returns of taxpayers, this sum to be held by the Chancellor of Financial Affairs for disposition by the Overseer.

Funds shall be distributed to parties in proportion to the respective number of votes cast for the President and Governors at the last election, except that new parties, on being recognized, shall share in proportion to their number. Party administrators shall make allocations to legislative candidates in amounts proportional to the party vote at the last election.

Expenditures shall be audited by the Watchkeeper; and sums not expended within four years shall be returned to the Treasury.

It shall be a condition of every communications franchise that reasonable facilities shall be available for allocations by the Overseer.

ARTICLE IV

The Planning Branch

SECTION 1. There shall be a Planning Branch to formulate and administer plans and to prepare budgets for the uses of expected income in pursuit of policies formulated by the processes provided herein.

SECTION 2. There shall be a National Planning Board of fifteen members appointed by the President; the first members shall have terms designated by the President of one to fifteen years, thereafter one shall be appointed each year; the President shall appoint a Chairman who shall serve for fifteen years unless removed by him.

SECTION 3. The Chairman shall appoint, and shall supervise, a planning administrator, together with such deputies as may be agreed to by the Board.

SECTION 4. The Chairman shall present to the Board six-and twelve year development plans prepared by the planning staff. They shall be revised each year after public hearings, and finally in the year before they are to take effect. They shall be submitted to the President on the fourth Tuesday in July for transmission to the Senate on September 1st with his comments. If members of the Board fail to approve the budget proposals by the forwarding date, the Chairman shall nevertheless make submission to the President with notations of reservation by such members. The President shall transmit this proposal, with his comments, to the House of Representatives on September 1.

SECTION 5. It shall be recognized that the six-and twelve-year development plans represent national intentions tempered by the appraisal of possibilities. The twelve-year plan shall be a general estimate of probable progress, both governmental and private; the six-year plan shall be more specific as to estimated income and expenditure and shall take account of necessary revisions. The purpose shall be to advance, through every agency of government, the excellence of national life. It shall be the further purpose to anticipate innovations, to estimate their impact, to assimilate them into existing institutions, and to moderate deleterious effects on the environment and on society.

The six-and twelve-year plans shall be disseminated for discussion and the opinions expressed shall be considered in the formulation of plans for each succeeding year with special attention to detail in proposing the budget.

SECTION 6. For both plans an extension of one year into the future shall be made each year and the estimates for all other years shall be revised accordingly. For non-governmental activities the estimate of developments shall be calculated to indicate the need for enlargement or restriction.

SECTION 7. If there be objection by the President or the Senate to the six-or Twelve-year plans, they shall be returned for restudy and resubmission. If there still be differences, and if the President and the Senate agree, they shall prevail. If they do not agree, the Senate shall prevailed and the plan shall be revised accordingly.

SECTION 8. The Newstates, on June 1, shall submit proposals for development to be considered for inclusion in those for the Newstates of America. Researches and administration shall be

delegated, when convenient, to planning agencies of the
Newstates.

SECTION 9. There shall be submissions from private
individuals or from organized associations affected with a public
interest, as defined by the Board. They shall report intentions to
expand or contact, estimates of production and demand,
probable uses of resources, numbers expected to be employed,
and other essential information..

SECTION 10. The Planning Branch shall make and have
custody of official maps, and these shall be documents of
reference for future developments both public and private; on
them the location of facilities, with extension indicated, and the
intended use of all areas shall be marked out.

Official maps shall also be maintained by the planning agencies of
the Newstates, and in matters not exclusively national the
National Planning Board may rely on these.

Undertakings in violation of official designation shall be at the
risk of the enturer, and there shall be no recourse; but losses
from designations after acquisition shall be recoverable in actions
before the Court of Claims.

SECTION 11. The Planning Branch shall have available to it
funds equal to one-half of one percent of the approved national
budget (not including debt services or payments from trust
funds). They shall be held by the Chancellor of Financial Affairs

and expended according to rules approved by the Board; but funds not expended within six years shall be available for other uses.

SECTION 12. Allocations may be made for the planning agencies of the Newstates; but only the maps and plans of the national Board, or those approved by them, shall have status at law.

SECTION 13. In making plans, there shall be due regard to the interests of other nations and such cooperation with their intentions as may be approved by the Board.

SECTION 14. There may also be cooperation with international agencies and such contributions to their work as are not disapproved by the President.

ARTICLE V

The Presidency

SECTION 1. The President of the Newstates of America shall be the head of government, shaper of its commitments, expositor of its policies, and supreme commander of its protective forces; shall have one term of nine years, unless rejected by 60 percent of the electorate after three years; shall take care that the nation's resources are estimated and are apportioned to its more

exigent needs; shall recommend such plans, legislation, and
action as may be necessary; and shall address the legislators each
year on the state of the nation, calling upon them to do their part
for the general good.

SECTION 2. There shall be two Vice-Presidents elected with
the President; at the time of taking office the President shall
designate one Vice-President to supervise internal affairs; and
one to be deputy for general affairs. The deputy for general
affairs shall succeed if the presidency be vacated; the Vice-
President for internal affairs shall be second in succession. If
either Vice-President shall die or be incapacitated the President,
with the consent of the Senate shall appoint a successor. Vice-
Presidents shall serve during an extended term with such
assignments as the President may make. If the presidency fall
vacant through the disability of both Vice-Presidents, the Senate
shall elect successors from among its members to serve until the
next general election.

With the Vice-Presidents and other officials the President shall
see to it that the laws are faithfully executed and shall pay
attention to the findings and recommendations of the Planning
Board, the National Regulatory Board, and the Watchkeeper in
formulating national policies.

SECTION 3. Responsible to the Vice-President for General
Affairs there shall be Chancellors of External, Financial, Legal,

and Military Affairs. The Chancellor of External Affairs shall assist in conducting relations with other nations. The Chancellor of Financial Affairs shall supervise the nation's financial and monetary systems, regulating its capital markets and credit-issuing institutions as they may be established by law; and this shall include lending institutions for operations in other nations or in cooperation with them, except that treaties may determine their purposes and standards. The Chancellor of Legal Affairs shall advise governmental agencies and represent them before the courts. The Chancellor of Military Affairs shall act for the presidency in disposing all armed forces except militia commanded by governors; but these shall be available for national service at the President's convenience. Except in declared emergency, the deployment of forces in far waters or in other nations without their consent shall be notified in advance to a national security committee of the Senate hereinafter provided.

SECTION 4. Responsible to the Vice-President for Internal Affairs there shall be chancellors of such departments as the President may find necessary for performing the services of government and are not rejected by a two-thirds vote when the succeeding budget is considered.

SECTION 5. Candidates for the presidency and the vice-presidencies shall be natural-born citizens. Their suitability may be questioned by the Senate within ten days of their nomination, and if two-thirds of the whole agree, they shall be ineligible and a nominating convention shall be reconvened. At the time of his nomination no candidate shall be a member of the Senate and none shall be on active service in the armed forces or a senior civil servant.

SECTION 6. The President may take leave because of illness or for an interval of relief, and the Vice-President in charge of General Affairs shall act. The President may resign if the Senate agree; and, if the term shall have more than two years to run, the Overseer shall arrange for a special election for President and Vice-President.

SECTION 7. The Vice-Presidents may be directed to perform such ministerial duties as the President may find convenient; but their instructions shall be of record, and their actions shall be taken as his deputy.

SECTION 8. Incapacitation may be established without concurrence of the President by a three-quarters vote of the Senate, whereupon a successor shall become Acting President until the disability be declared, by a similar vote, to be ended or to have become permanent. Similarly the other Vice-President shall succeed if a predecessor die or be disabled. Special elections, in these contingencies, may be required by the Senate. Acting Presidents may appoint deputies, unless the Senate object, to assume their duties until the next election.

SECTION 9. The Vice-Presidents, together with such other officials as the President may designate from time to time, may constitute a cabinet or council; but this shall not include officials of other branches.

SECTION 10. Treaties or agreements with other nations, negotiated under the President's authority, shall be in effect unless objected to by a majority of the Senate within ninety days. If they are objected to, the President may resubmit and the Senate reconsider. If a majority still object, the Senate shall prevail.

SECTION 11. All officers, except those of other branches, shall be appointed and may be removed by the President. A majority of the Senate may object to appointments within sixty days, and alternative candidates shall be offered until it agrees.

SECTION 12. The President shall notify the Planning Board and the House of Representatives, on the fourth Tuesday in June, what the maximum allowable expenditures for the ensuing fiscal year shall be.

The President may determine to make expenditures less than provided in appropriations; but, except in declared emergency, none shall be made in excess of appropriations. Reduction shall be because of changes in requirements and shall not be such as to impair the integrity of budgetary procedures.

SECTION 13. There shall be a Public Custodian, appointed by

the President and removable by him, who shall have charge of properties belonging to the government, but not allocated to specific agencies, who shall administer common public services, shall have charge of building construction and rentals, and shall have such other duties as may be designated by the President or the designated Vice-Presidents.

SECTION 14. There shall be an Intendant responsible to the President who shall supervise Offices for Intelligence and Investigation; also an Office of Emergency Organization with the duty of providing plans and procedures for such contingencies as can be anticipated. The Intendant shall also charter nonprofit corporations (or foundations), unless the President shall object, determined by him to be for useful public purposes. Such corporations shall be exempt from taxation but shall conduct no profit making enterprises.

SECTION 15. The Intendant shall also be a counselor for the coordination of scientific and cultural experiments, and for studies within the government and elsewhere, and for this purpose shall employ such assistance as may be found necessary.

SECTION 16. Offices for the purposes may be established and may be discontinued by presidential order within the funds allocated in the procedures of appropriation.

ARTICLE VI

The Legislative Branch

(The Senate and the House of Representatives)

A. The Senate

SECTION 1. There shall be a Senate with membership as follows: If they so desire, former Presidents, Vice-Presidents, Principal Justices, Overseers, Chairmen of the Planning and Regulatory Boards, Governors having had more than seven years service, and unsuccessful candidates for the presidency and vice-presidency who have receive at least 30 percent of the vote. To be appointed by the President, three persons who have been Chancellors, two officials from the civil services, two officials from the diplomatic services, two senior military officers, also one person from a panel of three, elected in a process approved by the Overseer, by each of twelve such groups or associations as the President may recognize from time to time to be nationally representative, but none shall be a political or religious group, no individual selected shall have been paid by any private interest to influence government, and any association objected to by the Senate shall not be recognized. Similarly, to be appointed by the Principal Justice, two persons distinguished in public law and two former members of the High Courts or the Judicial Council. Also, to be elected by the House of Representatives, three

members who have served six or more years. Vacancies shall be
filled as they occur.

SECTION 2. Membership shall continue for life, except that
absences not provided for by rule shall constitute retirement, and
that Senators may retire voluntarily.

SECTION 3. The Senate shall elect as presiding officer a
Congener who shall serve for two years, when his further service
may be discontinued by a majority vote. Other officers,
including a Deputy, shall be appointed by the Convener unless
the Senate shall object.

SECTION 4. The Senate shall meet each year on the second
Tuesday in July and shall be in continuous session, but may
adjourn to the call of the Convener. A quorum shall be more
than three-fifths of the whole membership.

SECTION 5. The Senate shall consider, and return within thirty
days, all measures approved by the House of Representatives
(except the annual budget). Approval or disapproval shall be by
a majority vote of those present. Objection shall stand unless the
House of Representatives shall overcome it by a majority vote
plus one; if no return be made, approval by the House of
Representatives shall be final. For consideration of laws passed
by the House of Representatives or for other purposes, the
Convener may appoint appropriate committees.

SECTION 6. The Senate may ask advice from the Principal

Justice concerning the constitutionality of measures before it; and if this be done, the time for return to the House of Representatives may extend to ninety days.

SECTION 7. If requested, the Senate may advise the President on matters of public interest; or, if not requested, by resolution approved by two-thirds of those present. There shall be a special duty to expressions of concern during party conventions and commitments made during campaigns; and if these be neglected, to remind the President and the House of Representatives that these undertakings are to be considered.

SECTION 8. In time of present or prospective danger caused by cataclysm, by attack, or by insurrection, the Senate may declare a national emergency and may authorize the President to take appropriate action. If the Senate be dispersed, and no quorum available, the President may proclaim the emergency, and may terminate it unless the Senate shall have acted. If the President be not available, and the circumstances extreme, the senior serving member of the presidential succession may act until a quorum assembles.

SECTION 9. The Senate may also define and declare a limited emergency in time of prospective danger, or a local or regional disaster, or if an extraordinary advantage be anticipated. It shall be considered by the House of Representatives within three days and, unless disapproved, may extend for a designated period and for a limited area before renewal. Extraordinary expenditures during emergency may be approved, without regard to usual budget procedures, by the House of Representatives with the concurrence of the President.

SECTION 10. The Senate, at the beginning of each session, shall select three of its members to constitute a National Security Committee to be consulted by the President in emergencies requiring the deployment of the armed forces abroad. If the Committee dissent from the President's proposal, it shall report to the Senate, whose decision shall be final.

SECTION 11. The Senate shall elect, or may remove, a National Watchkeeper, and shall oversee, through a standing committee, a Watchkeeping Service conducted according to rules formulated for their approval.

With the assistance of an appropriate staff the Watchkeeper shall gather and organize information concerning the adequacy, competence, and integrity of governmental agencies and their personnel, as well as their continued usefulness; and shall also suggest the need for new or expanded services, making report concerning any agency of the deleterious effect of its activities on citizens or on the environment. The Watchkeeper shall entertain petitions for the redress of grievances and shall advise the appropriate agencies if there be need for action. For all these purposes, personnel may be appointed, investigations made, witnesses examined, post audits made, and information required. The Convenor shall present the Watchkeeper's findings to the Senate, and if it be judged to be in the public interest, they shall be made public or, without being made public, be sent to the appropriate agency for its guidance and such action as may be needed. On recommendation of the Watchkeeper the Senate may initiate corrective measures to be voted on by the House of Representatives within thirty days. When approved by a majority and not vetoes by the President, they shall become law.

For the Watchkeeping Service one-quarter of one percent of individual net taxable incomes shall be held by the Chancellor of Financial Affairs; but amounts not expended in any fiscal year shall be available for general use.

B. **The House of Representatives**

SECTION 1. The House of Representatives shall be original lawmaking body of the Newstates of America.

SECTION 2. It shall convene each year on the second Tuesday in July and shall remain in continuous session except that it may adjourn to the call of a Speaker, elected by a majority vote from among the Representatives-at-large, who shall be its presiding officer.

SECTION 3. It shall be a duty to implement the provisions of this constitution and, in legislature to be guided by them.

SECTION 4. Party leaders and their deputies shall be chosen by caucus at the beginning of each session.

SECTION 5. Standing and temporary committees shall be selected as follows:

Committees dealing with the calendaring and management of bills shall have a majority of members nominated to party caucuses by the Speaker; other members shall be nominated by minority leaders.

Membership shall correspond to the parties; proportions at the last election. If nominations be not approved by a majority of the caucus, the Speaker or the minority leaders shall nominate others until a majority shall approve. Members of other committees shall be chosen by party caucus in proportion to the results of the last election. Chairmen shall be elected annually from among at-large-members. Bills referred to committees shall be returned to the house with recommendations within sixty days unless extension be voted by the House.

In all committee actions names of those voting for and against shall be recorded. No committee chairman may serve longer than six years.

SECTION 6. Approved legislation, not objected to by the Senate within the allotted time, shall be presented to the

President for his approval or disapproval. If the President disapprove, and three-quarters of the House membership still approve, it shall become law. The names of those voting for and against shall be recorded. Bills not returned within eleven days shall become law.

SECTION 7. The President may have thirty days to consider measures approved by the House unless they shall have been submitted twelve days previous to adjournment.

SECTION 8. The house shall consider promptly the annual budget; if there be objection, it shall be notified to the Planning Board; The Board shall then resubmit through the President; and, with his comments, it shall be returned to the House. If there still be objection by a two-thirds majority, the House shall prevail. Objection must be by whole title; titles not objected to when voted on shall constitute appropriation. The budget for the fiscal year shall be in effect on January 1. Titles not yet acted on shall be as in the former budget until action be completed.

SECTION 9. It shall be the duty of the House to make laws concerning taxes.

1. For their laying and collection:

a. They shall be uniform, and shall not be retroactive.

b. Except such as may be authorized by law to be laid by Authorities, or by the Newstates, all collections shall be made by a national revenue agency. This shall include collections for trust funds hereinafter authorized.

c. Except for corporate levies to be held in the National Sharing Fund, hereinafter authorized, taxes may be collected only from individuals and only from incomes; but there may be withholding from current incomes.

d. To assist in the maintenance of economic stability, the President may be authorized to alter rates by executive order.

e. They shall be imposed on profit-making enterprises owned or conducted by religious establishments or other nonprofit organizations.

f. There shall be none on food, medicines, residential rentals, or commodities or services designated by law as necessities; and there shall be no double taxation.

g. None shall be levied for registering ownership or transfer of property.

2. For expenditure from revenues:

a. For the purposes detailed in the annual budget unless objection be made by the procedure prescribed herein.

b. For such other purposes as the House may indicate and require the Planning Board to include in revision of the budget; but, except in declared emergency, the total may not exceed the President's estimate of available funds.

3. For fixing the percentage of net corporate taxable incomes to be paid into a National Sharing Fund to be held in the custody of

the Chancellor of Financial Affairs and made available for such welfare and environmental purposes as are authorized by law.

4. To provide for the regulation of commerce with other nations and among the Newstates, Possessions, Territories; or, as shall be mutually agreed, with other organized governments; but exports shall not be taxed; and imports shall not be taxed except on recommendation of the President at rates whose allowable variations shall have been fixed by law. There shall be no quotas, and no nations favored by special rates, unless by special acts requiring two-thirds majorities.

5. To establish, or provide for the establishment of, institutions for the safekeeping of savings, for the gathering and distribution of capital, for the issuance of credit, for regulating the coinage of money, for controlling the media of exchange, and for stabilizing prices; but such institutions, when not public or semipublic, shall be regarded as affected with the public interest and shall be supervised by the Chancellor of Financial Affairs.

6. To establish institutions for insurance against risks and liabilities for communication, transportation, and others commonly used and necessary for public convenience.

8. To assist in the maintenance of world order, and, for this purpose, when the President shall recommend, to vest jurisdiction in international legislative, judicial, or administrative agencies

9. To develop with other peoples, and for the benefit of all, the resources of space, of other bodies in the universe, and of the seas beyond twelve miles from low-water shores unless treaties shall provide other limits

10. To assist other peoples who have not attained satisfactory levels of well-being; to delegate the administration of funds for assistance, whenever possible, to international agencies; and to invest in or contribute to the furthering of development in other parts of the world.

11. To assure, or to assist in assuring, adequate and equal facilities for education; for training in occupations citizens may be fitted to pursue; and to reeducate or retrain those whose occupations may become obsolete.

12. To establish or to assist institutions devoted to higher education, to research, or to technical training.

13. To establish and maintain, or assist in maintaining, libraries, archives, monuments, and other places of historic interest.

14. To assist in the advancement of sciences technologies; and to encourage cultural activities.

15. To conserve natural resources by purchase, by withdrawal from use, or by regulation; to provide, or to assist in providing, facilities for recreation; to establish and maintain parks, forests, wilderness areas, wetlands, and prairies; to improve streams and other waters; to ensure the purity of air and water; to control the

erosion of soils; and to provide for all else necessary for the protection and common use of the national heritage.

16. To acquire property and improvements for public use at costs to be fixed, if necessary, by the Court of Claims.

17. To prevent the stoppage or hindrance of governmental procedures, or other activities affected with a public interest as defined by law, by reason of disputes between employers and employees, or for other reasons, and for this purpose to provide for conclusive arbitration if adequate provision for collective bargaining fail. From such findings there may be appeal to the Court of Arbitration Review; but such proceedings may not stay the acceptance of findings.

18. To support an adequate civil service for the performance of such duties as may be designated by administrators; and for this purpose to refrain from interference with the processes of appointment or placement, asking advice or testimony before committees only with the consent of appropriate superiors.

19. To provide for the maintenance of armed forces.

20. To enact such measures as will assist families in making adjustment to future conditions, using estimates concerning population and resources made by the Planning Board.

21. To vote within ninety days on such measures as the President may designate as urgent.

ARTICLE VII

The Regulatory Branch

SECTION 1. There shall be a Regulatory Branch, and there shall be a National Regulator chosen by majority vote of the Senate and removable by a two-thirds vote of that body. His term shall be seven years, and he shall make and administer rules for the conduct of all economic enterprises.

The Regulatory Branch shall have such agencies as the Board may find necessary and are not disapproved by law.

SECTION 2. The Regulatory Board shall consist of seventeen members recommended to the Senate by the Regulator. Unless rejected by majority vote they shall act with the Regulator as a lawmaking body for industry.

They shall initially have terms of one to seventeen years, one being replaced each year and serving for seventeen years. They shall be compensated and shall have no other occupation.

SECTION 3. Under procedures approved by the Board, the Regulator shall charter all corporations or enterprises except those exempted because of size or other characteristics, or those supervised by the Chancellor of Financial Affairs, or by the Intendant, or those whose activities are confined to one Newstates.

Charters shall describe proposed activities, and departure from these shall require amendment on penalty of revocation. For this purpose there shall be investigation and enforcement services under the direction of the Regulator.

SECTION 4. Chartered enterprises in similar industries or occupations may organize joint Authorities. These may formulate among themselves codes to ensure fair competition, meet external costs, set standards for quality and service, expand trade, increase production, eliminate waste, and assist in standardization. Authorities may maintain for common use services for research and communication; but membership shall be open all eligible enterprises. Nonmembers shall be required to maintain the same standards as those prescribed for members.

SECTION 5. Authorities shall have governing committees of five, two being appointed by the Regulator to represent the public. They shall serve as he may determine; they shall be compensated; and he shall take care that there be no conflicts of interest. The Board may approve or prescribe rules for the distribution of profits to stockholders; allowable amounts of working capital, and reserves. Costing and all other practices affecting the public interest shall be monitored.

All codes shall be subject to review by the Regulator with his board.

SECTION 6. Member enterprises of an Authority shall be

exempt from other regulation.

SECTION 7. The Regulator, with his Board, shall fix standards and procedures for mergers of enterprises or the acquisition of some by others; and these shall be in effect unless rejected by the Court of Administrative Settlements. The purpose shall be to encourage adaptation to change and to further approved intentions for the nation.

SECTION 8. The charters of enterprises may be revoked and Authorities may be dissolved by the Regulator, with the concurrence of the Board, if they restrict the production of goods and services, or controls of their prices; also if external costs are not assessed to their originators or if the ecological impacts of their operations are deleterious.

SECTION 9. Operations extending abroad shall conform to policies notified to the Regulator by the President; and he shall restrict or control such activities as appear to injure the national interest.

SECTION 10. The Regulator shall make rules for and shall supervise marketplaces for goods and services; but this shall not include security exchanges regulated by the Chancellor of Financial Affairs.

SECTION 11. Designation of enterprises affected with a public interest, rules for conduct of enterprises and of their Authorities, and other actions of the Regulator or of the Boards may be appealed to the Court of Administrative Settlements, whose judgments shall be informed by the intention to establish fairness to consumers and competitors and stability in economic affairs.

SECTION 12. Responsible also to the Regulator, there shall be an Operations Commission appointed by the Regulator, unless the Senate object, for the supervision of enterprises owned in whole or in part by government. The commission shall choose its chairman, and he shall be the executive head of a supervisory staff. He may require reports, conduct investigations, and make rules and recommendations concerning surpluses or deficits, the absorption of external costs, standards of service, and rates or prices charged for services or goods.

Each enterprise shall have a director, chosen by and removable by the Commission; and he shall conduct its affairs in accordance with standards fixed by the Commission.

ARTICLE VIII

The Judicial Branch

SECTION 1. There shall be a Principal Justice of the Newstates for America; a Judicial Council; and a Judicial Assembly. There shall also be a Supreme Court and a High Court of Appeals; also Courts of Claims, Rights and Duties, Administrative Review,

Arbitration Settlements, Tax Appeals, and Appeals from Watchkeeper's Findings. There shall be Circuit Courts to be of first resort in suits brought under national law; and they shall hear appeals from courts of the Newstates. Other courts may be established by law on recommendation of the Principal Justice with the Judicial Council.

SECTION 2. The Principal Justice shall preside over the judicial system, shall appoint the members of all national courts, and, unless the Judicial Council object, shall make its rules; also, through an Administrator, supervise its operations.

SECTION 3. The Judicial Assembly shall consist of Circuit Court Judges, together with those of the High Courts of the Newstates of America and those of the highest courts of the Newstates. It shall meet annually, or at the call of the Principal Justice, to consider the state of the Judiciary and such other matters as may be laid before it. It shall also meet at the call of the convener to nominate three candidates for the Principal Justiceship whenever a vacancy shall occur. From these nominees the Senate shall choose the one having the most votes.

SECTION 4. The Principal Justice, unless the Senate object to any, shall appoint a Judicial Council of five members to serve during his incumbency. He shall designate a senior member who shall preside in his absence.

It shall be the duty of the Council, under the direction of the

Principal Justice, to study the courts in operation, to prepare codes of ethics to be observed by members, and to suggest changes in procedure. The Council may ask the advice of the Judicial Assembly. It shall also be a duty of the Council, as hereinafter provided, to suggest Constitutional amendments when they appear to be necessary; and it shall also draft revisions if they shall be required. Further it shall examine, and from time to time cause to be revised, civil and criminal codes; these, when approved by the Judicial Assembly, shall be in effect throughout the nation.

SECTION 5. The Principal Justice shall have a term of eleven years; but if at any time the incumbent resign or be disabled from continuing in office, as may be determined by the Senate, replacement shall be by the senior member of the Judicial Council until a new selection be made. After six years the Assembly may provide, by a two-thirds vote, for discontinuance in office, and a successor shall then be chosen.

SECTION 6. The Principal Justice may suspend members of any court for incapacity or violation of rules; and the separation shall be final if a majority of the Council agree. For each court the Principal Justice shall, from time to time, appoint a member who shall preside.

SECTION 7. A presiding judge may decide, with the concurrence of the senior judge, that there may be pretrial proceedings, that criminal trials shall be conducted by either investigatory or adversary proceedings, and whether there shall be a jury and what the number of jurors shall be; but investigatory proceedings shall require a bench of three.

SECTION 8. In deciding on the concordance of statutes with Constitution, the Supreme Court shall return to the House of Representatives such as it cannot construe. If the House fail to make return within ninety days the Court may interpret.

SECTION 9. The Principal Justice, or the President, may grant pardons or reprieves.

SECTION 10. The High Courts shall have thirteen members; but nine members, chosen by their senior justices from time to time, shall constitute a court. The justices on leave shall be subject to recall.

Other courts shall have nine members; but seven, chosen by their senior, shall constitute a court. All shall be in continuous session except for recesses approved by the Principal Justice.

SECTION 11. The Principal Justice, with the Council, may advise the Senate, when requested, concerning the appropriateness of measures approved by the House of Representatives; and may also advise the President, when requested, on matters he may refer for consultation.

SECTION 12. It shall be for other branches to accept and to enforce judicial decrees.

SECTION 13. The High Court of Appeals may select applications for further consideration by the Supreme Court of decisions reached by other courts, including those of the Newstates. If it agree that there be a constitutional issue it may make preliminary judgment to be reviewed without hearing, and finally, by the Supreme Court.

SECTION 14. The Supreme Court may decide:

a. Whether, in litigation coming to it on appeal, constitutional provisions have been violated or standards have not been met.

b. On the application of constitutional provisions to suits involving the Newstates.

c. Whether international law, as recognized in treaties, United Nations agreements, or arrangements with other nations, has been ignored or violated.

d. Other causes involving the interpretation of constitutional provisions; except that in holding any branch to have exceeded its powers the decision shall be suspended until the Judicial Court shall have determined whether, in order to avoid confrontation, procedures for amendment of the Constitution are appropriate.

If amendatory proceedings are instituted, decision shall await the outcome.

SECTION 15. The Courts of the Newstates shall have initial jurisdiction in cases arising under their laws except those involving the Newstates itself or those reserved for national courts by a rule of the Principal Justice with the Judicial Council.

ARTICLE IX

General Provisions

SECTION 1. Qualifications for participation in democratic procedures as a citizen, and eligibility for office, shall be subject to repeated study and redefinition; but any change in qualification or eligibility shall become effective only if not disapproved by the Congress.

For this purpose a permanent Citizenship and Qualifications Commission shall be constituted, four members to be appointed by the President, three by the Convener of the Senate, three by the Speaker of the House, and three by the Principal Justice. Vacancies shall be filled as they occur. The members shall choose a chairman; they shall have suitable assistants and accommodations; and they may have other occupations. Recommendations of the commission shall be presented to the President and shall be transmitted to the House of Representatives with comments. They shall have a preferred place on the calendar and, of approved, shall be in effect.

SECTION 2. Areas necessary for the uses of government may

be acquired at its valuation and may be maintained as the public interest may require. Such areas shall have self-government in matters of local concern.

SECTION 3. The President may negotiate for the acquisition of areas outside the Newstates of America, and, if the Senate approve, may provide for their organization as Possessions or Territories.

SECTION 4. The President may make agreements with other organized peoples for a relation other than full membership in the Newstates of America. They may become citizens and may participate in the selection of officials. They may receive assistance for their development or from the National Sharing Fund if they conform to its requirements; and they may serve in civilian or military services, but only as volunteers. They shall be represented in the House of Representatives by members elected at large, their number proportional to their constituencies; but each shall have at least one; and each shall in the same way choose one permanent member of the Senate.

SECTION 5. The President, the Vice-Presidents, and members of the legislative houses shall in all cases except treason, felony, and breach of the peace be exempt from penalty for anything they may say while pursuing public duties; but the Judicial Council may make restraining rules.

SECTION 6. Except as otherwise provided by this Constitution, each legislative house shall establish its requirement for membership and may make rules for the conduct of members, including conflicts of interest, providing its own disciplines for their infraction.

SECTION 7. No Newstates shall interfere with officials of the Newstates of America in the performance of their duties, and all shall give full faith and credit to the Acts of other Newstates and of the Newstates of America.

SECTION 8. Public funds shall be expended only as authorized in this Constitution.

ARTICLE X

Governmental Arrangements

SECTION 1. Offices of the Newstates of America shall be those named in this Constitution, including those of the legislative houses and others authorized by law to be appointed; they shall be compensated, and none may have other paid occupation unless they be excepted by law; none shall occupy more than one position in government; and no gift or favor shall be accepted if in any way related to official duty.

No income from former employments or associations shall continue for their benefits; but their properties may be put in trust and managed without their intervention during continuance in office. Hardships under this rule may be considered by the Court of Rights and Duties, and exceptions may be made with due regard to the general intention.

SECTION 2. The President, the Vice-Presidents, and the Principal Justice shall have households appropriate to their duties. The President, the Vice-Presidents, the Principal Justice, the Chairman of the Planning Board, the Regulator, the Watchkeeper, and the Overseer shall have salaries fixed by law and continued for life; but if they become members of the Senate, they shall have senatorial compensation and shall conform to senatorial requirements. Justices of the High Courts shall have no term; and their salaries shall be two-thirds that of the Principal Justice; they and members of the Judicial Council, unless they shall have become Senators, shall be permanent members of the Judiciary and shall be available for assignment by the Principal Justice.

Salaries for the members of the Senate shall be the same as for Justices of the High Court of Appeals.

SECTION 3. Unless otherwise provided herein, officials designated by the head of a branch as sharers in policymaking may be appointed by him with the President's concurrence and unless the Senate shall object.

SECTION 4. There shall be administrators:

a. for executive offices and official households, appointed by authority of the President;

b. for the national courts, appointed by the Principal Justice;

c. for the Legislative Branch, selected by a committee of members from each house (chosen by the Convener and the Speaker), three from the House of Representatives and four from the Senate.

Appropriations shall be made to them; but those for the Presidency shall not be reduced during his term unless with his consent; and those for the Judicial Branch shall not be reduced during five years succeeding their determination, unless with the consent of the Principal Justice.

SECTION 5. The fiscal year shall be the same as the calendar year, with new appropriations available at its beginning.

SECTION 6. There shall be an Officials' Protective Service to guard the President, the Vice-Presidents, the Principal Justice, and other officials whose safety may be at hazard; and there shall be a Protector appointed by and responsible to a standing committee of the Senate. Protected officials shall be guided by procedures approved by the committee. The service, at the request of the Political Overseer, may extend its protection to candidates for office; or to other officials, if the committee so decide.

SECTION 7. A suitable contingency fund shall be made

available to the President for purposes defined by law.

SECTION 8. The Senate shall try officers of government other than legislators when such officers are impeached by a two-thirds vote of the House of Representatives for conduct prejudicial to the public interest. If Presidents or Vice Presidents are to be tried, the Senate, as constituted, shall conduct the trial. Judgments shall not extend beyond removal from office and disqualification for holding further office; but the convicted official shall be liable to further prosecution.

SECTION 9. Members of legislative houses may be impeached by the Judicial Council; but for trials it shall be enlarged to seventeen by Justices of the High Courts appointed by the Principal Justice. If convicted, members shall be expelled and be ineligible for future public office; and they shall also be liable for trial as citizens.

ARTICLE XI

Amendment

SECTION 1. It being the special duty of the Judicial Council to formulate and suggest amendments to this Constitution, it shall, from time to time, make proposals, through the Principal Justice, to the Senate. The Senate, if it approve, and if the President agree, shall instruct the Overseer to arrange at the next national election for submission of the amendment to the electorate. If not disapproved by a majority, it shall become part of this Constitution. If rejected, it may be restudied and a new proposal submitted.

It shall be the purpose of the amending procedure to correct deficiencies in the Constitution, to extend it when new responsibilities require, and to make government responsible to needs of the people, making use of advances in managerial competence and establishing security and stability; also to preclude changes in the Constitution resulting from interpretation.

SECTION 2. When this Constitution shall have been in effect for twenty-five years the Overseer shall ask, by referendum whether a new Constitution shall be prepared. If a majority so decide, the Council, making use of such advice as may be available, and consulting those who have made complaint, shall prepare a new draft for submission at the next election. If not disapproved by a majority it shall be in effect. If disapproved it shall be redrafted and resubmitted with such changes as may be then appropriate to the circumstances, and it shall be submitted to the voters at the following election. If not disapproved by a majority it shall be in effect. If disapproved it shall be restudied and resubmitted.

ARTICLE XII

Transition

SECTION 1. The President is authorized to assume such powers, make such appointments, and use such funds as are necessary to make this Constitution effective as soon as possible after acceptance by a referendum he may initiate.

SECTION 2. Such members of the Senate as may be at once available shall convene and, if at least half, shall constitute sufficient membership while others are being added. They shall appoint an Overseer to arrange for electoral organization and elections for the offices of government; but the President and Vice-Presidents shall serve out their terms and then become members of the Senate. At that time the presidency shall be constituted as provided in this Constitution.

SECTION 3. Until each indicated change in the government shall have been completed the provisions of the existing Constitution and the organs of government shall be in effect.

SECTION 4. All operations of the national government shall cease as they are replaced by those authorized under this Constitution. The President shall determine when replacement is complete.

The President shall cause to be constituted an appropriate

commission to designate existing laws inconsistent with this Constitution, and they shall be void; also the commission shall assist the President and the legislative houses in the formulating of such laws as may be consistent with the Constitution and necessary to its implementation.

SECTION 5. For establishing Newstates; boundaries a commission of thirteen, appointed by the President, shall make recommendations within one year. For this purpose the members may take advice and commission studies concerning resources, population, transportation, communication, economic and social arrangements, and such other conditions as may be significant. The President shall transmit the commission's report to the Senate. After entertaining, if convenient, petitions for revision, the Senate shall report whether the recommendations are satisfactory but the President shall decide whether they shall be accepted or shall be returned for revision.

Existing states shall not be divided unless metropolitan areas extending over more than one state are to be included in one Newstates, or unless other compelling circumstances exist; and each Newstates shall possess harmonious regional characteristics. The Commission shall continue while the Newstates make adjustments among themselves and shall have jurisdiction in disputes arising among them.

SECTION 6. Constitutions of the Newstates shall be established as arranged by the Judicial Council and the Principal Justice. These procedures shall be as follows; Constitutions shall be drafted by the highest courts of the Newstates. There shall then be a convention of one hundred delegates chosen in special elections in a procedure approved by the Overseer. If the Constitution be not rejected, the Principal Justice, advised by the Judicial Council, shall promulgate another, taking account of objections, and it shall be in effect. A Constitution, once in effect, shall be valid for twenty-five years as herein provided.

SECTION 7. Until Governors and legislatures of the Newstates are seated, their governments shall continue, except that the President may appoint temporary Governors to act as executives until succeeded by those regularly elected. These Governors shall succeed to the executive functions of the states as they become one of the Newstates of America.

SECTION The indicated appointments, elections, and other arrangements shall be made with all deliberate speed.

SECTION 9. The first Judicial Assembly for selecting a register for candidates for the Principal Justiceship of the Newstates of America shall be called by the incumbent Chief Justice immediately upon ratification.

SECTION 10. Newstates electing by referendum not to comply with recommendations of the Boundary Commission, as approved by the Senate, shall have deducted from taxes collected

by the Newstates of America for transmission to them a
percentage equal to the loss in efficiency from failure to comply.
Estimates shall be made by the Chancellor of Financial Affairs
and approved by the President; but the deduction shall not be
less than 7 percent.

SECTION 11. When this Constitution has been implemented the
President may delete by proclamation appropriate parts of this
article.

CHAPTER THIRTEEN

Conclusion:

I guess it is fair to say that I still have a lot more information to give you, but not enough time. I believe that if you do obtain a copy of this book, you will hopefully see that something wrong is truly going on around you. Time is short and you must act right away. Don't worry about convincing everybody, because you will not be able too. Remember it is written. I suggest you hold large meetings wherever you can, while you still can.

The Y2K problem is actually a curse and a blessing in disguise. The curse is, that many things will cease to function; allowing evil to run its course full speed ahead. The year of 1999 in numerology, represents Satan's final assault. It doesn't matter what your religion is, there is one Creator with a positive force, and there is Satan, one major evil force. Satan is just a name used here. Evil is evil.

The blessing is, that this problem is going to force people in the year 2000, to work together. People will need each other more than ever before. This bonding will be so strong, that the most evil of forces will not be able to take on the power of our unity.

The ignorant will perish, while the aware will prevail.

Understand readers, we have a war declared upon us. If you still think nothing is happening, or nothing is going to happen, or the government will save you, then you need to die! There is no room for the weak-minded in this battle, and you might as well be herded along like sheep and await your day of slaughter. Ask yourself one question, what is your purpose in life?

It is a must that you and any one you know learn the U.S. Constitution and its proponents backwards and forwards. Neither legislators nor law enforcement officials know or understand this powerful document. This document can save so many people grief and aggravation that it is not funny. Whether you are stopped on the highway unconstitutionally or incarcerated unjustly, you need to know your rights.

As to the militias all over the U.S., I make a call out to you; whether you are organized or unorganized. (As a small research project, I suggest all readers look up the definition of Militia in the U.S. Constitution) I know, that all of them are not racist radicals running around in the back woods without a purpose. It is the media that is responsible for their negative portrayal.

Many of them understand the U.S. Constitution, and many also are integrated with different races, nationalities and religions. I support the cause of many of them because of the fact that they demand freedom. Freedom by "any means necessary!" Since we all bleed the same blood, we are all in this fight together.

All of us need to put down our differences as human beings and fight our common enemy. Those organizations that hate Jews, African Americans, Whites, or whatever, need to put their feelings in the closet for this war that we must face. Otherwise, we do not have a prayer in the world. Whether or not you may want a separate state for your group, I suggest you get off that high horse for now and lets get busy. The devil is dancing and he would like nothing better than to see us all separated like churches of different religions on a Sunday; everyone goes their separate ways.

If these groups wish to return to their old ways after this is over, then so be it. If major events happen to begin today, many people will perish due to the fact that we will have been conquered and divided. I make a call upon all organizations that understand what is going on, to rise up, to share intelligence information, expertise, knowledge and resources to give the enemy the fight of their lives. This is not just a physical war, but a spiritual and physical war that needs our expression as a people to be the true voice of our government.

These evil conspirators truly believe that they will win. They fail to realize however, that Satan has no friends and pays no allegiance to those he promised great fortunes to. This is the weakness in all conspirators who believe they are protected in the light of Lucifer. Lucifer is real, and all the weak-minded will be captured in that light; eventually blinded until they fall into darkness.

If you are in need of a place to turn and an organization to turn to, a network will start here. However, I once again make a call out for those militia groups for support. Remain underground, unexposed to the elements of the All-Seeing-Eye and their satellites; and carry torches in their tunnels of darkness so they can be exposed. Evil hates light.

I have been blessed with this knowledge I lay before you, and it is my duty as an American citizen to share and/or depart this knowledge to you, to spread among your people. We do not need the help of the media to get our point across, and if you read my material, you can understand why. Remember the quote "The Revolution will not be televised."

No, I am not opposed to the government of these United States of America, but opposed to the "Invisible Hand" that is running it. No, I am not brainwashed, but an individual with better understanding of what this country represents. The power-elite, through the lenses of the controlled media, have distracted us from real important issues with O.J., Monica, the Impeachment Trial, Rodney King, Clarence Thomas, etc. long enough!

You have seen the ten planks of the Communist Manifesto. Doesn't it ring true that many of the things that are going on around you in this nation are representative of a Communist State? The Illuminati thinks so. That is their objective - a One World Government.

The quotes in this book are not to be represented as some of the most influential people in my life, but quotes from people that made meaningful statements. President Thomas Jefferson was a mason who followed Albert Pike's philosophy. Jefferson, one of the founders of the six men who constructed the back of the One Dollar Bill or Federal Reserve Note. He had nothing but evil intentions to be placed upon our sovereignty.

You can look at the back of the dollar bill and find that the truncated pyramid with the eye on the top. This is the "Eye of Lucifer;" as seen on the cover of this book. This represents the fact that you are always being watched. Just take a look at the surveillance cameras around you now. As for the rest of the symbols, notice how they all represent the number thirteen, the number assigned to Satan. Notice at the base of the pyramid the roman numerals, whereby if deciphered, represent May 1, 1776; the initiation of the Illuminati. Remember, the same as Law Day respected by the American Bar Association. That is no accident. Notice the Latin phrase NOVUS ORDO SECLORUM; this means the New Order of the Ages or New World Order. President George Bush mentioned this phrase many times in his speeches. The list goes on, but you need to see some of these things before it is too late.

Furthermore, if you are worried about receiving the mark of the beast on either the palm of your hand or your forehead, the one dollar bill with its symbolism represents the mark of the beast on it. Technically, many of you pass the dollar from hand to hand (palm to palm) already. You may now understand why Congress was correct in only authorizing gold and silver as the only coinage for this country.

In addition, you must denounce the United Nations and all of their activities. Do not let any one in legislative government support them either. You must also request a list of the members of the Council on Foreign Relations as well as the

Trilateral Commission and denounce all members. I truly mean all members, which also include legislators in Congress. They are out to destroy our sovereignty and the U.S. Constitution. You would be surprised that popularized political figures that are considered leaders by the media, are in the above organizations. Oh, do not forget about those Reverends that are supposed to be a part of the church. Reverends of all races and religions.

Remember, read the constitution and then look at your state and federal laws; perhaps you will then begin to understand. Study that document and make a call for all legislators in local, state and federal positions to know it by heart. You may contact me at any time, and I believe we will overcome this common enemy. Remember the Tower of Babel story? May peace be unto all of you.

About the Author

David E. Smith Jr. has been acknowledged in the field of Millennium prognostication. A noted Futurist, Mr. Smith is the president of Destech Press Inc. Having spent several years as a radio and television personality, Mr. Smith's recent endeavor is continue the study of American Jurisprudence and tax law.

David E. Smith Jr. received a B.A at the State University of New York at Oswego where he studied political science and business. From there, he received his J.D. from the State University of New York at Buffalo Law School.

Presently, Mr. Smith conducts seminars, fulfills speaking engagements, radio and television talk show interviews, as well as consultation for his expertise. He is also an author of three books and a newsletter, and has been widely acclaimed for his work.

Mr. Smith now resides in Westchester County, where he concentrates on his work. His future endeavors include writing more books that educate readers. Currently his "Spoonful of Knowledge Book Series"™ is being chartered into a Non Profit Corporation.

Mr. Smith enjoys hearing from his readers, and encourages them to participate in sharing information that can be useful for future projects.

"The Spoonful of Knowledge Series ™"

Presents Other Books:

FINDING YOUR PERFECT SOULMATE OR BUSINESS PARTNER
By David E. Smith Jr.
$14.95

DREAMS AND NUMBERS, NUMBERS AND DREAMS
By David E. Smith Jr.
$5.00

THE SECRET WORLD OF MONEY
By Andrew Gause

$14.95

Y2KAOS
By Andrew Gause
$14.95

Order Now! FOR MORE INFORMATION FILL OUT THE FORM BELOW.

Name _____

_____
            Last   First

Address _____

_____

Phone _(___)_____

Book of
Interest(s)_____

Destech Press Publishing Inc.
Suite 3
13 South Division St.
Peekskill, NY 10566
Ph: (914) 739-8053
Ph: (800) 431-1579 (Credit Card Orders Only)
Fax: (914) 739-8007
E Mail: destech@pcrealm.net

Web: www.destechpress.com